THE GOOD
DIVORCE

Books by Raoul Felder

Bare-Knuckle Negotiation
Schmucks! (with Jackie Mason)
Getting Away with Murder (with Barbara Victor)
Jackie Mason and Raoul Felder's Guide to New York and Los Angeles Restaurants
Jackie Mason and Raoul Felder's A Survival Guide to New York
Lawyers Guide to Equitable Distribution
Encyclopedia of Matrimonial Clauses
Divorce: The Way Things Are, Not the Way They Should Be

Books by Barbara Victor

NONFICTION

The Last Crusade
Army of Roses
Goddess
Le Matignon de Jospin
Getting Away with Murder (with Raoul Felder)
The Lady
A Voice of Reason
Terrorism

FICTION
Reckless
Coriander
Friends, Lovers, Enemies
Misplaced Lives
Absence of Pain

WITHDRAWN

THE GOOD DIVORCE

*How to Walk Away Financially
Sound and Emotionally Healthy*

RAOUL FELDER

AND BARBARA VICTOR

ST. MARTIN'S PRESS · NEW YORK

www.stmartins.com

Library of Congress Cataloging-in-Publication Data

Felder, Raoul Lionel.
    The good divorce : how to walk away financially sound and emotionally happy / Raoul Felder and Barbara Victor. — 1st ed.
        p. cm.
    ISBN 978-0-312-59296-7
1. Divorce.   I. Victor, Barbara.   II. Title.
HQ814.F453 2011
306.89—dc22

                                                              2010040216

First Edition: March 2011

10 9 8 7 6 5 4 3 2 1

CONTENTS

Authors' Note

Many people have been generous with their time, expertise, experiences, and knowledge in helping us write this book. Included in our list of people to whom we are grateful are lawyers, litigants, judges, psychiatrists, and those who comprise the "cottage industry" involving the discovery aspect of many matrimonials.

Most of these people have had no objection to our using their real names and titles in this book. Some have requested that we do not give them attribution and we have therefore changed their names to respect their wishes. In addition, there have been several extremely sensitive cases when we have made composites of situations.

There are several people who have helped enormously with the drudge work associated with producing a book, namely those working as paralegals, court clerks, researchers, and administrative assistants in law offices. To them we are touched and indebted for their willingness to help us understand all the intricacies of divorce.

INTRODUCTION

by Raoul Felder

IT WAS THE END OF THE DAY, everybody was very tough to each other, and our clients had left after a difficult negotiating session. My client, the husband, had displayed insensitivity to those concerns both real and imagined of a middle-aged woman whose prior experience in decision-making was confined to choices on the menus of better-class restaurants. Her perception was that she was about to embark on a journey that she believed would be to the endless emptiness of the life of a divorcée in a city where youth rules. Impatient and dismissive, her husband was like a man listening to a servant's side of the story after he had fired him.

We had gotten as far as we could toward a settlement without anybody coming to blows. Charitably, there was limited reference to real and imagined slights and indignities that took place twenty years ago.

The wife was a chatterbox, constantly talking. She was indifferent to points made or lost by the lawyers or the nuances of each of the parties' positions. Her basic response to each of her husband's positions was "No." She was as immutable and inflexible as the Hoover Dam.

The husband had two responses to any proposals coming from the other side. He announced his reason for not agreeing and then after the other side gave their retort, he simply kept repeating his reason in a progressively louder voice the way visitors to a foreign country do, believing that the volume of their voice can bridge the difficulties in translation. His other response was to simply sneer.

Mutual hatred and contempt suffused the room. These were not nice people but, for the lawyers, it was a job and the pay was good.

The clients left and I was alone with the other lawyer as he packed up his briefcase and I put my papers in order on my desk. For want of something better to say in the silent office, I said, "Well, we made some progress today."

"Yeah, but isn't she a whining bitch."

He was, of course, speaking of his own client. I was so taken aback that for a while I could not respond. Finally I said, "Did you ever think about going into another line of work?" He seemed to think my question was a feeble attempt at humor.

It was clear that my point had not penetrated. I tried again. "Well, you know that at her age—a fifty-one-year-old woman having to enter a marketplace peopled by nineteen- and twenty-year-olds—being suddenly single has to be pretty frightening."

"She'll have lots of money. You get better-looking the more money you have." He turned away, concentrated on packing his briefcase, and without looking up continued, "And what did she do for the money? Eat chocolates and warm a bed?"

The conversation was pointless. To him, his client was meat on a slab, waiting to be cut up or ground up, pushed aside when the next one was dumped on the cutting board.

I tried to explain but it was obvious that my colleague wasn't paying attention. I wanted to tell him that divorce does *not* have to be this way.

If we view the end product of the process, it is rare that one meets any divorced person who ever says he or she regrets being divorced. Most people say that it was a wise decision and many say it was the wisest choice they ever made in their lives. Regrets are usually about the process itself, the dramatis personae, or the results achieved. All of this can be changed, simply and painlessly. And it is the client who can effect this change. The easiest of all choices confronting the client is the choice of the lawyer.

When all is said and done and the theatrics are over, the lawyer is, to quote T. S. Eliot, "an attendant lord, one that will do/To swell a progress, start a scene or two,/Advise the prince; no doubt, an easy tool,/ Deferential, glad to be of use,/Politic, cautious and meticulous;/Full of high sentence, but a bit obtuse . . ."

There have been many times in my career when the opposing counsel is sensitive to both parties and is determined to shepherd his or her client through the process with sensitivity and understanding. I remember one case in particular. Another evening, another settlement conference.

The clock is the enemy of settlement meetings. Experienced lawyers arrange, if possible, for settlement conferences to take place at the end of the day. The thinking is that if one or the other attorney is heading toward resolution, it is best to keep things moving without having to run off to court or another client. Cynics say that the reason end-of-the-day meetings have a higher success rate is because people get worn down as evening approaches.

On that particular occasion, my client was the wife. My adversary, an experienced attorney whom I respected, represented the husband. We shook hands and greeted each other pleasantly. His client, however, kept his eyes lowered and seemed not only unhappy but guilt-ridden to find himself facing his wife and her counsel. My client, like her husband, was unable to look anyone in the eye. She was obviously frightened. While the lawyers conversed, both husband and wife concentrated on the entire landscape of my office: photographs, paintings, desk paraphernalia, the carpet.

During their long marriage, the wife had been little more than a puppet. Her husband had made all the decisions. Of course, once a puppet's strings are cut, it collapses.

There is always a prepared speech at the beginning of any negotiation, either by one of the lawyers or by the clients themselves. On this occasion, it was my opposing counsel. In a solemn tone that indicated he regretted having to take part in the dissolution of a marriage, he began by saying that his client wanted to do the "right thing." While the lawyer spoke, the husband nodded his head in glum assent, still avoiding his wife's eyes. Guilt is often a weapon more deadly than a thrusting dagger. I looked at the wife. In her eyes were many emotions: surprise, regret, sadness, and of course fury. At the end of my colleague's speech, which was crafted to avoid a protracted battle, I realized that he and his client intended to offer my client a fair settlement that obviously impinged on the husband's lifestyle. It was obvious to me almost immediately that the husband's lawyer had honestly and diligently calculated the legal cost of fighting my demands. It all boils down to one crucial sentence: "Better to give your wife and children than your lawyers."

Though there are lawyers who will feed a faint spark of anger, blowing enough air into it to cause a raging inferno, there are other lawyers who can convince a client to come to a fair resolution. All lawyers know that the best way to guide clients toward a land where there are no winners is to treat the process of divorce as an exercise in vengeance. We were lucky. My colleague was having none of this. Perhaps he was too tired, too old, and too rich to do otherwise, but more than likely, he was compassionate, fair, and capable of bringing common sense to the table.

The husband was a high-wage earner employed by a large public corporation. He had always filed honest tax returns, and had paid the family bills by check and credit card, which made his finances completely transparent. His lawyer's computation of my client's needs came within a small percentage of what our own computation had been. He also readily agreed to an equal share of the couple's assets. The deal was made. The lawyer was happy. His client seemed relieved as well, anxious to leave my office and get on with his life. I was happy, and my client breathed a sigh of relief. For the first time since this journey began, I sensed that she could see the road ahead as an adventure rather than a journey fraught with peril and uncertainty.

The key to getting the best out of the lawyer/client relationship is to stay in charge of the relationship and the divorce case. Initially, a lawyer is consulted to advise and explain. In this first interview and as the case progresses, it should be a matter of, to quote Frank Sinatra, "Suggest! Don't tell me." The initial meeting with a lawyer should be nothing more or less than an audition: a beauty contest where the lawyer explains what he can do for the client—and is hired or not. In polls taken of the public's perception of various professions and occupations, lawyers usually end up near the bottom, somewhere between used-car salesmen and ax murderers. But this is a bum rap. Lawyers basically reflect the panorama of society itself with all of its warts and splendors. Lawyers come in all sizes, shapes, sexes, ages, and levels of experience and intelligence. There are lawyers who are absolutely superb craftsmen and sensitive human beings and others who are merely second-class people in first-class suits.

Once hired, the lawyer then becomes the captain of the ship, the guide on a journey—short or long—through sometimes treacherous waters. But the client is the owner of the boat and it is the boat owner who decides how and where the boat is to go. Sometimes, along the way, the owner has to throw the captain overboard and hire a new one. A lawyer's job is to follow the client's wish and, as long as it is not illegal, unethical, or fattening, the lawyer should follow instructions.

The journey to divorce can be intellectually interesting, enlightening, liberating, and challenging, and, if a certain amount of dispassion can be mustered, to the game players it can even be fun. It is one of the few human endeavors, short of the havoc of war, where pretense and posturing is immediately stripped bare and one rapidly obtains an interior vision of a person's character, if not their very soul.

The beginning of the journey is its easiest part: the hiring of your lawyer. The next easiest is the firing of your lawyer.

Clients are consumers of legal services. Frequently, a consumer of produce takes more time picking a piece of fruit—squeezing it, sniffing it—than he does in choosing a lawyer. There are no printed warnings on the doors of divorce lawyers, as on a package of cigarettes. Perhaps this is a reflection of the fact that most legislators are lawyers.

During the initial interview, when a client is considering hiring a lawyer, the first question asked should be about those cases the attorney has already litigated, including the outcome of those cases. The client should also ask for copies of legal documents that the lawyer has prepared, if these are available.

In hiring a lawyer one must also rely on that most ephemeral of all things: intuition, even though the last time the client may have relied on intuition for guidance was when the unfortunate choice was made years earlier that ultimately resulted in the present visit to a divorce lawyer. Now that the client is older, wiser, and one hopes more skeptical, he or she is better equipped to choose the right lawyer.

Often, the key to a successful divorce simply means taking charge.

If a lawyer tells you something or writes something in a legal paper that doesn't make sense to you, it probably does not make sense at all. Law, notwithstanding its *pro hac vices, res adjudicates,* etc., uses basically the language of life, as opposed to medicine, where the terminology often obfuscates rather than illuminates. As a result of this, everybody is or thinks they are experts in the law, or at least qualified to give an opinion. The truth is, apart from courtroom skills that require an understanding of the rules of evidence, legal principals, and procedures, and the ability to marshal the facts in an effective way, anyone can become an expert in the individual aspects of their case. All of these seemingly disparate elements of a trial may appear daunting to a layperson, but if the process is adequately explained, the client can remain in charge. President Franklin D. Roosevelt, with no military experience or training (and interestingly a lawyer with little legal ability), was able to successfully run a world war. Part of taking charge is a client having the self-confidence to say, "Run that by me again, I don't fully understand it enough to make a decision."

Clients should question lawyers as to their proposed strategy, the propriety of what they're doing, and about their prior experience in similar matters. Once a lawyer has been retained, a key question should always be "What will happen if we do *not* do what you recommend?"

Since much of modern law is practiced by the written word rather than the spoken word, clients should ask to see drafts of all documents *before* they are submitted to the court, checking not only for accuracy but also for style, making sure that the document reflects what the client wants to say and in the way he or she wants to say it.

As time in the case goes by, the lawyer and the client should eventually be able to act as a team. At some point they should be like the old married couple. When one begins to say something, the other knows the rest of the sentence before it is spoken.

Divorce is a game that can be won, and won rather effortlessly. It takes focus and the willingness to bury the real and imagined wrongs that infect all of our lives. Instead, the client should be encouraged not to lose sight of the big picture, and to keep his eye on the ultimate goal. No lawyer or legal process can guarantee happiness or even a successful result. But, by following the simple rules of the road, the best possible result can be achieved without inordinate pain.

Divorce litigation should be a path to a much better place. People do not get divorced because they are bored. They get divorced because they are unhappy. Outside of a pardon, few things in life can offer a remedy to unhappiness that is accomplished merely by somebody signing a piece of paper. In matrimonial court, that is not only possible but guaranteed. Breaking up is not hard to do.

INTRODUCTION

by Barbara Victor

IN 1977 I MARRIED. IN 1979 the marriage was over. Back then, I was young, and had a child from a previous relationship, a good job, friends, a support system, and a lover. It never occurred to me that when my divorce was final my reaction would be as emotional as it was. Two years later, in 1981, standing in my kitchen and leafing through my mail, I came upon the official-looking envelope containing my signed and sealed divorce decree from a man I didn't love, and never thought about—or on the rare occasion when I did, remembered a violent and horrific marriage. Opening the envelope, I stared at those papers with the official seal from the supreme court, and the tears came without warning. Feelings of irreconcilable loss and grief that my marriage of only two years—no children, no community property, no reduction of my standard of living—was officially over.

What was it about those papers that caused such sadness?

What was it about finally being officially unmarried that caused those tears?

Those were rational queries to a reaction that was completely illogical—at least on the surface.

Thomas Moore's words come to mind. "We always expect love to be healing and whole."

That would be the ideal, but the reality of love is often quite different.

When love leads to marriage, it is nearly impossible to separate the legality of marriage from the emotion of love. Most people fall in love with their hearts. Marriage, though a legal contract, carries with it feelings that are rarely found in other legal conventions. People sign a marriage contract based on love, passion, money, loneliness, desperation, fear of being alone, desire for children, or religious beliefs. When love dies, and marriage goes stale, the result is most often divorce.

The end of a love affair is heartbreaking enough. When people face the prospect of divorce, they not only suffer the emotional upheaval, but are often shocked to realize that their futures and those of their children are subject to the binding and enforceable rules imposed by the legal system. Seeing those divorce papers in my kitchen that day, reading the legal language that officially made me a divorced woman, was the final shock in an episode in my life that I thought I had already coped with emotionally and managed to bury away in my memory. Suddenly, the law was involved, advising me that my marriage, a personal, private, and intimate decision I had made based on emotion, had been terminated by a court of law. At the time, the first thought that occurred to me after I had calmed down was that as long as a marriage is intact, husband and wife don't usually think of their union as a legal and binding contract. Rather, most people view it as a commitment to love each other, raise a family, and make a life together based on whatever feelings prompted them to marry in the first place. It is atypical for a couple to live their everyday lives according to the laws and tenets of a marriage contract. Only when the marriage disintegrates does the reality of the law enter into what had been an intimate relationship. Only then do people realize that feelings are not part of the equation because the law will govern the dissolution of their union, their futures, and those of their children.

When Raoul Felder and I decided to write this book, we discussed what we wanted to convey to our readers. Based on his experience as one of the preeminent divorce lawyers, his first instinct was to define the obstacles in the legal system, explain how they could be avoided, suggest new ways to level the legal playing field, and guide people through divorce— a process that is both foreign and frightening. After beginning to research and interview, we understood that part of our book would indeed be to educate people about what or what not to expect when embarking upon the process of divorce. We also knew that we could not prevent them from going through all the normal emotions that accompany a dying or, as in my case, a dead relationship. When people become involved in the entanglements of divorce, the first emotion felt is usually fear of many imagined or real possibilities—fear of losing assets and income, custody of children, social status, luxuries, and even basic necessities. Those fears result in people feeling rage, rejection, betrayal, and vengeance. What we wanted to convey was that divorce, similar to marriage, is a process. The first reaction—usually fear or rage—should evolve into pragmatism and ultimately into acceptance that divorce, though painful, is the only way to terminate an unhappy marriage. Unfortunately, many people do not behave according to what the ideal process should be.

Felder knows the law. Based on his more than ten years of experience as a prosecutor for the federal government, and then many more years as a matrimonial lawyer in private practice, he has seen it all—in his office, in court, during trial, and through countless post-trial motions that often result in months and years of unrelenting anguish. His experience has shown him that the emotions connected to divorce often cause people to act irrationally. When that happens, the best remedy is a lawyer who is out for the best interests of the client.

My skill as a journalist who covered the Middle East throughout the last thirty years of my career had given me an insight into the absence of women's rights, and the problem of domestic violence. Though I too had seen it all, it was from a very different perspective than Raoul Felder. My experience was more international, focusing on people throughout the world who were in dire straits—whether the cause was political, cultural, economic, or personal. My specific interest in divorce evolved from the way women are abandoned and abused in certain countries where their religions allow men to make unilateral decisions to divorce, abscond with the children, and leave their wives without support. Focusing on family battles in the United States and other developed countries, the rules are far different yet potentially no less fraught with grief that can, in most cases, be avoided. When, along with Felder, I wrote a book about domestic violence after the O. J. Simpson trial, what shocked me was that these women, who had been abused, beaten, and tortured, systematically refused to press charges against their abusers. It took a near-fatal experience or the brutalization of a child to convince them to put their husbands or partners in jail. During hundreds of interviews, one of the most difficult tasks was to persuade women that life would get better once they had the courage to leave an abusive relationship.

When it came to this book on divorce, Raoul and I believed we had the ability to define how the legal system had failed the poor, the middle class, and the rich. Between us, we had innumerable sources who could recount their experiences concerning divorce, whether they were lawyers, judges, forensic accountants, law guardians, psychiatrists, life coaches, real-estate appraisers, and everyone else involved in the cottage industry associated with breaking up a marriage. The most important sources, however, were the litigants themselves who had done battle in their lawyers' offices, and in the courts. These were the walking wounded who could barely function after the fray was over.

Nothing surprised Felder, not even the occasional violent episode that erupted in his office during negotiations.

What never ceased to amaze me were the number of people who, after the decree was final, still dedicated their lives to taking revenge and keeping track of every perceived injustice resulting from the demise of their marriages. Their trauma was often every bit as severe as what one suffers at the death of a loved one, with one major difference. Eventually, people adjust to death, even in the most horrendous cases where a child dies or a spouse or parent is the victim of a violent crime. The usual stages of loss are rage, which becomes grief, which ultimately turns into acceptance. The loss is always there but somehow people cease reliving the trauma and move on with their lives. For those who manage to accept the tragedy, there is usually an absence of bitterness and self-pity. Curiously, divorce elicits some of the most violent and destructive emotions. For some, divorce seems harder to accept than the death of a loved one. There are myriad complicated reasons for this, which we discuss in detail in this book. For one thing, when the death of a loved one does not implicate the one who is left behind, there is no guilt or regret on any real level. When it comes to divorce, there is always blame, recrimination, and self-doubt that one or the other spouse could have done something to prevent it.

After months of research and interviews, we soon became convinced that though it was vital to reveal and explain the intricacies of the legal system to help people make the right choices, it was equally crucial to help people view divorce as a positive rather than a negative step. Based on all my conversations with people who had or were about to experience the realities of breaking up a home, this book had to impart a critical reality that many people often ignore.

When a marriage has gone bad, divorce is the only remedy that allows people to have a chance at a happier life.

Feelings of sadness, failure, rage, rejection, betrayal, and fear are all normal reactions in the beginning. Adjusting to the fact that a marriage is irretrievably broken takes an ability to understand that living in hell with a partner is far worse than living happily alone. We wrote this book to assure people that all the negative and destructive emotions they feel during the separation, negotiations, and court appearances are normal. We were determined to help people understand that millions have gone through what they are going through. There is no denying that it is tough. We needed to assure our readers that with the right attitude and perspective, life will be better—with or without another husband, wife, or partner.

This book not only discusses and dissects the process—from an emotional and legal perspective—but also offers hope, based on actual cases, that there is life after divorce.

Another important lesson to learn is that life after divorce does not necessarily include finding another partner. Those who believe that happiness and self-fulfillment can only be achieved if a divorced person finds another spouse or partner are destined to be disappointed. The notion that finding another partner is the only solution after a marriage has ended also is a recipe for disaster. Healing after divorce takes time. But time does nothing for those who are determined not to heal. Healing comes from within, with the help of friends, family, and above all, a wise divorce lawyer who does not stoke the fury but rather calms the fear.

Beginning a new relationship can only work when people are able to transform the negative emotions connected with divorce into a positive outlook toward the future. Talking to hundreds of men and women revealed to us that one of the dreads people have is that their spouse will remarry before they do—as if that is proof that the husband or wife who remarries is blameless for the divorce. The reasons are steeped in cultural and societal judgments. From ancient times until recently, unmarried people are suspect because of bias against their lifestyle or because it is assumed that they are neurotic, misanthropic, and somehow not desirable enough to attract a mate. Gender inequality usually follows that kind of thinking. A divorced man is considered a commodity, a trophy at a dinner party. Divorced women are frequently ignored. Another inequity is that women are often seen as the biggest losers emotionally, while men are viewed as the biggest losers financially. Neither is true. There are no automatics.

Just suppose, as I stood in my kitchen that day in 1981, I had received a letter from court, announcing that a pending legal case with an employer, for instance, had been settled and I was free to find another job without the threat of suit for conflict of interest. Would I have felt the same overwhelming sense of sadness, loss, and grief that the legal case was finally over and I was free to move on? The answer is no.

After talking to so many people, and writing for so many months, the answer to my own question about why I had such an emotional reaction when I received my officially stamped divorce papers two years after the fact became apparent. Every situation is different. In my case, I had never mourned the demise of my marriage. It took a piece of paper—an official document—to make me finally face the fact that I was now, like millions of others, a divorced woman. I could no longer avoid accepting that I had miscalculated, used bad judgment, and caused pain to someone whose expectations had never been fulfilled.

When Raoul Felder and I began thinking about a title for this book, we wanted to convey the message that there could be "the Good Divorce." And the only way to make this true is to embrace a certain philosophy.

Each individual owns his or her life.

Finding happiness and fulfillment begins and ends by making the necessary changes in life to reach those goals.

Our hope is that this book gives people pragmatic and realistic advice about the process of divorce. Given the profoundly personal nature of many of the stories we use in our book, we hope readers will realize that their feelings and reactions are normal. Ending a marriage is never easy. Living in a miserable marriage is unbearable. Doing what it takes to terminate an untenable marriage successfully is worth the effort. There is nothing better than a good marriage. If a marriage is bad, there is nothing better than a good divorce. This book proves that life really does get better if people learn from their mistakes and take advantage of the opportunity for another chance.

PART ONE

DANCE
OF DEATH

1

STARTING OVER

If you want to know about love, ask a divorce lawyer.
—RAOUL FELDER

MARRIAGE IS NEVER AS BLISSFUL as people expect. Divorce is never as devastating as people imagine.

Divorce is a process that includes emotional, financial, and legal steps that ultimately end in the litigants being unmarried. Once the legalities are over, the hope is that the individuals involved will walk away, determined to begin a new and better life.

Whatever the motive to marry, it is always a conscious decision that happens from the inside out. Regardless of the reasons, marriage is an exercise in optimism. If divorce were viewed as an exercise in optimism as well, divorce lawyers would make less money. People would not waste years of their lives fighting over meaningless issues, which are remnants of a relationship that is already dead and only waiting to be buried.

The question divorce lawyers often ask potential clients who walk into their office is a variation of "To what do I owe the pleasure of your company today?" The answer would probably be that the client wants the attorney to represent them in a divorce. Perhaps a more precise question posed by lawyers should be "Why are you here today and not five years ago or six months ago or twenty years ago or last week?"

Most of the time, people focus on a mindless event that brought them to the point to begin divorce proceedings. They might respond that they have reached the end of their tethers. Many people would say the same thing: "Not one day more" or "I just couldn't take it any longer." Curiously, when asked to describe the "it" they are referring to, things become jumbled into disjointed memories, confusion, and an inability to pinpoint time.

Unless there has been a volcanic act of violence, when people finally decide to end a marriage, it is always a calculated act usually preceded by years of unhappiness, a change of circumstance, an emotional upheaval, or a fissure that becomes a canyon of regret.

Whatever the circumstances, fantasizing about a divorce will not result in freedom.

Consulting a lawyer about divorce does not mean the marriage is over.

Fighting, slandering, and whining during divorce negotiations only make it more difficult to walk away from the legal entanglements of marriage without unnecessary trauma.

In many cases, all the reasons why people marry are usually the same reasons people dread the idea of divorce. Whatever the age or gender, some will fall back on religious teachings that it is far better to sacrifice one's own happiness in order to save the "sacred" institution of marriage. Others cite children as the reason for marrying and staying together. Many will claim that money was the motivation to marry and the reluctance to divorce is because finances are too complicated and intermingled to sort out a viable solution so that both could keep the same standard of living. Some marry and remain in a bad marriage because of habit. The majority, however, marry out of fear and avoid divorce out of fear—fear of living and dying alone. The truth is that there are far worse fates than being young and single or old and alone. Young or old and married to an incompatible or violent partner is a guarantee that life will never be better. Sacrificing for the sake of children usually means that offspring suffer the same or similar anxiety living in a home that has an absence of love, respect, and joy. Growing old with a partner where life is suffused with resentment, indifference, and a lack of respect and caring is a life wasted. Living in a marriage where love, respect, friendship, and compatibility are gone is a life without hope. Regardless of the reasons, many believe that nothing is perfect and living with someone whose flaws they know is more comfortable than trading the known for the unknown with someone new.

There is nothing more fulfilling than a good marriage. There is nothing more debilitating than a bad marriage. Divorce is a wrenching experience for everyone, whether you are the one leaving or the one being left. The choice, however, between a bad marriage and a good divorce would seem to be apparent. Obviously, for many who dread the idea of breaking up a home, or those who actually terminate a marriage, there is often regret, bitterness, and rage. If people really thought about the goal line, after the messy negotiations and arguments are over, they would realize that divorce gives people a fresh start to lead better lives. Approaching divorce as an adventure means viewing a bad marriage as a reparable mistake. One thing is certain: It takes courage, self-examination, confronting reality, and a sense of optimism to embark upon a process that will forever change your life and the lives of your children and spouse.

There are no perfect circumstances for embarking upon the process of divorce. Even if one or both litigants want the divorce, and no paramours are involved, and there are millions of dollars available to support two households in the same style as when there was one, people still suffer excruciating pain when they break up. That doesn't mean that a good divorce lawyer or mediator who knows the law, understands a bit about psychology, and who is out for the best interests of the client does not make a positive difference when navigating the labyrinth of the judicial system. The problem about divorce is that it is never only a matter of breaking a legal contract or dividing up assets, or even adjusting to life without a familiar partner. It involves so many other emotions that not even a competent matrimonial lawyer with years of experience is able to convince clients that the anguish they feel is normal and only one part of the process. Matrimonial lawyers are also often unable to persuade their clients that their trauma, which renders them paralyzed, angry, or depressed, will disappear with time. Almost all the predictable irrational and vengeful reactions from litigants have little to do with the bureaucracy of the legal system, but rather are because people are consumed with their own failure, sense of rejection, and the harsh reality that life as they know it will forever change. It is difficult to assure those going through divorce that fault and self-loathing are useless emotions that only prolong the agony. It is often complicated to explain to people that there isn't anyone, including a professional, who can *force* a man or a woman who has been left, or worse, left for another, to understand that divorce is the best alternative to beginning a new life. Nor can anyone, including a professional, force someone to love another. There isn't anyone, regardless of how smart or skilled, who can compel another human being who faces financial ruin, inaccessibility to children, the loss of a home, routine, and the habit of waking up every morning with the same person, to comprehend that divorce is the only chance to start again. Those realizations must come from within the individual involved in the divorce. Only the individual himself or herself has the power to heal and take control of his or her life, with or without the help of a lawyer, therapist, friends, or family.

There are many obstacles on the way to recovery. Usually, when love dies, it is not a mutual happening where both parties wake up one morning and decide they don't love each other anymore. The tragedy is that more often than not, one partner decides the marriage is over, for myriad reasons that begin and end with a loss of love, respect, caring, and a desire to work things out to keep the union and the home intact.

Another impediment is that people are unable to approach divorce as merely a matter of breaking a legal contract. Though divorce *is* a broken contract, covered under the law, monitored and adjudicated by attorneys and judges, it is one that is based on the most primal emotions, such as love, pride, ego, self-respect, and countless other feelings that color the reactions of the litigants, preventing them from making productive decisions.

The reality is that almost everybody knows about contracts, as they are made and broken every day. Most people have been involved in some kind of contract or employment agreement, partnership arrangement, or purchase understanding. Even when a dog is bought from a breeder, there is a contract of sorts governed by the American Kennel Corporation that either allows or forbids the owners to breed the dog. There is a modest price to register the dog with the promise of spaying the animal, or a higher price if the dog's thoroughbred credentials will be used to reproduce puppies. Opening up a charge account at a local cleaners or department store, or having a credit card, involves a contract where the cardholder signs an agreement that he or she will be responsible for all bills. Most people understand that if a contract is broken without the agreement of the other party, there is some kind of penalty and ultimately a settlement for loss of income or services rendered. If an agreement is not reached, there are legal consequences.

Most people don't become rabid when they break an employment contract or a lease, or any other legal accord. If a contract could never be broken, would anyone in their right mind ever sign one? What would happen if the contract of marriage could never be broken? Think about being forced to stay married to someone who was abusive, physically or emotionally, who shirked all responsibility and offered nothing in the relationship except to argue, ignore, or criticize. Think about living in a house where the atmosphere was constantly tense, hostile, unfriendly, and detrimental to the emotional well-being of the children. Obviously, if there were no divorce, people would be far more reluctant to marry. Common sense, therefore, would dictate that everyone who marries is aware that if the marriage doesn't work out, there are legal ways to terminate the relationship.

Other than those who are not marrying for the first time or who are older and wiser, most people refuse to admit that the possibility of divorce entered their minds at the time they recited their marriage vows. But just as people sign other contracts knowing they can always break them, it would seem that an awareness of the possibility of divorce at the time of marriage is a normal, albeit unpleasant or fleeting, thought. Not that people marry with the idea that "this is the first step to divorce." According to many divorce lawyers, people who are at the stage where they are actually considering divorce will admit that they fantasized about it for years before they finally had the nerve to consult a matrimonial attorney.

Though the act of marriage between two consenting individuals is highly personal, when it ends, it is an act ultimately controlled by laws. Couples in the throes of divorce find they are not only facing the death of love but also a loss of control over how they choose to end the union. Suddenly, often for the first time in their lives, courts, lawyers, and judges are in charge of their financial and emotional future, as well as those of their children. Acting out of revenge or the need to punish their spouse guarantees lifelong repercussions. Even those who have had experience in the divorce arena or have had contact with lawyers suddenly realize how unprepared they are to recount their entire lives to a total stranger. As they become increasingly involved in a bitter fray, it is even more shocking to learn that their spouses have also revealed intimate details about their habits, sexual preferences, financial practices, or other indulgences, and idiosyncrasies that they practiced in the privacy of what was once the marital home.

During the process of divorce, in addition to the legalities, people often leave a trail of misery in their wake—children, friends, and colleagues who will have definite reactions and judgments. The trick to having a good divorce is to accept the situation as irrevocable, sort out the true friends who lend support, ignore those who decide to judge you harshly, and, with the help of those loyal friends, family, a competent lawyer, and perhaps therapy, to work toward turning an ugly situation into a happy ending.

Taking steps to end a marriage is one of the most difficult decisions anyone can make. All the negative and destructive emotions people feel during the separation, negotiations, and court appearances are normal. Understanding these emotions at the beginning allows people to move beyond them to more rational thinking as the process evolves. Finding happiness and contentment after divorce is also a process. It is important that people understand that millions have gone through what they are going through and it is tough going. With the right attitude and perspective, even if that means cutting off from those who judge negatively or those who have sided with the enemy, it is not only possible but probable that life will be better—with or without another husband, wife, or partner.

When people choose the magic date to begin the dance of death, it is always premeditated. Though people often claim they were shocked to learn their spouse wanted a divorce, most had slipped into a routine where fighting, lack of communication, living separate lives, estrangement, and an absence of sexual relations became the normal components of their marriages. If they had reflected on their lives, most would realize that the surprise or shock they felt when they found themselves in a lawyer's office was only that they were forced to face the reality—that their marriages had been a convenience at best, a sham at worst.

There is accidental birth.

There is accidental death.

There is never accidental divorce.

When someone enters a lawyer's office with the intention of ending a marriage, it usually means that he or she has stopped dancing around problems and dissatisfactions, boredom, frustration, hatred, resentment, and despair and has made a conscious decision to take aim and begin the procedure that will kill the relationship. The moment of truth in any marriage is in some ways like the moment when the matador in the bull-ring stops his dance, ceases taunting and menacing the bull, and takes his sword to go in for the kill. For the matador, it is the passion for the sport and the adulation of the crowd that drives him to a flawless finish. Anything less than perfection and the matador is injured, killed, or humiliated. But unlike the moment of truth in a bullring, there is never a swift, clean kill to break up a home.

Everyone is curious about the travails of others. When celebrities divorce, details of the breakup are far more newsworthy than their marriages were. Even when noncelebrities divorce, the particulars about the process are a source of local and family gossip. Witnessing the unfolding of a divorce from the safety of an intact marriage is much like slowing down to gape at the gory remnants of a car accident. Grateful they are not the ones lying on the road, people still know, somewhere in the backs of their minds, that they are neither immune to nor exempt from becoming victims and ultimately statistics. Just as road accidents don't always serve as cautionary examples of the consequences of speeding or drunk driving, however, the ugly and messy divorces of friends, family, or celebrities rarely give people an incentive to rein in their emotions so their divorces remain civilized and clean.

Statistics gathered in 2008 by the American Bar Association show that one out of two marriages ends in divorce. According to those figures, it is safe to say that marriage is a failing institution. If you add the married couples who live apart, for which there are no reliable statistics, those battling it out in divorce court who have not yet become statistics, litigants who opt for a quick divorce in the Dominican Republic or Haiti, or couples who simply live together in misery for economic, religious, or social reasons, the marriage failure rate must be far in excess of 50 percent. Yet marriage endures. People recite their vows every day. To quote the song made popular by Frank Sinatra, "love and marriage go together like a horse and carriage . . . you can't have one without the other." But then again, horses and carriages are no longer in style.

Not believing in marriage is acceptable. Not believing in love is tantamount to not believing in the Easter Bunny. Love is life. Marriage is an institution. Some people, however, question the wisdom of living their lives in an institution. Yet for the majority of people throughout the world, the culmination of love, falling in love, being in love, is marriage.

There are many who claim that when they fell in love they were thinking with their hearts (or other portions of their anatomy) rather than their heads. They talk about love at first sight, having been overtaken by emotions that provoked myriad sentiments, how lust and attraction overcame them and they simply succumbed to those feelings. Others claim that their decision to marry was not governed by hormones or sentiments. Those people insist that they entered into marriage after much thought and decision, based on loneliness, habit, financial security, compatibility, procreation, the formation of a family unit, the education and nurturing of children, the legitimization of sexual relations, a public declaration of love, or the desire to obtain citizenship or tax benefits.

All kinds of people marry and all kinds of people marry for different reasons.

Christie Brinkley is the supermodel who was married to Billy Joel. Most recently, she was the focus of an ugly divorce from Peter Cook. Her middle husband was Richard Taubman, whom she married on December 22, 1994, in Telluride, Colorado. Their marriage ceremony was near where, according to press reports, they were both in a helicopter crash in March of that same year. For Brinkley and Taubman, their marriage was based on having survived what could have been a deadly accident. Taubman proposed while Brinkley was still married to Billy Joel. Brinkley and Taubman married, had a son, and less than a year into the marriage, they divorced. According to press reports, in the end, Brinkley was obliged to pay Taubman $2 million as a "parting gift." When their divorce was final, both Brinkley and Taubman admitted, in their own words, that their marriage had been an impulsive act motivated by a "celebration of life."

Elizabeth Taylor's last marriage, to a construction worker named Larry Fortensky, was based on their mutual addictions. The media explained that they had met at the Betty Ford Clinic in Palm Springs, where both were determined to expiate their respective demons. It was Taylor's second stay at the clinic, where she had been treated for addiction to prescription drugs. Fortensky had been ordered there by the court after a conviction for drunk driving. Their worlds spun at different corners of the universe. Taylor was an Oscar-winning actress and by virtue of her seven previous marriages (she married Richard Burton twice) owned some of the world's most famous diamonds. Fortensky, as Taylor liked to describe him, was an employee of a "large engine equipment company."

Despite the chasm that separated their emotional, cultural, and intellectual sensibilities, Taylor proclaimed that this was the real thing and "this time was forever." If Fortensky was swept away by the wealth and glamour or had motives that were less than pure, it did not impact on Taylor's decision to walk down the aisle yet again. Whatever anyone says about Taylor, when it comes to marriage, she is an optimist.

Famous, infamous, ordinary, rich, or poor, people who marry can be divided into three categories: optimists, pessimists, and pragmatists.

Those who are optimists believe that love is the most fundamental and crucial aspect of a marriage. For them, love is the glue that will keep them together forever as they share joys and weather adversity. They assume that comfort, convention, and routine will ward off the desire to forge new intellectual or sexual frontiers, or quell dreams of what could have been. To the optimist, marriage is an act of faith. Divorce is an unthinkable and terrifying alternative.

Pessimists believe that love is ephemeral and marriage is an unnatural state that comprises but one stage of life. There is birth, childhood, adolescence, adulthood, career, and the vow to share a life, procreate, retire, and die. To the pessimist, love is an unrealistic emotion. Divorce is a probability. If and when divorce becomes a reality, it creates an irrational fear of accelerating the life process toward certain loneliness and death.

Pragmatists understand that love must be nurtured to make the relationship solid and enduring. They understand that expectations about love are often exaggerated and though passion may wane, with care, devotion, and friendship, the bond of marriage can remain unbroken. The pragmatist knows that love takes effort and marriage means constant work, tooling and retooling the various components of a relationship. To the pragmatist, marriage does not guarantee "happily ever after." If divorce happens, it is tantamount to a broken contract that nonetheless often produces fear of the unknown.

When optimists are confronted with divorce, they often wallow in self-pity. Everything they believed in has been proven wrong, as some had never considered the possibility of facing life unmarried. Fear turns to grief and becomes rage at themselves and ultimately at their partner for destroying their sense of order.

When pessimists are in the throes of divorce, there is a sense of relief that they are finally living their own self-fulfilling prophecy of failure.

Despite any psychological preparation for an eventual collapse of the union, they still experience anger at themselves for going against their own instincts, which turns to rage at their partner for his or her complicity in the failure.

When pragmatists meet with a matrimonial attorney to terminate a marriage, they fool themselves into thinking that their emotional clarity has rendered them blameless. As the process unwinds with all its complications and land mines, confidence turns into vengeance, which results in blame, which becomes fear that their judgment could be seriously flawed in every other area of their lives.

Whether faced by an optimist, pessimist, or pragmatist, the demise of a marriage begins with the breakdown of all rational communication, leading to arguments, recriminations, sometimes even violence, until the final death blow when one or the other partner walks into a lawyer's office to begin divorce proceedings.

Despite the pain and acrimony that usually accompanies divorce, slugging it out in court in a rancorous battle is not only unnecessarily humiliating, but inordinately costly. Given the statistics of divorce and the fact that the majority *are* hostile, it would seem that regardless of why people married, when they divorce it is often a fight to the death.

The power, success, and financial rewards that divorce lawyers enjoy come about because the majority of people complicate what is already a complex course of action—the dissolution of a legal union.

The truth is that many of those embroiled in divorce can barely remember why they married in the first place, in the same way they are incapable of answering the question that might be posed by a matrimonial attorney: "Why do you want a divorce now and not six months ago or five or twenty years ago?" Most people refuse to confront the dynamic of their relationships. They are often unwilling to admit, even to themselves, that divorce was inevitable given that they had been living empty lives.

Extricating oneself from a dying or dead relationship should produce a sense of relief that divorce has the potential to be a life-affirming experience rather than proof of a failure. Yet the mystery remains why love and marriage, despite the statistics of failure, remain a celebration, while divorce often ends with social ostracism, criticism, misery, and alienation from friends and family.

Divorce is liberating. Liberation affords people choices. To have a positive divorce, people must learn how to use their impending freedom wisely. If the inevitable happens and people find themselves as defendants or plaintiffs in divorce cases, the first step is to take control of their lives. Taking control means thinking ahead, keeping the end goal in sight, and making rational decisions that are not colored by self-pity, vengeance, or spite.

Back to the original question a lawyer will ask a potential client during that first encounter. "Why are you here today and not five years ago or six months ago or twenty years ago or last week?" As explained, most people can't answer that question. Before the process of divorce goes any further, people should understand when, rather than why, the time has come to consider ending the marriage. Perhaps even more important would be to identify what prospective brides and grooms expected out of marriage.

2

What Men and Women Expect Out of Marriage

Men and women certainly want admiration and
respect, but their deepest desire is to be loved.
                                        —Tony Bennett

BEFORE DIVORCE BECOMES AN OPTION or an alternative, and inequity becomes a glaring aspect of the legal entanglements leading up to
separation, negotiations, and a final decree, it might be beneficial to understand what men and women expect out of marriage. Even more important
would be to figure out how disappointment or hope led to a breakdown of
dialogue and ultimately to divorce. Though these topics are highly individual, there are certain differences between men and women and their
respective expectations of marriage.

Marriage is like the child's game of "hit the crack." The two partici-
pants stand a sidewalk square away from each other. The object is to
bounce a ball and hit the crack. Once the ball finds its mark, one never
knows which way it's going to bounce. When two people with different
histories and memories vow to live together as man and wife, sharing
decisions, problems, joys, and failures, it is impossible to predict the reaction or action of either husband or wife after a problem is solved, a decision is made, or a goal is achieved.

Sharing a life with another human being is complicated. First-time
couples rarely contemplate the next twenty or thirty years of day-in-and-

day-out living, loving, fighting, making up, weathering good and bad times, tragedies, and celebrations. Those who are venturing into marriage for the first time don't always consider that marriage is not just about two people setting up a life together. Fears, adjustments, and conflicting emotions often result because of myriad outside influences and individuals that can destroy the union. When a couple gets into bed, there are at least four other people present—each set of parents as well as that intangible and elusive enemy that is memory. How many people have ended up in a lawyer's office complaining about in-laws, former lovers and girlfriends, ex-spouses, stepchildren, and jealousy over friends who are too much a part of the couple's life? Too many to count!

Even the veterans of marriage who should be more aware of the possible land mines than those marrying for the first time can't predict problems that might cause a rupture. Experience does not necessarily mean tolerance. The veterans might say "Life is too short" or "Who needs this?" or "I've suffered through one or two bad marriages. Why put myself through a third time of misery?"

The reality is that more than half of all marriages never reach that stage when two people become so intertwined that they can accept that excitement is replaced by comfort, anticipation becomes trust, and enthusiasm settles into pride.

Love entails risk and marriage guarantees strife. Unconditional love does not automatically happen over the long term of a marriage. To keep love alive and a marriage intact and thriving, agreements, conditions, tolerance, and understanding are the keys to avoid ending up in divorce court.

Ideally, the way it's supposed to work is that two people who have made a decision to marry make an investment in each other for the long term. But with new medical advances that prolong life, the notion of "till death do us part" can be a nightmare scenario, or at best, far too long.

What people believe they want in the beginning and what is important to them—dreams, hopes, expectations—are usually irrelevant as the years pass. Still, from a purely statistical point of view, to hear what men and women want and expect out of a spouse and marriage is interesting, if only because it shows how gender defines the internal hardwiring of each individual.

Based on an online survey of one hundred men and one hundred women who were questioned about marriage, there was a big difference in the responses of both men and women based on age. For example, twenty percent of one hundred men ranging in age from twenty-one to thirty-five believe that women do not expect their husbands to provide for them financially. Fifty-seven percent of men between the ages of forty and seventy-five believe that women want them to take charge, be aggressive, and function as patriarchs when it comes to having the last word on family decisions. Obviously, younger men responded far differently.

The typical groom today is twenty-seven years old, compared to 1960 when he was twenty-three. Younger men who marry today are far more aware of what today's women want in a spouse than the last generation of men. In fact, today's prospective grooms are seeking women who are the complete opposite from their mothers and are citing traits in a wife that are diametrically opposed to what their fathers looked for.

Since the turn of the twenty-first century, perhaps because of the unstable economy or the fear of random terrorist attacks, men are looking for women who are more nurturing as well as more independent. According to a Gallup Poll commissioned by the National Marriage Project, 94 percent of men between the ages of twenty and thirty want to marry someone who could fulfill their emotional needs. These men explained that they wanted a "psychological companion," a partner who shared their aspirations and was "spiritually" compatible. One of the men interviewed in our online questionnaire was especially specific.

"I don't need a wife who changes diapers or does dishes. I can pay someone to do that. I want a soul mate. Times are tough. It's hard enough to make a living and expect my wife to do battle in the workplace. The pleasure comes from marrying an equal who can share my problems as I can share hers, as well as celebrate our successes."

In 1939, a Gallup Poll was taken where men were asked if they would allow their wives to work, and 63 percent answered in the negative. Even as recently as 1977, according to a General Social Survey at the University of Chicago's National Opinion Research Center, nearly 70 percent of men still believed that their wives should stay at home and care for the children.

According to a Gallup Poll taken in 2002 of teenage boys, 94 percent responded that they planned to marry one day and to have children. Those numbers are up by 10 percent from 1977. Beyond that, men today are not only marrying later than they did in 1960, when the average age of a bridegroom was twenty-three. In that same Gallup Poll, young men between the ages of twenty and twenty-four said they wanted women who were financially independent, employed, and who had their own interests, hobbies, and friends.

Of those one hundred men interviewed about what they wanted in a spouse, 64 percent had been married before. More than half of these maintained they wanted a younger woman, a wife who was sexually experienced, and who made them "proud." The other half of the previously married men said they wanted a woman who had compatible tastes, could be a distant but friendly stepmother, and who had the same goals and aspirations for their "golden years."

Of those men questioned, almost 76 percent claimed that while they hoped their wives would be "understanding friends," they also stated that their need for friendship and intimacy could be satisfied by male friends and other family members. When asked to be specific, 90 percent reiterated that they expected their wives not only to be caregivers but also guaranteed sexual partners. Forty percent of those men who were between the ages of twenty and forty stated that marriage assured the paternity of their children, and that fidelity was not as big an issue with men as with women. When questioned on the meaning of that response, that same percentage explained that cheating for a man was virtually "meaningless," while if a woman was unfaithful, that was far more serious a threat to the marriage.

Women who were questioned on the online survey focused more on the romantic and emotional aspects of marriage. Approximately 84 percent defined the traits that made a good partner and lifelong companion as being sensitive and loving, offering compliments, being aware of how hard their wives worked both at home with the children and at outside jobs, and how much respect, fidelity, and attention their husbands gave them. Financial support, aggression found in the typical alpha male, taking charge, and functioning as the patriarch were not attributes that were high on the list of women's priorities for a husband. Also, when questioned on the online survey, 92 percent of women expected their husbands to function as their "best friends." Of the one hundred women questioned, 76 percent believed their marriages would last.

By nature, women are far more optimistic than men about marriage.

Those women who were optimistic about their marriages also believed that if "their husbands loved them enough to marry them, they would not want to break up the home." They also felt that if their husbands strayed, they would return, especially if there were children. Those same women also believed that men "ease" into monogamy and ultimately "abide by moral or religious conventions." Women between the ages of forty and sixty felt that if they kept themselves in "good physical condition," and were "intellectually up to date," their husbands would not run off with a younger woman. They also maintained that after forty, their husbands were more interested in making money than having "acrobatic sexual relations."

It is always difficult to take statistics and generalize what men and women want out of marriage. People pick their spouses for a variety of reasons, and when questioned about what they want in a wife or husband, they will invariably respond based on the characteristics and assets their mates actually have.

Everyone is a package. Define the package and then compare it to other packages and that is how most people decide whom they want to marry or with whom they want to cohabit.

British prime minister Benjamin Disraeli's wife said about him, "Dissy married me for the money but if he had it to do all over again, he'd do it for me."

Whatever the bond that brings two people together—and it is different for every couple—it either cements the marriage or tears it apart.

More recently, the young wife of a famous and infirmed industrialist/public figure filed for divorce. When she had married her husband, who was thirty years her senior, he was already physically impaired. After several years, he became mentally incompetent. She filed for divorce. During negotiations, her husband's attorneys accused her of marrying him for money. She demanded an apology. As it happened, her lawyer was one of the coauthors of this book. He adhered to her wishes and asked the adversary lawyers to apologize to his client. They refused. When he told her there would be no apology forthcoming, he also offered his opinion.

"Of course she had married her husband for money, but she had chosen him and he had chosen her because of a total package of what each offered the other—money and prestige in exchange for youth and beauty. It could have been anyone. Thousands of beautiful young women would have been delighted to marry the older infirmed public figure and probably many old and sick men would have been grateful to have a beautiful young wife. But each chose the other because of motives that went beyond the obvious."

Divorcing for reasons that are not obvious can be as frequent as marrying for unobvious reasons. Terrianne is attractive, articulate, and ambitious. Though she only had one year of college, her intention was to finish and train for a career in nursing. Terrianne grew up in a troubled home in a small town near Milwaukee. All through high school she dated the same boy, a strapping and popular football player who was "everything I wanted in a boyfriend." When the pair graduated high school, Terrianne enrolled in a community college while her boyfriend, Emil, went to work, learning to repair engines in his father's garage. When Terrianne ran out of money to continue college, and after her mother married for the third time and informed her there was no room in the house for her, she, along with her boyfriend, moved to Chicago. Once there, the couple settled into a run-down studio apartment and Terrianne managed to save enough money to go to school to learn how to be a bartender. After she got her license and found a job at a small pub on the outskirts of Chicago, she enrolled in another community college. Her boyfriend found a job at a local garage. Their relationship continued for two years. On Terrianne's twenty-second birthday, her boyfriend began putting pressure on her to marry.

"I didn't want to get married," she explains. "I had a goal. I wanted to finish college and go to nursing school. It wasn't that I didn't love him but marriage was just not part of my plan. I had seen it go bad too many times with my mother and father, who each married three times after they divorced. I knew the key to my success was independence."

Alone in a strange city, working and going to school, Terrianne's only security and frame of reference was her boyfriend. "He wasn't just a boyfriend," she continues. "He was someone who knew me when . . ."

After a while, Emil threatened to leave her if she didn't agree to marry him. They married and for another year, their routine continued. Several weeks after their first anniversary, Emil came home and confessed that he had been unfaithful.

"There was this girl who lived in our building. She was ugly and stupid and had no teeth. That wasn't the point, I guess," Terrianne explains.

"But my boyfriend chose her to cheat on me. And then he came home and told me because he couldn't stand keeping his own dirty secret."

Predictably, she took him back. There was no doubt, however, that their marriage was doomed, at least in Terrianne's mind. In the end, after another year, she threw him out and continued on with her work, school, and life goals.

There is wisdom in her story, as well as lessons to be learned. One of the lessons is that marrying young when one or the other has little or no experience sets up a scenario where the husband or wife can lament his or her lack of sexual experience and do something to rectify that loss. The wisdom in Terrianne's story is that though women can and often do suffer more after a divorce, they are by far more able to take care of themselves and their children when they decide to leave or are left. Coming from the mouth of a twenty-three-year-old, Terrianne's philosophy is as sophisticated and knowledgeable as that of any trained therapist:

"Women will pick up and leave a guy whether or not they've got another man waiting in the wings. Men won't usually do that. They need someone to take care of them. The problem is that single women are not such sought-after commodities as single men. I remember how women chased after my father after he divorced my mother. I also remember how women were afraid to invite my mother to dinner because she was divorced. That's the bummer for women. But I'd rather be a woman than a man—at least I know I can be alone and not be lonely."

Since statistics demonstrate that at least 50 percent of all marriages end in divorce, it is obvious that divorce is part of the process of marriage in more than half the legal unions. Yet people are less afraid of marrying than they are of divorcing.

If people could somehow use whatever means they could afford or had at their disposal to overcome the fear of the unknown when it comes to divorce, they would find themselves halfway on the road to recovery. They would also view ending an unhappy marriage as a positive step. The reality is that people are either paralyzed, so they waste years of their lives living in misery, or they take the step to separate and end up experiencing trauma, fear, regret, guilt, or anger. Indecision accounts for many of those negative emotions.

One of the initial dilemmas when contemplating divorce is to know when hope is gone. The law is complicated within itself. To uncomplicate the process, people should perhaps look inward to understand the balance of good and bad in their relationships. There are no set rules, as everyone has different values, standards, expectations, and desires. There is, however, certain behavior that should signal the end. Ultimately, the decision is highly individual. What is universal, however, is realizing that certain transgressions rank high on the scale of knowing with absolute certainty that it is time to call it quits.

3

Knowing When to Call It Quits

Some of us think holding on makes us strong; but sometimes it is letting go.

—Hermann Hesse

EVERY MARRIAGE HAS PROBLEMS. Every husband and wife experience frustrations concerning habits, behavior, or character traits that annoy or even enrage them.

Marital disputes, when they are rational, can be productive. Often an argument, if it is fair and balanced, brings to the surface issues that can and should be resolved. If the words used are not incendiary or insulting, arguments should not normally escalate to the point where there is emotional or physical abuse. If things escalate and every disagreement becomes a barrage of insults, the relationship is in danger. Repeated attacks on a spouse's intelligence, looks, character, dreams, desires, or sexual prowess fall under that heading of emotional abuse and, depending on the self-control of the person abused, can lead to divorce.

The question that many people ask themselves or ask therapists, marriage counselors, priests, ministers, rabbis, or lawyers, is how to know when there is an absence of hope and it is time to call it quits. We have devised a scale that carries with it a number for each transgression and fault committed by one or the other spouse. To simplify, we have used a technique in which each letter in the word *divorce* carries with it a specific number that would be assigned to a specific fault and pattern of behavior. The total number of the value of each letter in the word *divorce* is twenty-four. If and when each spouse makes a list of conduct and actions that he or she deems unacceptable or dangerous and that number reaches or approaches twenty-four, perhaps it is time for the couple to consider that there is an irretrievable breakdown of the union.

Based on the numeric values that numerologists assign to every letter in the English alphabet, each letter in the word *divorce* has the following numeric value: D is four, I is one, V is six, O is seven, R is two, C is three, and E is five. While the calculation is simple enough, every individual is different. Some will put higher numbers on transgressions or faults that others might consider benign or inconsequential. For example, during a survey administered by the authors to one hundred men and women, all were asked to list what they considered to be the most egregious to the most tolerable or inoffensive behavior. Of the women between the ages of twenty and sixty who were polled, 100 percent indicated that domestic violence carried a score of twenty-four, while 35 percent said that infidelity would lead to divorce only if it was habitual. Forty-five percent said that infidelity, even if discovered only once, did not necessarily mean their spouse had strayed only once. One woman said, "Once caught could be one hundred times not caught." What the authors knew from the survey was that some women were merely hypothesizing, while others had actually experienced the betrayal.

Not surprisingly, depending on the socioeconomic level of the women interviewed, there was almost an even split between those who were rich, not only in income but also in assets, when it came to their reactions about their spouse's adultery. Almost half claimed they would "take their husbands to the cleaners," while the other half said they would close their eyes and "up their spending habits." Those who were poor to middle income were more inclined to confront their husbands. More than half of these said that they would "throw him out of the house, but would take him back if he promised not to do it again." One woman put it like this: "All men cheat but I'll be damned if I'm going to give in so some other woman can play stepmother to our children." Another woman said, "I'd confront the bitch. I'd blame her before I'd give up my life."

Of the men between the ages of twenty to sixty questioned, 95 percent responded that "an unfaithful wife" carried a score of twenty-two, while 5 percent said that infidelity carried a score of twenty-four.

Depending on the standards and levels of tolerance of an individual as to what he or she expects in a partner, the divorce scale differs drastically. There are some men and women who cannot abide a spouse who is overweight, a disinterested sex partner, one who is slovenly, a bad housekeeper, a distant parent, or a spouse who is habitually unemployed. Drug abuse, alcoholism, harassment, and public humiliation were all high on the "unacceptable" list of those men and women interviewed. Women gave alcoholism, drug abuse, and habitual unemployment the highest scores— between sixteen and twenty-four. Interestingly, women were far more tolerant of a spouse who was a distant or absent parent, as well as a husband who was overweight and slovenly. Men rated public humiliation, being overweight, and disinterest in the children between fifteen and twenty—much higher than women. The most minor faults from both female and male perspectives were bad housekeeping habits, sloppiness (men who drop their clothes throughout the house or don't help with the dishes), and a less than exciting sexual partner.

Of those interviews conducted of one hundred men and women who represented a cross section of society—socially, economically, and culturally— some were in the process of divorce, others were already divorced, and still others were married and contemplating divorce.

Notwithstanding people's different levels of tolerance, the authors believe that domestic violence carries with it an automatic score of twenty-four, as does inflicting harm or abuse on children.

Other transgressions, only in the opinion of the authors, carry with them the following numbers:

Infidelity carries with it a score between five and fifteen. That is highly subjective as there are some couples who have an understanding or arrangement that monogamy is not a prerequisite for devotion, respect, and love.

Not caring about personal appearance might be a ten, unless there are medical issues that cause someone to gain weight or be unable to lose weight. In those cases, the number might be reduced to zero. Not bothering to wash or wear clean clothes, however, falls into another category that hovers around nine. Partners who have no self-control or discipline to make an effort to keep themselves in reasonably good condition are not mindful of their responsibility to stay healthy and attractive for their spouse and children.

Bad housekeeping habits are five on the scale, considered to be minor transgressions, especially if both husband and wife work. There are exceptions. Even if both partners work, there should be a discussion about organization and responsibility to share chores. Children, if they are old enough, should be included in talks concerning division of household jobs.

The majority of those polled, both men and women (78 percent), stated that indifferent parenting skills is a fifteen, even if husband and wife both work. There were exceptions. The key is communications. In those cases where working parents discuss and agree as to how they will share the responsibility of raising their children, there are few recriminations and strife. Of those polled, 85 percent of women who did not work outside the home suggested that their husbands should be put on a weekend schedule where they would be responsible for the children. Of those women who worked away from the home, 65 percent stated that a prearranged schedule of shared child care was fair. Of the men polled, 80 percent stated that even if both parents worked, the one who earned less money should have more child-care responsibility. Working wives and mothers disagreed and claimed that regardless of who earned more, if both parents had jobs outside the home, the child care should be shared equally.

In all cases, whether both parents worked and regardless of which parent earned more money, 95 percent agreed that without discussion and agreement concerning child-rearing and other household responsibility, there was resentment. Accusations of disproportionate responsibility led to fighting.

Alcoholism and drug abuse are each an automatic twenty-two, if the addicted partner refuses to seek help. If he or she is willing to be treated and makes an effort, alcoholism and drug abuse should be considered a disease and the score falls to zero.

In the case of habitual unemployment, especially with the current economy and downsizing and forced retirement, the score is five. The score jumps to twenty, however, if either spouse makes no effort to find work, or if he or she refuses to take work that is part-time or below their level of training. Both husband and wife must make every effort to contribute financially to maintaining the household. For the very rich, if one or the other partner does not work with the agreement and sanction of his or her spouse, the score is also zero. If husband or wife prevents the other from working, the score jumps again to fifteen. In that situation, both parties are culpable—he or she that restricts the professional career of the other, and he or she who goes along with that kind of unilateral decision-making.

Overspending carries a ten as it points to a lack of responsibility as well as deceit. Marriage is a partnership. If a budget is put into place and one or the other does not stick to it, it is tantamount to a betrayal or breaking a promise. Husband and wife should consider that they are "in this thing together" for the good of their relationship, their futures, and the futures of their children.

Irresponsibility covers a wide range of transgressions. If the irresponsibility involves child care, finances, lack of loyalty, or lying, the score is twenty-four. If irresponsibility is due to forgetfulness, disorganization, or simply a professional overload, the score drops to five.

Public humiliation is an automatic twenty. There is no excuse for humiliating husband or wife in public or in front of friends and family. Criticism, correction, and airing grievances should only happen in private.

Possessiveness or jealousy counts for ten. Constant accusations or denying a spouse permission to see friends and family often fall under the heading of emotional abuse, which frequently becomes physical abuse, both of which are an automatic twenty-four. There are some women who were interviewed who maintained that a husband's jealousy or possessiveness is a sign of his love. The excuse men who batter their wives often give is "If I didn't love you, I wouldn't bother to correct you or get angry." Or, "I only hit you because I love you so much that it drives me crazy when you talk to anyone else." These reasons are not acceptable. The most prevalent obstacle to terminating abusive relationships comes from the women themselves. It takes a lot of courage to admit privately, or to others, that they are indeed the victim of domestic violence. It is for this reason that many women, approximately 80 percent who report their spouses for domestic abuse, fail to press charges when the time comes to appear in court. Even if the marriage can be saved with appropriate therapy for both partners, pressing charges or seeking safe shelter is the first step.

Boredom is an emotion rather than a transgression and ranks only at number three. The irony about boredom is that it is often the reason people give for breaking up a marriage. Obviously, if either husband or wife makes no effort to interest the other or take an interest in the other's hobbies, work, or future plans, their problem is bigger than the monotony and tedium of a day-in, day-out relationship where nothing changes and there is little to look forward to or there is a lack of stimulation between the couple. Perhaps a better term on the scale rather than boredom would be lack of effort to help the relationship survive, which carries with it an eight.

Emotional abuse or repeated attacks on a spouse's intelligence, looks, character, dreams, desires, or sexual prowess are worth twenty-three points. If the relationship becomes a constant barrage of insults where any one of the above traits or characteristics dissatisfies either partner enough to provoke vicious slurs, the marriage is irreparable without help. That help could be religious, spiritual, or psychological, but in all cases, it is urgently needed to try to save the union.

REGARDLESS OF WHICH transgression listed above occurs, with the exception of physical or emotional abuse, communication is the key. People have different morals, religious beliefs, personal agendas, and emotional histories that all contribute to their level of leniency or intolerance of all the above-cited problems in their marriages. Ideally, discussion about differences and similarities should be broached before marriage. Unfortunately, according to those men and women polled, discussions around dissatisfaction usually take place when the situation has gone so far that it is barely possible to have a civil conversation. If expectations were broached at the very beginning, there could be a frame of reference or baseline to bring up failures or transgressions in a more rational manner.

Many couples who close their eyes to certain behavior and plod along in loveless, boring, or disappointing marriages by cutting themselves off emotionally will ultimately reach a point of no return. Often the most egregious behavior is tolerated for years so that it becomes an acceptable pattern.

Women or men who are in abusive relationships might blame themselves for provoking their partners. Or, they accept the abuse rather than admit to it or react to it proactively out of embarrassment or fear of reprisal. When the aggression escalates to the point where family or friends intervene and force them to react, or if people suffer near-fatal injuries, only then will divorce become a reality—often when it is too late.

Less lethal but nonetheless offensive conduct such as sloppiness, weight gain, disinterest in children, or boredom are all traits that usually result in sporadic arguments or nagging.

Drug or alcohol abuse is often a matter of one partner enabling the other or joining in. This too might go on for years until one or the other is arrested or admits to the addiction and goes into therapy, leaving the other with no partner in the game of self-abuse.

Infidelity is complicated for a variety of reasons. There are serial philanderers, reactive cheaters, and recreational players. Whatever the impetus for infidelity, often what began as a game, habit, or retribution develops into a life-changing event.

One man, a well-known sports figure, admitted that his infidelity was, in his mind, only a momentary physical attraction that he acted on but never considered harmful to his marriage or meaningful to his life. Until it was.

"I met my future wife when we were both freshmen in college. It was love at first sight for me. After a couple of months, she was in love with me as well. We were each other's first lover, engaged before we graduated, married a year later, and parents at twenty-five. We have two beautiful daughters. To anyone who knows us, we appear to be the happiest of couples. Yet I find myself wanting out. What could have happened to bring me to this point in life? The short answer is simple. I met someone a year ago, and what began as a simple affair (not my first) has evolved into something much deeper. We are consumed by passion and desire for each other. We both realized over time that while our physical relationship was great, the emotional and intellectual connection was every bit as strong and fulfilling. I went outside my marriage to find what had been missing with my wife. I didn't intend to find love. Life is short and I felt if I stayed in this marriage, the resentment I would feel toward my wife and my life would eventually destroy us both."

The couple went into therapy. The sports icon confessed that there was someone else in his life. To his surprise, his wife admitted that she had known for over a year that he was having an affair but thought it would eventually end. But while she was prepared to forgive him and keep the marriage together, he was not. Another several months in therapy and the husband agreed to break off with his girlfriend and, for the sake of history and their children, to give their marriage another chance. Then, again to everyone's surprise, the wife said that after therapy she realized how she had changed and, as a result, had outgrown him. "We married too young," she said. "Never had the chance to know other people and now, at this point in my life, I'm curious. I want my independence and I want to go back to work."

Over the years, while the sports figure had gained fame and adoration from his fans, she had also changed. She was no longer willing to be the "wife of . . ." but rather wanted to recapture her identity. Self-awareness or self-knowledge allows people to see their lives with more clarity so that ultimately they realize that their only chance for happiness is to dissolve a legal union.

Couples who go into therapy are often able to face the reality of divorce as more of a relief than a tragedy. Talking things out allows them to realize that the marriage is not working, that they feel out of place, no longer needing or getting the security they once hoped marriage would bring. In the end, marriage counseling works on one of two levels.

In some cases, the couple learns how to communicate with each other and go off with new tools to express themselves and to be aware of behavior that causes their spouse to react negatively. Husband and wife make a commitment to be open and honest and discuss their grievances in a civilized and noncritical manner.

In the other type of case, the couple admits that being married is not fulfilling any of their expectations. They are able to see that love has died, physical attraction has waned, and their goals have changed. Therapy enables them to see that divorce is a chance to begin again to find fulfillment and happiness.

In the 1970s, the pop culture definition of love was "never having to say you're sorry." In the twenty-first century, perhaps the new pop culture definition of love should be "doing what you don't want and feeling good about it." The trick to a *good divorce* is not to consider that phrase an oxymoron or impossible to achieve.

If people entered a lawyer's office to begin divorce proceedings remembering the qualities that drew them to their spouse in the beginning rather than what drove them apart, half the battle would be won.

Remember the good rather than the bad. It is the opposite of what therapists teach addicts in many treatment centers—remember how bad they felt the morning after a binge, rather than how euphoric they felt while they were drinking or drugging.

The best advice a divorce lawyer can offer a client during that initial meeting is to remember that the person on the other side of the litigation was once a lover, friend, and spouse, and, if there are children, remains the parent of those offspring. This advice from a lawyer should not be construed as an attempt to bring the couple back together and avoid the divorce. Rather, it should be seen as an attempt to make the couple realize that though they no longer want to be man and wife, they still have a history of love, affection, and respect, and in some cases will be sharing custody and the upbringing of their children. It is a reminder that divorce should not necessarily cause the couple to view each other as mortal enemies.

Just as marriage is a dual decision to experience all that life brings and not just a series of edited highlights that are only positive, divorce should be approached as an event that is not just a series of negative edited highlights.

Many divorce lawyers, when interviewing clients, understand that they have fallen into the habit of treating their spouses differently than they do friends and colleagues.

In professional and social situations, people apologize and compromise.

In any relationship, including marriage, ups and downs are part of the rhythm of the dynamic.

Once people are in the middle of divorce negotiations, many refuse to compromise, apologize, or make concessions.

If divorce was viewed as a journey, and lawyers were considered guides who helped people navigate new and distant places both within themselves and externally, those facing divorce might be more amenable to setting their sights on the goal rather than making plays that cause fumbles on the field.

There is a natural sequence to love, marriage, and divorce, though they are distinct in their definitions.

Love is an abstraction.

Marriage is an act of faith.

Divorce is a broken contract.

It is correct to assume that most people don't wake up one morning and decide to end their marriages. Whether or not they use our suggested divorce scale or concoct their own, alone or with the help of a therapist, friend, or religious mentor, there are only two possible results—work to keep the marriage intact or divorce. Neither option is guaranteed to be the final decision. If the conclusion is to divorce, the next step in the process is choosing the right matrimonial lawyer. In the end, it is the attorney who is responsible for the client's ability to view things more objectively. If the attorney puts the welfare of the client before his or her gain, the legalities become less frightening and emotions more tempered. Well-intentioned and honest attorneys will explain options to clients, help them to understand certain realities of the system as it exists, describe the consequences of rage and irrational behavior, and counsel them to eliminate a portion of the fear of the unknown. Only then can those taking steps to break up a family find themselves on the right path toward recovery.

4

CHOOSING THE RIGHT LAWYER

*Choosing the wrong lawyer means just one more
disastrous union after another.*
                                        —RAOUL FELDER

ON THE SURFACE, THE ANATOMY OF A divorce is predictable and
transparent. Papers are exchanged, whether they are summonses, complaints, answers, counterclaims, or replies—each party accuses the other of
doing something that predictably is denied (and both often feel that their
version of events is accurate). Then the fight begins about the real core of
the case. It could be the children—who gets them, who visits them, who
can twist their minds, who hates the other spouse enough to use them as
weapons. In reality, usually the rancor is all about money—money real or
imagined; money in checking or savings accounts, stock certificates, under
mattresses, ensconced in pension funds or tiny banks on second-floor offices in exotic Caribbean islands; money borrowed or lent; or the monetary
value of "things" such as homes, cars, jewelry, Grandma's wedding presents,
mortgages, furniture, art, trading card collections. Like Edgar Allan Poe's
Annabel Lee, who was "loved with a love that was more than love," to
some people "money is money that is more than money." It is the force of
life. They will covet it as they would a neighbor's wife, steal it, caress the
thought of it, hide it, and easily lie about it under oath in a divorce case.

Though divorce lawyers have a moral obligation to temper the emotions of their clients, they are often rendered helpless. Matrimonial attorneys never come into the process at the beginning, when their clients are friends, deeply in love, impassioned by each other, when they have no desire to consider that their emotions, complicity, or feelings will ever change or diminish.

The involvement of a matrimonial lawyer happens at the end of the marriage when bitterness, disappointment, humiliation, hurt, anger, or just plain boredom have caused the demise of the union. The crippling consequences of an ugly divorce are instigated by spite, greed, and revenge. Money and emotions are inextricably linked in any matrimonial.

It is as wrenching to split up a double-wide trailer as it is to divide up Mar-a-Lago. Rich or poor, there are no winners in adversarial divorces. Everyone involved falls into the failure trap. According to many lawyers and judges, the only way to have a civil divorce is if litigants accept certain inevitable realities before they hurl accusations or hold steadfast to punish their soon-to-be ex-spouse. There are three facts to remember when going through a divorce.

People cannot force another to love them.

People cannot oblige another to live with them.

Nothing is forever.

When litigants have uncontrollable emotions, and matrimonial attorneys feed those heightened feelings of hatred, rejection, and vengeance, the process of breaking up a marriage often results in a contest where neither litigant is left standing. Given the irrational feelings of those involved, divorce is almost always a battle that ends with two losers or with both parties victims of a painful process where the price—emotionally and financially—is far greater than they imagined.

When potential clients have their first meeting with a matrimonial lawyer, after they are unable to answer why they decided to divorce now and not months or years earlier, the next question the lawyer might ask is, "Why do you think you will be happier unmarried to this person rather than married?"

The usual response clients give is to cite all the injustices, transgressions, and faults of their spouses. Often, the list is so horrendous that lawyers wonder why it took so long to decide. Even if clients admit to adultery or violence, the excuse is inevitably the fault of their spouse. Or, the reason given has nothing to do with the actual facts.

MARK GOTTLIEB IS A forensic accountant who is hired by divorce lawyers representing either side in any given matrimonial, or he may be appointed by the court as a neutral investigator to go through the litigants' financial records. The work that Gottlieb and other forensic accountants do is to trace assets of litigants. Forensic accountants do what a good IRS agent is trained to do: discover the real financial worth of a taxpayer. They also trace the money in a divorce case, value businesses, issue reports, and, if necessary, ultimately testify in court. Some litigants who are subjected to the scrutiny of a forensic accountant in a divorce have submerged or hidden those assets, not particularly to cheat their spouse in anticipation of a divorce, but rather long before divorce has been contemplated, to cheat the IRS. Once hired by a divorce lawyer, forensic accountants also ascertain which assets are commingled or individual in order to know what will or will not become part of any eventual divorce settlement.

Several years ago Gottlieb was in court in Rockland County in New York State. The Rockland County Courthouse is old, with no elevators and narrow courtrooms. Unlike most courtrooms in large cities, the plaintiff's table is directly behind the defendant's instead of the usual configuration where prosecution and defense are seated at separate tables side by side with a considerable space between them. The court clerks in that antiquated courtroom in upstate New York, Gottlieb says, are also relics from the past as they are almost all elderly women in their seventies or eighties who can barely make it up the stairs to the courtroom. On that occasion, Gottlieb had been hired by the defendant, who happened to be the wife. When the court's afternoon session was due to begin, he, along with the defendant and her lawyer, had just returned from lunch. Seated between the wife and her lawyer, Gottlieb waited for the judge to appear to reconvene the hearing. Seated in front of them were the husband and his counsel, who were also waiting for the session to begin.

"I was going through my notes," Gottlieb recounts, "and the lawyers were reviewing their papers when all of a sudden the husband turned around and said to his wife, 'Do you want to know why we're getting divorced?' In response, the wife stood up, poised for a brawl. 'As a matter of fact, I would like to know why you're filing for divorce after twenty years.'" Gottlieb smiles. "The husband didn't hesitate. He told her that for twenty years she never learned how to boil water. He never got a decent meal at home."

According to Gottlieb, "The wife shouted, 'So, the fact that you came home with gonorrhea has nothing to do with it?' And with that, she threw everything at hand from her attorney's table—pitchers of water, files, paper, staplers, book bags, binders, hole punchers. She just emptied the table and threw everything at her husband—one item at a time. The elderly court clerks tried to break up the melee but were just too feeble to help. It was like *Jerry Springer,* except the couple was anything but the typical contestants on *Springer.* They were two educated people that if you met at a social function would be charming, interesting, and well-mannered."

GOOD LAWYERS ACT not only as legal experts, but also as therapists, social workers, life coaches, and detectives. Ideally, they will handle their clients with a combination of tough love and compassion. As legal experts, they will shepherd them through a complicated legal system with a minimum of trauma. If attorneys have the skills to function as pseudo-therapists or psychologists without training or portfolio, they will try to make their clients realize that divorce can be a positive experience. They might also tell clients that divorce could be a chance to delve within to see what, in their history, caused them to make certain choices. George Santayana noted that those who do not understand their pasts are doomed to relive them. With patience and understanding, matrimonial attorneys will guide their clients toward making correct decisions that can benefit them, rather than making bad decisions intended solely to punish their spouse. By encouraging people to express their doubts or uncertainties, divorce lawyers can respond to each one individually in order to demystify the unknown so negotiations are less acrimonious.

Attorney Ken Burrows, who practices both in New York and in Connecticut, believes that going into the mode of therapist is the best way to understand a client. "Most people who come to me haven't been analyzed, or at best [have been] imperfectly analyzed," Burrows says. "Unless people have gone through some kind of therapy, they are going to have a difficult time separating historical issues from their divorce. If I had to describe my job, I'd say it was giving people the opportunity to find happiness when they make new lives. I try to make my clients understand that divorce can be a life-affirming experience. I also help them to understand why the marriage didn't work. Why couldn't she make you happy? Why did he want to leave? I ask them, what does that say about you? If people understand that it's not their fault, that simply they were incompatible or the other person had needs which couldn't be fulfilled or that she or he was incapable of changing to their spouse's liking, it makes things easier. Look at divorce as a way to exit a bad situation. There are times when a man or a woman client will begin to see what they lacked. Often, for the first time, they are willing to make certain changes within themselves for the next time around. It can actually be liberating to admit that if they changed, they would be better people. Once they get to that point, they can let go of the anger and hurt and consider themselves lucky to have another chance."

The first step for any attorney facing a client in the throes of a divorce is to gain his or her trust. If lawyers are astute detectives, they will seek to understand and unravel the complicated dynamic that defined the marriage. They should also come to understand the need their clients have to hang on to a situation that only causes them humiliation and pain. Choosing a good divorce lawyer who is morally compatible allows those who are about to embark on the process to view the end of a marriage with hope rather than with despair.

Ken Burrows believes that if he could meet the parents of any one of his clients, he could better understand why a client chose a wife or husband who turned out to be wrong for them. "History has a lot to do with someone's choice of a spouse," Burrows claims. "People tend to repeat their parents' mistakes because it's all too familiar. And that also falls under the heading of a good attorney being psychologically astute enough to understand why a marriage failed, what are the delicate issues, and what are the sensitive points that should be avoided to make the negotiations go smoothly."

Those who can afford to hire a lawyer will be required to give a retainer. In a large city this can range anywhere from twenty to seventy-five thousand dollars. Also in a large city, the hourly rate for attorneys can range between two hundred and a thousand dollars, depending on whether the litigator is a partner in the firm or a junior member.

Generally, most states consider legal fees, including retainers, to be the obligation of the husband in a divorce, whether he is the plaintiff or the defendant. In divorce court, the financial merits of a divorce are judged on income rather than assets. Since men are usually the major wage earners in a marriage, they are typically responsible for their own and their wives' legal fees, as well as for the appraisal of property and any forensic accounting necessary for the financial discovery aspect of a case, even if their assets are less than those of their spouse. There is nuance to this rule. If a man is self-made, he has enough confidence in his own ability to generate new income. Men who have inherited their money often have little faith in their own prowess to earn a living. As a result, it is much more difficult for an attorney to deal with the latter in terms of settling cases where each litigant has to give and take based on income and assets.

If fees are a delicate subject between client and lawyer, an even more sensitive issue is what they can expect for their money. Smart clients will ask their prospective attorneys several important questions.

> How much will the total divorce cost?
> How long will it take?
> How far is the lawyer willing to go if the case goes to trial?
> Has the lawyer actually tried cases before, and if so, how
>   many?
> Will the lawyer try the case or relegate it to a junior member
>   of the firm?
> If necessary, will the lawyer appeal a final decision, as well as
>   appeal any intermediate court orders along the way?

If the client is a woman, she should also ask that if the court awards her legal fees, will her attorney refund the retainer she has advanced?

Once the fees are agreed upon and the client and lawyer have determined that they can work together and have the same goals, the lawyer who has been retained needs to contact the client's spouse by letter. The purpose of the letter is to inform the husband or wife that his or her spouse has retained counsel and that he or she should do the same so that both attorneys can be in communication. Depending on how quickly the adversary spouse seeks counsel, the lawyers will begin a dialogue by e-mail, letter, or phone. Lawyers will discuss in broad terms the demands of their respective clients.

From then on, it is up to the client to be as forthright as possible when the lawyer begins his questions that will have a direct impact on how he or she approaches the case. One main subject will be a marital history in order to prepare the complaint for divorce or appropriate responsive pleading, and in order for the lawyer to know the relevant issues that exist between the client and his or her spouse. The lawyer will ask the client to provide a narrative on the following topics: educational backgrounds of the couple; medical history and present medical condition of the couple and their children, if any; employment history of both parties, including present employment, periods of employment, nature of employment, and the amounts earned.

More personal questions are asked by the lawyer, such as the circumstances surrounding the first date, engagement, and marriage, and whether it was a religious ceremony, and if the couple lived together before marriage.

After the lawyer has all the details of the events leading up to the moment when the client has sought legal counsel, the next series of questions are the most pertinent. The lawyer will want to have a chronological narrative of the events leading to the breakdown of the marriage, such as inappropriate behavior on the part of the client or the spouse, including any emotional, verbal, or physical violence. It should also include financial misdeeds, fraud, crimes, and any other legal problems that resulted in a trial and condemnation or even an accusation of wrongdoing. This is necessary in order to determine the basis for a cause of action for divorce.

Once these points have been addressed, the client will be asked to reveal the number of marriages between them, children from those unions, and children from the present union, as well as a list of all, if any, mental and physical health issues. One of the last questions requires the client to reveal the names of accountants, therapists, doctors, and all other professionals that they (the couple) have retained, hired, or consulted throughout their marriage.

During those first few meetings between lawyer and client, the discussion will also focus on whether or not the couple is already living in separate houses, and, if there are children, discussion centers on child support, custody, and visitation.

In other words, the matrimonial attorney needs to know everything about the marriage, even details that might seem irrelevant or inappropriate to the client.

Costs can rise dramatically if there is resistance and acrimony from the beginning.

Opposing lawyers will have a conversation to see if there is a chance of settling the case without going into court. The issues raised in that conversation might be how close or far apart their respective clients are when it comes to money, grounds for divorce, if any, and other issues of a financial settlement and custody. If the finances of the litigants are complicated, or if one or the other refuses to reveal assets and income, a forensic accountant can be called in to determine the actual income and net worth of each litigant. If custody cannot be negotiated reasonably or either party is against sharing custody, the court will frequently appoint a law guardian, representing the children, to investigate the home situation in order to determine the best interests of the children. Other experts might be called into court to testify concerning issues such as worth and ownership of real estate, art, jewelry, and any other finances that could be considered commingled. (See Appendix A.)

These experts comprise a kind of cottage industry connected to divorce and include forensic accountants, real estate appraisers, life coaches, parenting coordinators, business evaluators, therapists, attorneys for the children appointed by the court, and social workers, all of whom become part of the process. These experts are costly. For example, forensic accountants, whose job it is to sift through all financial records and data from the beginning of the marriage to understand what is deemed separate or joint property, charge up to four hundred dollars an hour. Real estate appraisers may charge according to the value and size of the apartment, house, and properties if there are multiple dwellings, since size and value may be a factor in cost, reflecting an eventual settlement.

Though there is no-fault divorce in all fifty states, a good attorney will insist upon knowing particulars of the opposing spouse, such as spending habits, attributes, strengths, weaknesses, and how he or she will react to an impending divorce. It is essential for anyone seeking legal advice in a divorce to be completely honest with an attorney. There is nothing worse for the client than if his or her lawyer walks into an ambush in the courtroom. Yet most experienced lawyers know that after traveling a long and difficult road, even on the eve of the trial there is always one more thing the client has not revealed.

AUSTIN WRIGHT WAS THE EPITOME of the starched, prim Englishman; vest buttoned, collar stiff, posture erect. He came to New York to take over the American branch of his family's import-export business, which handled the importation of Japanese video and photographic equipment. Austin Wright's wife accused him of having an affair with a Japanese girl who worked as his secretary. When his wife locked him out of their apartment, Mr. Wright sued her for divorce.

When Mr. Wright's lawyer contacted Mrs. Wright's lawyer, he heard a most incredible story. According to the wife's attorney, Wright was not only having an affair with the Japanese woman in his office but had asked his wife if he could bring her home, along with her sister, and have sexual relations with both of them while his wife watched and ministered to his needs. Further, he told his wife that he intended to sponsor the woman and her sister for American citizenship and had already purchased the cooperative apartment next to the marital home so they could all live together.

To look at Mr. Wright, it was difficult to believe that this proper Englishman was capable of such insanity. Wright denied the story and his lawyer believed him without the slightest doubt. When questioned by his attorney as to how and why his wife could possibly make up such a story, Wright simply said, "She's crazy. Her charges are a figment of a very sick imagination." It was plausible, since the more the wife embellished the story of the Japanese sisters and the construction to break through to the newly purchased neighboring apartment, the more unstable she sounded.

Wright's lawyer was convinced that the wife was indeed nuts, but he also believed she was telling the truth. When they finally got to court and the case began, it turned out that the workers who were doing renovations on the new apartment claimed the Japanese women were there but swore that it was Mrs. Wright who initiated the renovation and instructed building workers to move certain pieces of furniture from one apartment to the other. The doormen also testified that they only saw the Japanese women enter the apartment when Mrs. Wright was present. By that time, the court was not only convinced that the wife was telling the truth but was also certain that she was mentally unstable.

Mrs. Wright might have been crazy, but she wasn't stupid. When she sensed that the judge and lawyers thought her to be crazy, she picked up the inkwell on the judge's desk and threw it at her husband, screaming, "He even revised his will so the girl would be the main beneficiary." Turning to his client, the lawyer asked Mr. Wright, "Is this true?" With a smile and calm demeanor, Mr. Wright responded, "Why, of course it is." In the end, despite the woman's violent outburst or perhaps because of it, the judge advised her to seek psychiatric help while awarding her a disproportionate share of her husband's assets, including the new apartment under renovation. Outside the courtroom, the lawyer asked his client why he had lied. "My wife was making the accusations," Wright replied evenly. "I thought in this country the burden of proof was on her. Why should I admit to something before she could prove it?"

ONCE THE LAWYER understands what his or her client is willing to accept or pay when it comes to the financial portion of the case, and what he or she is prepared to agree to as it concerns the children, understanding one litigant's side of the case may be only the beginning.

The total cost of a divorce involves more than just attorney fees or payments to those in the cottage industry connected to the discovery aspect of a case. If a divorce is complicated and there are millions at stake, expenses can also include stenographic minutes, filing fees, jury and witness fees if there is a trial, and the fees of all the other specialists that could be involved in the process. Professional witnesses—psychiatrists and other mental health professionals, forensic witnesses of all sorts—all charge fees, usually substantial, if they are required to appear in court.

Divorce lawyers and those involved in the cottage industry connected to the dissolution of a marriage see people at their absolute worst and are privy to the unfiltered hatred and rancor of the litigants. From the inception, it is not a pretty set of circumstances that is conducive to forging an agreement without strife.

While the overburdened courts have an interest in coming to a resolution quickly, let us be brutally frank: there is little incentive for some attorneys to move quickly to achieve a settlement for their clients. When litigation is unnecessarily prolonged, only those with unlimited funds can unfairly tie up the courts with issues such as temporary support, custody, and division of assets. Most people can't afford the cost of such a prolonged process.

Finding a lawyer who understands that divorce usually boils down to a matter of arithmetic is the ideal.

Lawyers who specialize in the rich and famous get exorbitant retainers and huge hourly fees. The reason, of course, is that the very rich have the means to pay for and prolong a case.

The most vulnerable are the middle class, those who are salaried and whose income is a matter of public record. As employees, they are accustomed to taking orders, advice, and suggestions, and are easier to handle as they will take a lawyer's counsel without too many questions or too much resistance. When they opt for divorce, a decent lawyer will try to arrange a settlement before their meter runs to an impossible price where the lawyer will get more than the spouse and children. As always, the notion of right or wrong, victim or victimizer, or guilty or innocent is the basis for the rage that transmogrifies into irrational and intransigent behavior. There is where the lunacy begins. If the attorney does nothing to temper the lunacy but rather encourages it—or even acts as an enabler—nobody suffers more than both litigants and their children.

There are two distinct types of matrimonial lawyers. There are those who put the interests and well-being of their clients before their own gain. And there are those who make false promises, incite dissension, and are determined to nurture their own reputation of being tough and unyielding. These lawyers should be avoided at all costs—and usually their costs are exorbitant.

5

When to Run, Not Walk, out of a Lawyer's Office

*Why bother to get married? Find somebody you hate
and pay them one half of everything you have.*
—Mel Brooks

DIVORCE IS LIKE A PENDULUM. At one end, usually at the very beginning of the divorce process, the husband says the wife is a wonderful person. "I'm sorry I screwed up," the husband will say. Then the pendulum begins to swing, and the thinking is "My wife's a good person, but so am I, and I'm entitled to live also." After all the so-called friends and family begin telling the husband all the things the wife did that he didn't know about—spending, cheating, talking about him behind his back—or when the husband falls in love with another woman, the mindset of the husband is "That bitch. I'm not going to give her anything."

The trick is to begin and end negotiations before the pendulum starts to swing too far, and whether a lawyer understands that is one of the best indicators that he or she is out for a client's good rather than his own personal gain.

Good lawyers know the weaknesses and strengths in any case they take on, and they understand their clients' vulnerabilities. An intuitive lawyer knows when to be reasonable and when to be intractable. Lawyers who don't consider their clients' best interests as paramount may well mislead them if they tell them that negotiation shows weakness and standing firm will ultimately win the case. Whether a client is rich or poor, victim or victimizer, they can and often do fall upon a lawyer who is not out for their best interests. Those attorneys can be court-appointed and have no incentive to fight for justice as their fees are minimal, or they can be litigators known to represent the rich and famous who are willing to suffer aggravation and wasted time and will prolong a case for obvious financial reasons. Realistically, there is no way to empirically prove or disprove these allegations.

The curious thing about matrimonial lawyers is that they have no specialized background that qualifies them, other than "on-the-job" experience. In comparison, a criminal lawyer has usually served in the office of a district attorney or public defender before going into private practice. Negligence or accident lawyers have backgrounds either as employees of insurance companies or with large negligence firms before they embark on their own. Lawyers who specialize in administrative law generally have served in a government agency. No such training exists for a divorce lawyer. Usually he or she has stumbled on the specialty through a series of referrals and a word-of-mouth reputation. The key attributes of a competent divorce lawyer are his or her integrity, personality, and an ability to keep up with divorce reform laws that ultimately change procedure—not to mention that mysterious gene that makes one lawyer better than another.

All matrimonial attorneys understand that encouraging litigation results in unnecessary and exorbitant legal fees. Those lawyers who are intent upon profiting from a divorce will react in the following way when they find clients sitting in their offices, bemoaning their fate and crying as they recount the alleged indignities and abuse that led to that moment in time.

"Count on me," that type of lawyer says. "We'll destroy the bastard [or bitch]. We'll humiliate him [her] until he [she] begs for mercy. He'll [she'll] be on his [her] knees. Trust me."

Hearing those words from a divorce lawyer should automatically set off an alarm in a client's brain. Run, don't walk, out the door, and find a lawyer who projects sanity rather than venom, who will calm instead of incite rage. Any good lawyer will try to diffuse a potentially acrimonious situation if the goal is to resolve the matter as quickly as possible. Attorneys who guarantee results or who promise to annihilate their opponents have doomed their clients before the fight even begins. Every time lawyers tell clients that they can make repeated visits to court for one motion or another are stealing months or years from someone's life. Lawyers who neglect to explain that short-term sacrifices or losses could result in long-term gains are acting out of ego, greed, or their own personal experience with divorce that causes them to want to "settle a score." If a lawyer boasts that he or she will win the case, it is a patent lie. There are no guarantees in divorce cases. There are no winners.

New Jersey attorney Gary Skoloff says, "I will say to a male client, for instance, 'Pay your wife, not me.' When I said that to one client, he said his shrink told him the same thing. All those court appearances where nothing gets accomplished make people bitter against the system. The truth is that when a lawyer is forced to go to court, judges seldom believe that the case couldn't be settled through negotiation. Bringing litigants back to court over and over may be a way of exhausting them so they will ultimately settle. Frankly, going into full trial mode is the dumbest way to spend money. Burning it in Central Park is just as good as spending it on a divorce."

New York divorce lawyer Eleanor Alter agrees with Skoloff and maintains that 95 percent of divorces are settled outside the courtroom. "Only five percent are litigated," Alter says. "The reality is that the system could not handle more than five percent. Most of the time, even when a divorce goes to trial, people get exhausted or simply can't keep paying the hourly rate for a lawyer to make repeat appearances before a judge."

At best, going through the stages of divorce that will end in the dissolution of life's most binding emotional contract is traumatic enough. The sole goal of a lawyer should be to help the client avoid the pitfalls that await the unwary, and that, if ignored, could sink a client into a mire of misery for years to come.

By the time people consult a lawyer, it is usually too late for the marriage to be saved. By then, people have been through seeking advice from therapists, clergymen, guys at the bowling alley, or girlfriends at the hairdresser. The lawyer's office is usually the crossing of the Rubicon, from which there is no return. It is not too late, however, to manage a divorce where there are minimal emotional and financial scars.

Joan Lipton is a forensic accountant who consults with many divorce lawyers to ascertain assets of the litigants as well as evaluate the profits, losses, and worth of a business. She has seen firsthand the rage that goes along with negotiating divorce settlements. She has also witnessed lawyers who are more rancorous than their clients.

"Some people are better at separating the emotional from business," Lipton says. "All in all divorce is a horrible experience but people have to get through it. They have to be assured that life goes on. They have to know that a slash-and-burn tactic only prolongs the agony. People think it's more frightening for women but the truth is that fear has to do with someone's sense of whether they feel they're the victim, and that's gender neutral. It also has to do with resiliency. I've seen men cry as well as women. What surprised me most of all were two attorneys who got so angry, they were ready to punch each other and take their fight outside to a parking lot. It's interesting, but when people cry, it's not about the money. When they get angry, that's about the money. When lawyers get angry, it's about ego."

One example of a lawyer who impeded a settlement in a divorce case demonstrates how the client, more than the opposing counsel or litigant, became an inadvertent victim.

During divorce negotiations, Jason S. was willing to allow his wife to live in what had been the marital home, along with their two children. The original agreement called for Jason and his wife, Susan, to split the expenses of the apartment until they decided to sell it, when they would again divide the profits equally. Things changed in the middle of negotiations. A job that Susan thought she had fell through. Through her attorney, Susan asked if her soon-to-be ex-husband would be willing to pay the entire mortgage and maintenance for six months until she found another job and could resume her career.

"It seemed reasonable to me," Jason explains. "There was no doubt that Susan needed some time. My lawyer's immediate reaction was to tell my wife's lawyer that I would never agree to pay all the expenses for six months. When I told him that I actually was willing, he began screaming at me that I wouldn't let him do his job. You'd think it was his money, his family, or his divorce. He told me to let him handle it. The mistake I made apparently was to contact my wife without the knowledge of my attorney and explain that I was agreeable but I would have to call off the dogs—meaning my attorney. She wasn't supposed to tell her lawyer about our conversation but she did. When my lawyer found out, he fired me.

Not only did I have to pay my entire bill up until that point, which went way over the retainer, but I also had to pay my wife's attorney because he had spent time on the phone with my lawyer. The divorce stalled. I had to find another lawyer, start over again, give another retainer, and all because my lawyer refused to let me compromise with my wife. In the end, it was for the best. I found an attorney who was reasonable. My wife and I agreed on the terms and the divorce went through without a lot of unnecessary grief."

LAWYERS FIGHT FOR A LIVING.

Until people realize that it is their divorce and their decision what to ask for and what to give, they will never get the chance to lead better lives.

Honest lawyers will never promise to deliver every single point their client wants. If the client insists on fighting "fire with fire," and instructs his lawyer that the marching orders are an eye for an eye and burn for burn, a decent lawyer will suggest that the client find other representation. Someone who assures a client that every demand made out of fury, distress, or revenge is possible to be met, rather than cautioning them about spending money needlessly, is not out for the client's best interests. Experienced attorneys know that any client who is willing to pay the lawyer anything just so their future ex-spouses get nothing has a divorce that can potentially last longer than the marriage itself.

The prevalent assumption among the legal profession is that men with means are able to give their wives money to compensate for "years lost." Not everyone, however, is a person "of means." Men who are in lower or middle-income brackets often find themselves in dire financial straits in order to adhere to a court's ruling for maintenance and child support. When a lawyer encourages a client to give in at all costs, that advice is as detrimental as urging someone to fight all the way up to appeals court.

The other side of that equation is that women who are left have a "take them [their husbands] to the cleaners" mentality. Most people don't realize that they are billed for every phone call to their lawyer, each court appearance, and even letters written or conversations between their attorney and their spouse's litigator. Every inch of the way carries with it an enormous price tag.

Many experienced lawyers and judges believe that the first offer a woman has from her spouse who has left the marital home is the best she'll ever get. In the very beginning, the husband, filled with remorse and guilt, has not yet been confronted with mounting legal fees, court costs, and time consumed with the divorce. At that moment, when he sees his future ex-wife as a victim—alone, shocked, humiliated, and sad—he is ready to make life easier for her in exchange for his freedom. Within days or weeks, when he sees her turn vindictive and raging, he is no longer in a pitying mood. Unfortunately, the majority of women are reluctant to accept the first offer. If they have a lawyer who convinces them that the first offer is only the "floor" and the amount will go up, the meter clicks on without an end in sight.

All too often divorce ends in a miscarriage of justice for either side. Lawyers who take up the cause of ruining a husband in order to win an overinflated settlement for the wife are guaranteeing their own future fees when the husband takes the wife back to court to amend the agreement. Lawyers who represent the husbands and manage to deprive the wives of sufficient money to live are also only thinking of their own financial gain. If there are children, lawyers who care most about money and ego are dooming the offspring to unnecessary involvement in an ongoing parental bloodbath.

Judge Tommy Zampino, the chief judge in the supreme court in New Jersey, has presided over hundreds of divorces. According to him, "Divorce could be easy for the rich and poor alike if people did not let their lawyers get in the way of common sense.

"One man, Paul Z.," Judge Zampino relates, "was a high-profile television executive who dragged out his divorce for years. His lawyer and his wife's attorney hated each other, though they both admitted that their clients were hysterical, violent, and incapable of reaching a negotiated conclusion. At one point, Paul and his wife, during an appearance before the judge, launched into a polemic concerning the time Paul would pick up his children for a weekend visit. The point of contention involved a difference of fifteen minutes. Finally, I slammed my hand down and said, 'Do not tie up my courtroom for this kind of nonsense. Both of you should be ashamed of yourselves for doing this to your children. And your lawyers should be ashamed for allowing this nonsense.'"

Though Judge Zampino took matters in hand when it came to a ridiculous argument over fifteen minutes, he could do little to control the primitive rage that consumed these two people. Upon leaving the court, the couple, accompanied by their attorneys, suddenly began punching and clawing each other. At one point, Paul's wife bit him on the hand. When the wound became infected, Paul went to a hospital emergency room. The doctor put him on a course of antibiotics. Two days later, Paul, through his attorney, sued his wife for assault.

Emotional distress can be infinite.

Revenge is a full-time job.

The reality of divorce is that no one can right the wrong committed in any marriage, not even the most talented and brilliant matrimonial lawyer. Regardless of the bitterness or anger, alimony can never be a panacea for the emotional pain that divorce causes, especially if a lawyer manages to win a case by breaking one of the two litigants either financially or emotionally. Lawyers who advise their clients to confront the drama on a daily basis merely to drive their spouse crazy are only fostering misery. Matrimonial attorneys who convince their clients that their actions during negotiations will be the last time in their lives when they will have a direct impact on the futures of their soon-to-be exes are promoting resentment that will take years to heal.

The incentive for lawyers to encourage, promote, or incite clients to behave in any of the ways mentioned above is twofold: their fees will increase by the hour, day, week, and month, and their clients will spend precious time in a misguided effort to be the center of negative attention. Those people who get bad advice from their lawyers and either consciously or subconsciously wrangle over money for years as a way of keeping a memory or their presence in the spouse's life alive, or prolonging an emotional hold on their husband or wife, are destined to wallow in the divorce rather than celebrate their freedom.

Gary Skoloff has handled hundreds of divorces, representing both men and women. According to Skoloff, unless it is a matter of custody or assets that are not all revealed, most of the time if the lawyers representing each side are honest, they can sit down and settle any case in about fifteen minutes.

"Forget the craziness of the clients," Skoloff says. "Both lawyers know the facts if they're presented out in the open, and we know where the case will end, even if it goes to trial. If our clients listened to us, they could avoid spending millions on lawyers and all that anger that goes with litigation. And, if they avoided lawyers who encouraged that kind of craziness, divorce would be a more simple and less traumatic event."

The rational client who is buoyed by a cautious attorney will tell their spouse that they are not interested in a protracted battle. They will remind him or her of the emotional price the children will ultimately pay if they witness their parents harming each other financially, physically, or mentally. If they have chosen a matrimonial lawyer who is intellectually honest and morally compatible, they will try to reason rather than direct their legal representatives to communicate everything from financial matters to who picks up the children at what time. The objective of both client and attorney will be to get the divorce done as quickly and as fairly as possible without using children as weapons or hurling baseless and untrue accusations at each other.

A civilized divorce is about compromise.

A divorce court is not a boxing ring.

No one, not even someone who is represented by an attorney who has a reputation for destroying the opposition, can get blood from a stone, and that is underlined by the hardships of the current dismal economic situation which ultimately affect divorce.

In Delaware, financial adviser Carol Arnott maintains that rising job losses are responsible for a decrease in child support payments. Losing jobs also results in a loss of health insurance. Both these issues are considered when couples are contemplating divorce. Arnott claims that families planning divorce know that health insurance will become low on the list of necessities compared with things such as rent, mortgage, food, and utilities. "Health insurance payments can't be put on a credit card," she has noted. "When employer-provided health insurance is gone and you're looking at spending hundreds of dollars a month that you don't have on an insurance premium, your first priority is going to be putting food on the table, not buying insurance. Unfortunately, the result can be financial devastation in the event of a serious accident or illness."

Throughout the country where Wall Street and General Motors as well as other large companies have been overrun by layoffs, people are thinking of other alternatives to hiring divorce lawyers.

Michelle Smith, a financial planner and regional director for the Institute for Divorce Financial Analysts, has seen casualties at the investment bank and brokerage of Bear Stearns result in her clients needing to make a complete psychological and lifestyle readjustment.

"Lifestyle that's been built up in over a decade is literally, within the span of one week, getting wiped out," said Smith.

The more rational couples are reevaluating their options.

Even in the best of times, just as marriage tends to be seasonal, with fashion magazines and resorts catering to the typical June bride, so too is divorce seasonal. It is also respectful of family occasions. People do not usually divorce when holidays are approaching, such as Thanksgiving, Christmas, New Year's, or Easter. Birthdays are difficult as well, as are graduations from high school and college. During these times the air is suffused with the joys of family and good feelings. Divorce, predictably, takes a backseat. Still, getting through memorable events before one or the other announces his or her intention to break up the home rarely cushions the shock. On a more pragmatic level, postponing divorce until bonuses, inheritances, and salary increases are handed out is a futile attempt to protect assets and income.

People must remember that the rules of marriage remain in effect until a separation agreement is signed, or a formal divorce action is commenced.

There are always good and bad in every profession. At the very beginning, lawyers must decide how they want to run their legal practice and their lives. Given the cost of retaining legal counsel, those without large sums of money simply can not afford to commit themselves to spending tens or hundreds of thousands of dollars even for an attorney who is scrupulously honest.

Lawyers are paid by the hour. Negotiations cost money. For the poor, low income, middle class, and even the rich who are determined to divorce without spending inordinate sums on lawyers, there is another alternative to hiring an expensive attorney. Unfortunately, there are certain conditions that make this option possible for only a minority of couples.

6

MEDIATION

A mediator ridiculing mediation is a healthy exercise.
With humor any conflict is a source of entertainment;
clowns are funny because they deal with conflict.
—LUIS MIGUEL DIAZ, MEDIATOR

MEDIATION IS A PROCESS that eliminates the prospect of going to court to litigate a divorce. It is not only more cost-efficient, but it also encourages husband and wife to establish communication that is not filled with rancor, anger, or vengeance. Those couples who choose mediation do not have to spend endless hours with lawyers in or out of the courtroom, where the meter is running and the cost goes up by the hour. In addition, couples who end up in divorce court find themselves excluded from most discussions between their lawyers and the judge. Mediation is a positive means to open a dialogue between husband and wife where they are involved in their divorce and decisions concerning their financial futures and the lives of their children. That said, there are very stringent emotional conditions for mediation to be an option and to work.

How easy life would be if husbands and wives decided to divorce at the same time and agreed to simplify the terms of the divorce so each could get on with their life. In reality, of course, that is usually not the case. It is sad but true that there are few litigants who are able to enter into mediation. Even more distressing is that there are few litigants who

think dispassionately enough to realize that finding civilized ways to resolve issues will not only save money and spare children from unnecessary trauma in an already fraught circumstance, but will also allow both
parties to heal. It is rare to find people who realize from the inception
how costly litigation can be financially and emotionally in terms of losing control over their lives.

Unfortunately, according to the Hoover Institute's Policy Review in
2009, 80 percent of divorces are unilateral and not mutual decisions.
Rarely do two people have an epiphany at the same time that tells them
to get divorced. When that does happen, and it is indeed rare, couples can
save money, negotiate calmly, and move on toward divorce that at least
eliminates the drama though not always the scars. Those are the couples
who are ideal candidates for mediation.

A mediator does not necessarily have to be an attorney. A mediator
must be skilled in negotiating and also have some background in psychology, and—often the hardest requirement—must be skilled in the art
of science of matrimonial law in order to achieve positive results.

The work of a mediator is to moderate discussions with the couple as
they work out their needs, demands, and desires, and to guide them toward compromise that will avert months or years in court. If and when
there is agreement, husband and wife are required to consult separate
lawyers, who will review the settlement before each signs. In some media-
tions, when both sides are represented by lawyers, the lawyers agree, or the
rules provide that if the mediation fails, neither lawyer can represent the
respective clients in a subsequent divorce. The object, obviously, is not
to give either lawyer a vested interest in the mediation failing.

Why would a lawyer mediate in addition to or in place of representing
clients in a divorce?

Too often, mediators are lawyers or psychologists, social workers and
others, who may not be earning what they feel is a sufficient or adequate
income, and to supplement their income, transform themselves into mediators. A lawyer who earns sufficient income, and is in demand by clients, will not decide to become a mediator unless it pays better—and it
does not—to the benefit of the client.

Bruce Kogan is a professor of law at Rogers Williams University in
Rhode Island. Previously, he was interim dean of the law school, as well

as dean of the Harvey Rishikov Law School. Currently, in addition to his duties as law professor, Kogan is the director of the University of Rhode Island Mediation Clinic.

Kogan views the principal point of mediation as one of convincing two people who might be on opposite sides of an argument to move toward the center.

"Most mediators aim for a 'yes' to bring the parties to the center for compromise," he says. "Usually one or the other is incapable of budging, which means that my job to make the mediation work is to get the saner and nicer of the two to move toward the center and then some. I've had couples where the wife was sweet and compliant and the husband wanted the divorce but he wanted it on his terms. In those cases, I will direct my attention mostly to the wife. Before I take on a mediation, however, I have certain little tests that I perform. For instance, I study the body language of the couple. If they talk directly to each other, there's hope. If they only look at me and talk through me to their partner, that's not encouraging. Often, I'll go out of the room. If they're sitting next to each other and communicating when I come back in, I know there's a chance to make it work."

A mediation usually costs between twenty-five hundred and three thousand dollars, and takes about four or five hours of talking and negotiating, which is done over several days. Generally, mediation is not only considered economical but also chic. Many people believe it is sophisticated to be able to work out a divorce without the hysterics and emotions that turn them into raging animals.

"There are concerns," Kogan explains. "Because it's considered the 'new thing' and cheap and chic, a lot of people who love the idea are completely incapable of actually sitting down and talking things out rationally. They are not adult enough to know that in the end, compromise is the only way to make a mediation work."

As mediators, lawyers, and their clients gain more experience with mediation, it is possible that many disputes will not be settled by the process. The positive side of that reality is that even if the dispute is not settled, mediation improves the litigants' ability to communicate, define their objectives, and narrow the areas of contention. A knowledgeable mediator is there to guide people to evaluate their options and determine whether their goals are realistic.

Los Angeles divorce attorney Neal Hirsch has also done many media-tions. While they are cost-effective and less emotional, they entail risk. "The problem is that often, six months later," Hirsch says, "the accommodator in any mediation will wake up and they're screaming at the mediator and their lawyer, saying they were pushed into a settlement and it's all the mediator's fault. The curious thing is that the couple with fifty million at stake is more willing to work things out and not have regrets afterwards than couples with far less money. They're the ones who are lucid enough not to throw money at lawyers."

The court does not have the right to appoint a mediator. A mediator, however, has the power to bring the settled case before a judge if the couple is agreeable.

Mediation could be considered the ideal divorce scenario for both financial and emotional reasons. The big caveat is that both husband and wife have to be agreeable to end their marriage in a civilized way. Each has to put his or her emotions on hold and guard a pragmatic approach. If one half of the couple agrees, and the other does not, mediation is out of the question.

There are several different styles of mediation, but also several certainties regardless of which style mediators use. One thing is guaranteed. Mediation is confidential, flexible, and the mediator remains neutral. During a session, a mediator can and will point out areas where each spouse is more equipped to control, settle, and give in. The hope is that since the couple is working with basically the same information and facts concerning their marriage, a mediation approach will ultimately require far less time to negotiate a resolution that makes sense than more traditional divorce proceedings would.

Mediation is voluntary. It can go on for as long as the couple and the mediator believe there is a chance to come to a viable and mutual conclusion. However, if one or the other spouse chooses to end the mediation and opt for an adversarial divorce, the mediator automatically severs his or her relationship with the couple.

The main advantage of mediation is that it allows the couple to be in control of their own divorce. Not being at the mercy of matrimonial law in the event of a court battle, or of a judge, or especially of lawyers who are self-interested, couples can and often do get through the divorce with less conflict and more disposable income. (To find a mediator near you, visit www.divorcenet.com/mediation.)

While there are lawyers who are often not out for the best interests of their clients, the only criteria for mediators is that they are experienced and skilled at fostering and urging agreement. Since mediation is often difficult to approach unless people are willing to put their emotions aside, and lawyers—good or bad—are expensive, it is also the responsibility of clients to enter into the process of divorce with a sense of acceptance and lucidity. The truth is that many clients will make life hell for their attorneys, either because they can afford to, or because they were irrational even before they found themselves in the middle of a divorce.

7

CLIENTS FROM HELL

*Have you heard of the new divorced Barbie doll? She
comes with all of Ken's stuff.*

—ANONYMOUS

HOLLYWOOD HAS TACKLED the subjects of marriage, divorce, infidelity, and even the premise that people would rather die than divide a house, assets, or other property. The movie *The War of the Roses* is one example. Though a fictional account of a particularly acrimonious divorce, that scenario has been played and replayed in real life with people who would rather destroy their own lives and those of their children and sabotage a chance to make new lives rather than reach a compromise to divide their assets. In *The War of the Roses,* the couple fight to the death for their house. In the last scene when the brawl becomes out of control, both cling to a massive crystal chandelier that ultimately falls to the floor and kills them.

Just as lawyers should be carefully vetted by potential clients, so should lawyers decide if they can work with and handle a prospective litigant in a divorce case. Though it is difficult, any lawyer has the right to refuse to take a case if he or she senses that the potential client is unmanageable and inordinately vengeful.

In some cases, crazy people who retain lawyers and are willing to pay them unnecessarily high fees can afford to be crazy. They buy the right. Often lawyers who represent crazy clients will find themselves facing their client's spouse, only to realize that he or she is just as crazy. The question that always comes to mind is how did these two people, both obviously unstable and violent, manage to stay together for decades before deciding to divorce? What happened?

The explanation is much like the old Arab tale of the camel. First the camel sticks his nose in the tent, then his head, and pretty soon you're sleeping with a camel. Those couples who are equally disturbed don't wake up one morning and discover they are living with a lunatic. The process is incremental. Psychiatrists call it habituation. A grandfather clock with a pendulum that swings back and forth making a loud ticking noise becomes soundless to the person who has been hearing that clock for years. People who lived over the Third Avenue El simply didn't hear or feel the rumbling and shaking in their apartments that the train made. In the same way, people get habituated to each other's peculiarities. When they finally decide to divorce, it is either because of an act of violence or a large unauthorized withdrawal from a joint account, or something that upsets the usual dramas in the relationship. Then the fight begins and for these people, the court becomes the boxing arena.

The only exceptions are those wealthy people who are fodder for the press, as they often engage in bizarre behavior. Though they have an innate wish to gratify their every desire, if the marriage is bad, they leave it and usually prefer to settle out of court for fear that their future ex-spouse will reveal their peculiarities.

Often, it is simply not economically viable or emotionally sound for a lawyer to take on a case which in the end is neither worth the time spent, money earned, or aggravation. Any sensible lawyer can tell during the first meeting that the client facing him across his desk is either intent on getting divorced with the least amount of trauma and pain, or determined to bring their wife or husband "to their knees." They are the same ones who consider their spouse as the enemy and blame him or her for everything. They are the Captain Ahabs of divorce.

As Herman Melville wrote, "He piled upon the whale's white hump the sum of all the general rage and hate felt by his whole race from Adam down; and then, as if his chest had been a mortar, he burst his hot heart's shell upon it."*

* *Moby Dick* (New York: Oxford World Classics, 2008), Chapter 41, pp. 164–165.

During negotiations, those who refuse to accept any responsibility for the demise of the marriage remain defensive, inflexible, and controlling. They are hell-bent on winning every argument at all costs and resist any form of cooperation with their soon-to-be ex-spouse. Some refuse to communicate with their spouse, and will only talk through their lawyer, which results in unnecessarily high legal fees. Their goal, however, is not to save money. They are out to punish and get revenge, whether by becoming embroiled in a custody battle or accusing their spouse of sexually abusing the children or committing acts of domestic violence.

From an attorney's viewpoint, the worst male clients are those who are used to controlling the destinies of others. For example, a self-made businessman who accumulated his fortune through hard work may resist giving his wife any money. To him she is nonexistent. Being forced to part with hundreds of thousands or millions of dollars is anathema to a man who wants nothing more than to forget he was ever married to a woman who is about to become an ex-wife. These are the same men who, when asked to produce a tax return to prove what their income is, may occasionally go through the following exercise.

The false-income-tax scam begins with the client, usually the husband, who will go to the most reputable and large accounting firm in town to ask them to prepare his income tax return. The information he supplies is false. Operating in good faith, the accounting firm prepares the tax return based on the bogus information. When the return is complete, the man will ask that the firm give him the return (now containing the name of the preparer, a respected accounting firm) and tells them he will mail it to the Internal Revenue Service. Instead of submitting it, the man puts it in a drawer and consults another accountant, sometimes a small neighborhood one-man office. The man supplies the second accountant with the correct information and sends that one in to the IRS.

When the divorce begins, each side requests financial information. The man will supply the wife's lawyer with the false revenue return that was never filed. Since the false return was prepared and stamped by the prestigious accounting firm, the lawyer and the wife will accept it as truthful. Usually, unless someone discovers that the false form was never submitted to the IRS, the figures on that form concerning income and assets are accepted and negotiations resume based on those false figures.

Another type of client who may be difficult to work with as a litigant—
in fact lawyers often assume as much even without meeting them—are
physicians. They are the men and women who often have difficulty taking advice as they are so accustomed to controlling peoples' lives and
destinies. They may resent being told what to do by an attorney as much
as they resist taking business advice from their brokers or money manag-
ers. Doctors often feel they know everything, probably because they deal
in life and death. Strangely enough, among doctors, psychiatrists tend to
have a high degree of emotional and intellectual instability.

One client, a woman who was the wife of a noted psychiatrist, began
divorce proceedings against her husband. When her lawyer called the
husband, he calmly told him that the woman was not his wife but a patient who had the delusion that she was married to him. A year later, a
judgment of divorce was handed down with a handsome settlement in
favor of the wife and children. By then, the psychiatrist must have realized that indeed the woman was married to him.

There was also the case of a famous forensic psychiatrist whose wife
came home from a movie and saw a stack of separation agreements waiting to be signed on one side of the dining room table. On the other side
was a hunting knife. The psychiatrist told his wife to take her pick, the
inference being if she didn't sign, she would get the knife. Prior to that
incident, that same psychiatrist was accused of domestic violence. His
wife called the police, but when they arrived, the psychiatrist presented
his credentials and, like his colleague described above, told the police that
the woman was not his wife. He informed them that she was a sick and
delusional patient who had invaded his home and believed she was his
wife. The police took him at his word and left, escorting the wife from the
home.

Another group of difficult clients are actors and other stars who are
surrounded by minders and sycophants who tell them, no matter how
crazy an idea is, that they are right. It's the "yes, baby, you're the boss"
syndrome. One well-known actor, unbeknownst to his lawyer, one of the
coauthors of this book, arranged for his slavish assistant to hire detectives
disguised as deliverymen, washer repairmen, and phone company people
to spy on and follow his wife. He also had her home surreptitiously surrounded by cameras. The only way the actor's lawyer found out about it
was after the fact, when his client refused to pay the detectives' bill. The

detectives called the lawyer and demanded payment. That is one extreme of the rich and famous. The other side of that scenario is that often those in show business are willing to give in quickly, as they live in a world of delusion and make-believe and often have lots of money. When they are faced with the realities of life involving divorce, settlements, and custody, they frequently settle quickly to avoid bad publicity.

Another group of difficult clients is other lawyers and judges. Though the rate of divorce among those in the legal profession is low, and generally they strive to avoid litigation in their own divorces, they tend to be intransigent. Even if the lawyers' fields are corporate or admiralty law, when it comes to their own divorces, they will research relentlessly and come up with bizarre proposals and theories.

Judge Tommy Zampino, the chief judge in the supreme court in New Jersey, heard one case where both litigants were attorneys. Much to his amazement, the battle was over custody of the family dog. Not only did each want the other to pay "dog support," but each wanted full custody of the dog. That in itself was not unusual, as any lifestyle budget includes pet care, but neither was willing even to share custody of the pet. Despite efforts by the judge to bring the two litigants, whom he had known professionally, into his chambers, accompanied by their respective counsels, there was no reasoning with either of them. Each recited obscure laws and both threatened to take any decision Judge Zampino made that was not favorable to the appellate court. (In this case, the legal fees would undoubtedly have been minimal, as each would have represented him or herself.)

Finally, Judge Zampino told the husband and wife to bring the dog to court. He instructed the lawyers that both defendant and plaintiff would stand on either side of his courtroom armed with as many treats and toys as they wanted. The dog, which happened to be a male poodle, would be released into the courtroom, and the one the poodle went to first would have full custody.

"The day of reckoning arrived," Judge Zampino relates. "The litigants were on either side of my court, on their hands and knees with all the toys and treats spread before them. On cue, my clerk carried in the poodle and let him go. The first thing the dog did was to pee on the floor before running straight to me and jumping up into my arms."

In the end, when all the more important issues were settled and the anger had subsided, Judge Zampino says that the custody of the dog was resolved. "No, I did not get the family pet," he says. "As I recall, the wife got the dog and the husband was able to buy another dog and deduct the cost of the animal from the entire maintenance package."

The general rule should be that if you need brain surgery, go to a neurosurgeon; if you are casting for a film, hire an actor; if you need therapy, see a psychiatrist; if you want a divorce, consult a matrimonial lawyer. The trick is not only to *consult* the attorney, but to listen to his or her advice and follow his or her lead, as the attorney knows how to extricate people from potential legal disasters. The other tip to remember is that doctors should not cure themselves and lawyers should not represent themselves or second-guess their own attorneys.

Unfortunately, even if there are decent attorneys in the fray and a sensible and experienced judge, clients can be unmanageable for a variety of reasons—anger, insanity, and even drug and alcohol abuse. It takes a self-confident and knowledgeable attorney to know whether to deal with a "special case client," or if that is impossible, to resign from the case.

Within the parameters of lunacy, there are differences between men and women who are embarking upon a divorce. By the time a woman walks into a lawyer's office to defend or institute divorce proceedings, she can be unhinged, or at least extremely upset. A man will often cover his anxiety with aggressive behavior. Then there are some cases when divorce lawyers are confronted with graphic sexual descriptions, bold-faced lies, and irrational demands when clients come to them for help. Some of these clients—of both genders—are not unhinged because of a divorce but have had previous psychological problems, some serious, all their lives.

A celebrated Los Angeles attorney recalls one case where his client, the wife of a wealthy and powerful movie executive, claimed that her phones were bugged, messages were being sent through the television, and her soon-to-be ex-husband had planted a transmitter in her head. At one point, when the lawyer was riding in the client's car, she stopped short and motioned to the lawyer to get out. As the attorney got out of the car, he asked her what happened.

"They bugged my car," she said. "They put a tape recorder in my car so everything we say will be used against me in court."

That same client would call her attorney at all hours of the night, rambling on and on about what she expected as a settlement, listing her expenses and possessions in excruciating detail.

"Why are you telling me all this in the middle of the night?" the attorney asked her. "It could wait until the morning when you're in my office."

Quite seriously, the woman replied, "Because they bugged your phone. The quickest way to get a message to my husband is to tell you what I want over your home phone."

Another lawyer tells a harrowing story about a male client who was, based on solid evidence, having an incestuous relationship with his daughter. This was a moral issue for the lawyer.

"I sat my client down and let him know that I had hard evidence," the lawyer begins. "I informed him that his wife's attorney would present that evidence in court and even if he were to be exonerated, the damage to his reputation would be terrible. His image as a substantial member of the community would crumble, his position on numerous boards would end, and his career in banking would be shattered. I gave him a choice. Either he settles with his wife with the proviso that he would never see his daughter again unless she requested it, and if so, only in the presence of his wife, or I would resign from the case."

The man agreed with his lawyer's advice. He settled with his wife and promised never to see his daughter unless the teenager requested it and then only in the presence of her mother.

In theory, an experienced lawyer can control the client, especially if the client has something to hide. In practice, lawyers sometimes are faced with clients who are so disturbed that it is best for the lawyer to resign from the case. One attorney recounts an experience that was completely untenable.

The client, the wife of a successful real-estate developer in Florida, focused on the sexual activities she and her husband participated in during their marriage. As time went on, her descriptions became increasingly graphic. The problem was that the woman was French and her command of English was limited. When her lawyer had trouble understanding her, she would pose for him in his office and assume the positions of the sexual acts she claimed her husband forced her to perform. Finally, the lawyer suggested that instead of a show-and-tell in his office, she might write down all the peculiar sexual acts, even in French, and if necessary, he would have them translated into English. For the next month, the lawyer received a letter every day by messenger, each one more detailed and pornographic than the next. In desperation, the lawyer told her that unless she produced a medical certificate corroborating these practices, he could no longer represent her. A week later, the woman arrived at her attorney's office with a certificate from an orthopedist who obviously was trying to help. In his report, he concentrated on the callus formation on her knees. The lawyer politely told the woman that she would be better off seeking other counsel.

Just as there are no typical clients, even among the sane and insane, there are also no typical marital histories. Some people seeking divorce have been married for decades, others for months. Some have children. Others are childless. Some are young. Others are middle-aged or elderly. Often, husbands and wives both work and have charged professional careers. Just as often, while husbands work in offices, wives work at home, raising children and overseeing domestic duties. The opposite can happen as well. Wives work in offices while husbands stay home to care for the house and family. There are also myriad reasons that lead to divorce, though there are no ironclad rules. First wives are not systematically left for trophy wives. Men are not always dumped for tennis pros or personal trainers.

One eighty-three-year-old man who is a legend in the advertising business left his sixty-two-year-old wife of thirty years for an eighty-three-year-old woman.

According to the American Bar Association, 80 percent of women leave their husbands simply because they are unhappy, while 76 percent of men leave for another woman or man. According to a Pew Research Institute survey in 2008, 80 percent of women over the age of fifty who divorce will not go on to marry or have a serious relationship. Conversely, 75 percent of men over the age of fifty will go on to marry or cohabit with a woman who is ten or more years younger. There is no doubt that if proof of life after divorce means finding another mate, women are at a distinct disadvantage compared to men.

Though many clients from hell were difficult, disruptive, and deranged before they found themselves either plaintiff or defendant in a divorce, some were driven crazy by their spouses, who did everything to humiliate and harm them. In those cases, it takes an extremely sensitive and astute lawyer to manage the client while at the same time protecting the client from a partner whose sole aim is to demolish his or her future ex-spouse during and after negotiations and a final decree. In those cases, the lawyer will see a client when a specific event related to the separation but not incident to the divorce has already taken place.

FORGET MUTUAL DECISIONS to end a marriage. Forget two relatively civilized and calm people who are willing to sit down together to work out the terms of their divorce. Instead, focus on something more realistic—two people who are angry, bitter, and hurt, and have been together for several decades, the parents of children, who have shared possessions, real estate, stock, retirement, and bank accounts. Consider that one spouse has fallen in love with someone else and wants out of the marriage. Think about the one left behind who has invested years of his or her life in the relationship, gone through tough times, nurtured, supported, encouraged, and loved the other. Reflect upon the years of history the couple has shared where suddenly every blade of grass in a country house is a reminder of better times, how every empty space on a bookshelf or blank wall where once a painting hung is like a knife through the heart. Imagine an empty closet or desk devoid of papers as signs of some crippling emotional failure on the part of the one left behind.

This is the most usual state of mind of most people who are on the receiving end of the process or are forced to respond to the process. These people need to choose their lawyer carefully. Because they are already damaged, the worst thing for them is to fall into the grip of a professional who plays on that pain for his or her own monetary gain. These people, though wounded, also fall under the heading of "clients from hell." They take care, nurturing, patience, and understanding from their attorneys.

Litigants who have suffered the shock of being left will often consult a lawyer after they have been summarily notified without warning that their spouse is leaving.

Wanda Rupert's husband left a voice mail informing her that he was leaving her and their three daughters because his mistress was pregnant with his child. "Divorce is not a family decision that is discussed and arbitrated by a majority vote," Rupert explains. "When I came home from work and heard my husband's message, I almost collapsed. My first thought was what the hell was I going to tell our children? My next thought was how I was going to torture this bastard until there was no breath left in my body. This was the ultimate insult. What did he expect—that I wouldn't fight back? I had no idea he even had a girlfriend. Right then and there I made up my mind that I would break him. What stopped me?" She smiles. "My lawyer, thank God."

In another case, a man was coming out of his office when a uniformed and armed sheriff's deputy appeared and served him with divorce papers. His reaction was to rush home to try and talk to his wife. When he arrived at his house, he found that his wife had changed all the locks. The experience of rejection is bad enough, but rejection without warning is as brutal as being tossed naked into freezing Arctic waters.

"I called my lawyer who handled all my corporate work," Joseph Patrillo explains. "He told me to come right over to his office. When I got there, all I did was cry. I couldn't even speak. Within an hour, I was furious. I banged my hand so hard on his desk that I broke the glass top. If I could have killed my wife and gotten away with it, I would have done it."

Upon learning that her husband had consulted an attorney, one woman cut up all her husband's clothes. In another case, a husband threw his wife's jewelry into the East River while on a business trip to New York City. As it happened, these two victims of divorce consulted the same lawyer from a large Midwestern city. Speaking at his request without attribution, the lawyer tells the following story.

"They consulted me on the same afternoon," he says. "Two different meetings with two people who were completely out of control. At that point, they needed a doctor more than they needed a lawyer. I've seen just about everything, but the violence and lunacy coming from these two individuals—otherwise, I imagine, perfectly normal people—was just pathetic. In the end, all I did for the two hours I spent with each of them was to listen and calm them. If I could've prescribed meds, I would have."

There are even more humiliating scenarios. After seven years of marriage and working two jobs to put her spouse through the police academy, including typing all his assignments, Betsy was told by her husband that he had fallen in love with someone else.

"That was bad enough, but my husband's girlfriend happened to be someone I had met and who had always been so sweet and nice to me. In fact, Gina worked with my husband and would hang out at our house and would even talk to me about the troubles my husband and I were having trying to conceive a child. At that point, I was in the middle of intensive medical treatment after having three 'female' surgeries. Gina was our number one fan when it came to encouraging us to have a family. Well, one Thanksgiving, after [I had been] working out of town, my husband begged me to fly home early to be with him at Thanksgiving. Naturally, I did because I loved him. I flew home and we had a lovely family dinner at my parents' house and then went home to relax and digest the meal. We were lying around the living room, completely happy, having had a wonderful holiday, when all of a sudden, my husband turned to me and told me he wanted a divorce. Shocked and in tears, there was no way to change his mind. Not being able to afford my newly purchased/redecorated home on just my income, I moved into an apartment which didn't accept pets. I had to give my dog away, which was heart-wrenching. Two months later my husband called to tell me he had great news. Gina had moved in with him and she was pregnant. They were planning on getting married. Believe it or not, he told me they were going to name their baby the same name we were going to name ours when we were planning a family. It was surreal. Since he kept the house, he told me they planned on using the nursery I had decorated and painted because they loved the colors and thought I did such a good job. I was speechless!"

Months later, after having the benefit of a lawyer who encouraged her to enter into therapy, and with the support of friends and family, Betsy made an important step toward recovery. She realized that even though she had lost her husband, relinquished the marital home under duress, and moved into an apartment without her beloved dog, she was not yet insulated from her husband's spite and rage.

"It took a while until I realized this wasn't about me or my failure as a wife. This was about him. I believe he was more furious with himself for having made a mistake—marrying me—and I believe that given his personality, he basically hates women and will do the same thing to this wife. His rage at me, the desire to humiliate me and hurt me even after everything was settled and he had moved on to another life, was a symptom of his own self-loathing. My lawyer was a wonderful woman who had gone through a similar experience. She taught me that being bitter or wanting to get even would only destroy me. I needed to get on with my life."

Ordinary people go through extraordinary circumstances when confronting divorce. Sometimes lawyers go through extraordinary circumstances with their not-so-ordinary clients. Somehow, perfectly intact people facing divorce become undeniably irrational.

Donna Hanover was a high-powered television personality when she became enmeshed in divorce proceedings with her husband, then mayor of New York, Rudy Giuliani. When Giuliani and Hanover separated, it was the only time a sitting New York mayor had been involved in a divorce. A further aspect of the divorce was that after they had been separated for some time, Giuliani acknowledged that now there was another woman in his life, whom he would ultimately marry. Even more newsworthy was that toward the end of the divorce, he became an international figure as a result of the terrorist attack on the World Trade Center on September 11, 2001. All of the above resulted in relentless media coverage that made it difficult for the attorneys on both sides to go about the mundane legal process of simply getting two people divorced. What made things even more complicated for his legal counsel was that the mayor refused to use any government personnel to handle the media, thereby creating an enormous practical burden for the lawyers. The co-author of this book, who represented Giuliani, found that his phone service was inundated with media calls from all over the world. Media was camped outside his office, which meant that other clients would come to a divorce lawyer expecting privacy, and instead face television crews waiting outside of their lawyer's office building and sometimes outside his office door.

As the divorce negotiations dragged on, Hanover made it publicly clear that she considered the mayor's official residence, though a government-owned building, as the marital home. Although nobody had elected her to anything, and she resided in Gracie Mansion only as a result of her husband's elected position, she objected to his being allowed to invite guests to the public portion of the building even though that was separated from the living quarters.

In the course of a legal argument to the court, Giuliani's lawyer predicted that Hanover would stay there until "the last minute of the last hour of the last day of his term." In short, his lawyer felt, for her, it was more about the emoluments of office than it was about the more human issue in the divorce.

Several months after the settlement was reached and the divorce was over, the prediction made about when Hanover would leave Gracie Mansion turned out to be correct. As the ball dropped in Times Square to signal in the New Year, Hanover posed for a battery of cameras as she and her children were about to depart the mayor's official residence.

It was the last minute of Giuliani's term as mayor of New York.

LAWYERS ARE CRUCIAL to the intricate legal process of divorce. Clients often sabotage their lawyers' best efforts to settle a case without litigating in court. As we explained, mediation is not the usual course when embarking upon negotiations that will ultimately settle a divorce. In all cases, however, unless the circumstances are unusually amicable, which is often not the case, what is a wife or husband, or worse yet, a wife or husband with children, to do until the case is finally settled and he or she receives support?

Since the first appearance in divorce court usually involves a hearing for pendente lite or emergency support, it is curious that there is no system in place to separate the rich, middle class, and poor. In a democracy, this prospect, on first blush, sounds awful. Thought out, however, it actually becomes fairer than the present system. For example, real emergencies regarding food and shelter could be heard immediately in a separate arena where lesser proof is required. Those cases where the litigant is demanding luxuries to maintain a "standard of living," a separate venue or part of the court could hear those cases after review and verification of expenses by state-funded professionals. In this way, at the end of the divorce process when actual testimony is required, the differential between temporary maintenance and permanent maintenance would not be glaringly different.

When a litigant demands temporary maintenance to keep up a "style of living" until a permanent settlement is reached, the process grinds to a crawl. If a judge has four hundred cases to move through the system and is forced to be stuck on several dozen cases where people are fighting for a European vacation allowance or weekly flower arrangements, it is unfair to those in real need, as well as to judges who are underpaid and overloaded. A natural separation based on financial need would speed along the process for everyone. It would also discourage this mechanism that provides for temporary support—pendente lite—which is frequently a license to steal.

8

PENDENTE LITE

*Marriage changes passion. Suddenly you're in bed with
a relative.*
                    —MARK GOTTLIEB, FORENSIC ACCOUNTANT

IT IS ALL WELL and good to say to a wife and mother, or husband and
father, that his or her case will be heard in eight months. Unfortunately,
the courts seem to have the same notion of time as decorators, so that
eight months usually turns into two years. That suggests that if one has
only six months to live, the hope is that the person giving the amount of
time left would be a decorator or a court clerk.

The problem with waiting such a long time to have a case heard, never
mind settled, is that often the husband or wife doesn't have the means to
pay for the rent, food bills, and other necessities of life until he or she is
summoned to court to end the process, which, by then, may be too late.

In the supreme court or its equivalent for married couples, and in the
family or "everyman's" court for unmarried couples, an emergency temporary support mechanism is set up to provide—theoretically, at least—
instant relief for those who cannot survive financially until a final
settlement is reached. As it was originally conceived for indigent women
and men with small children, the purpose of pendente lite was to award
emergency funds for clothes, food, and shelter until a final divorce settlement could be granted. It was also a way for women or men in real need

to be awarded maintenance without having to go through a lengthy process of providing certified bills and receipts to prove that their requests were legitimate. In some states, the application for temporary relief is made orally. In others it is made based on skeletal papers and, in other rare cases, by detailed motion papers, supported by affidavits and documentary evidence. In rare cases it requires a full hearing or trial even to set temporary support and custody.

In the majority of divorces, the first motion lawyers make is for temporary support or pendente lite. There are several initial steps when the process begins. If the wife or husband in the case needs emergency temporary support, and the litigants can't or won't agree on the terms, each side appears in court for the pendente lite hearing.

Lawyers for the plaintiff and defendant draw up a set of papers, stating the amount that is needed weekly or monthly for their client to survive. If it is the wife's lawyer, he or she may say she needs a thousand dollars a week for support. The husband's lawyer may submit a set of papers saying she needs fifty a week, and a judge who, at this early stage of the case, really doesn't know who to believe since actual trials or hearings are not usually conducted on pendente lite motions, comes to a figure somewhere in between. The judge's decision is a sort of "rude justice," which means that the figure is generally either ridiculously too low or too high.

To re-create the scene, "rude justice" can be best described as follows.

It is usually the wife's lawyer who comes to court and says, in effect, "Your Honor, you have no real way of knowing if what I say, in terms of my client's needs and her husband's income, is accurate or if the other lawyer's version is the truth. But this wife and these children cannot wait eight months to eat or to pay the rent and all the other family bills that have and will accrue in the interim. We therefore ask you to render rude—but hopefully fair—justice on an emergency basis until some months later, when you hear all the evidence and witnesses, and can do perfect justice."

Rude or perfect, if the woman or man in question is in dire need of housing, food, heat, and whatever other necessities, pendente lite relief is a moral and crucial precursor to eventual permanent support. Depending on the situation, the good or bad news is that the appellate courts usually do not like to review such interim awards, and they almost have a virtual—but not actual—intelligence stamp prepared that says the best remedy (for an inequitable temporary award) is a speedy trial. Speedy trials, however, are not that speedy.

There are numerous other problems and obstacles that can and often do occur in court, and not just concerning the system but also the litigants themselves. For instance:

What if there is no trial?

What if there is a settlement that is presented to the court months after a temporary support order has been handed down?

What if judges, litigants, and their lawyers are eventually aware that the emergency support granted was based on knowingly inflated and erroneous living expenses?

What if the emergency support order was granted based on fraudulent representations and documents?

What if everything the litigants say under oath in the court is a lie?

One lawyer from Ohio answers those questions. "So what?" she says. "The discovery papers are used to cross-exam people at trial. Temporary support is only temporary."

A glamorous German woman married a well-known industrialist. The marriage fell apart and she appeared before a judge for temporary support. During a break in the hearing, she shouted out in the court, "What kind of place is this? They stand up and hold up their hands and swear to tell the truth, and then immediately proceed to lie."

She was echoing the sentiments of many people who are used to another legal system, particularly Western European countries. Though testimony taken under oath is taken seriously in America, since perjury in all jurisdictions is a felony and in some jurisdictions even has a mandatory jail sentence involved, sadly, back in the real world, a trial is often a contest between two liars who both lie under oath. In those cases, their lawyers are constrained. They cannot order their clients to take lie detector tests. Unfortunately, they are forced to basically accept their client's view of the world and the dispute, and they become helpless, unknowing accomplices to perjury. Obviously, if a lawyer believes his or her client is lying, the lawyer cannot, as an officer of the court, be party to perpetuating its perjury. Usually, however, the lawyer has no way of knowing or even suspecting that his or her client is lying.

A lawyer has to decide how to live his professional life. Either he or she is prepared to lie for the sake of winning a case, or he or she is determined to be scrupulously honest from the beginning to the end. From a purely efficient point of view, morality and legal obligation aside, lawyers who lie ultimately get caught. Most states have begun making lawyers do what federal laws require. Lawyers must certify that each document they present is true to the best of their knowledge, including what clients put on a financial statement or on a list of expenses that will keep them afloat until a case is settled or tried. The problem is that what is required of an attorney to certify what a client claims is not much of a certification. All the attorney has to do is take the client's word and sign off on the papers that will be submitted to the court. This system, in effect, rewards a lazy or noncurious lawyer. There is no bright line or Richter scale that dictates the degree of searching cross-examination the lawyer must undertake in questioning his or her own client. Having said that, all experienced lawyers have, at one time or another, had their internal lie detectors go off and have shown some clients the exit and returned their retainer.

There are no automatics in these situations. It is up to the judge, and the determination of the litigants, to be honest. It is also up to the lawyer to make sure the client is providing the court with papers that reflect a realistic list of basic necessities or luxuries as the case may be.

Based on research we did concerning the mechanics of emergency relief, we found several important observations made by Judge Nancy E. Gordon. Judge Gordon has presided over countless pendente lite hearings where one or the other litigant is living with a new partner and the living arrangements become part of an eventual order for temporary maintenance.

"When a woman or a man comes to court to ask for emergency relief," Judge Gordon says, "and it is a legitimate claim that requires urgent attention, the court will ask for a list of monthly expenses for each party. I'm thinking of one case in particular when the man claimed his rent was twenty-five hundred dollars and therefore he was unable to pay his wife's rent, which was three thousand dollars a month. What tilted the scales in that particular case was that the man was living with a woman who was sharing the rent and other expenses such as gas, electricity, and telephone. As a result, his monthly costs were reduced by half. I took that into consideration when I awarded the wife the full amount for her rent without prejudice, meaning that if his situation changed, he could come back to court to ask for relief."

Often, the results of a pendente lite application in a matrimonial litigation will set the tone for the rest of the case and may very well affect the ultimate outcome. If an unequal or unfair result occurs early on in the case, it could spell disaster for one party. It is usually through pendente lite motions that the judge who will likely be assigned to the matter will first become familiar with the parties. This will also be the first time that the judge will learn the critical facts regarding the parties' marriage, separation, children, and other pertinent facts relevant to the dissolution proceedings. This first impression is one of the most critical aspects of any matrimonial litigation.

From the impoverished wife and mother who needs food for her children to the unimaginably rich who require six figures a month to "survive," the examples of those who ask the court for pendente lite or temporary support are as diverse as the people themselves. There are women who appear in supreme court for temporary support and present a list that includes a personal trainer; hairdresser; clothes allowance; money for the upkeep of clothes; appointments for manicures and massages; dining out; fine wine and champagne; and airfare to travel to multiple homes throughout the world. Obviously, what are necessities to one woman are luxuries to another. What is sustenance for survival for one man—country club dues, maintenance on a cooperative apartment, chauffeur, upkeep for a Ferrari, and a valet—are unheard-of self-indulgences to another.

When a final settlement is reached and it turns out that the ultimate maintenance award was far less or more than what was awarded during the emergency hearing, the judge who made the temporary award is considered to have simply made a mistake. Unfortunately, in most cases, there is little or no recourse for either the provider or the one who has been awarded that inflated or deflated, exaggerated or undercalculated monthly sum. To demand a refund or an adjustment is usually impossible, and in any event, entails time in court, which involves legal fees that often negate any money that can be credited to the benefit of the litigant. To further complicate matters, many jurisdictions have a rule that even if a temporary award is overturned on appeal, the one who overpaid during the period the appeal was pending, prior to the appellate decision, is not entitled to a refund, and the recipient does not have to give back any monies. The rationale is simple and pragmatic.

If a wife/mother or husband/father has received an award that is too high and is subsequently reduced, in virtually all cases the wife/mother or husband/father has spent all of the money he or she has received. To create a payback situation may be impossible. To force a settlement in that case would be quite unfair to the wife/mother or husband/father. As for the husband/father, if he has underpaid his wife and children based on erroneous financial information, often, though not always, he is at a distinct disadvantage, especially if he left for another woman.

Some marriages have lasted for decades, with each partner approaching or past middle age, while others are relatively new marriages with young partners. Some are second or third marriages where husband and wife are also deep into middle or even old age, with children and grandchildren. Regardless of the many possible combinations, assets and earnings are the two key ingredients when judging who pays what to whom, how much, and for how long. Determining which spouse leaves or abandons the marriage and the marital domicile is often tricky. Is the one who slams the door and walks out the one who abandons the marital home? In some cases, one partner simply cannot take the physical or emotional abuse any longer and decides to leave.

In theory, pendente lite awards are gender neutral, especially now that men, more than women, are losing their jobs or taking salary cuts in a dismal economy. For the most part, however, it is still men who are required to support their wives, who usually have custody or at least shared custody of the children. Given that alimony and maintenance are based on income and not assets, and while it is true that women may control more wealth than men (by virtue of outliving their husbands), the unfair truth is that in any broad sampling, women earn less than men.

Pendente lite is not only gender neutral, but it is also impervious to class. Rich, middle class, or poor, no one is exempt from falling prey to a miscarriage of justice.

IF EVER THERE WAS A COUPLE who are the perfect example of how a divorce can go bad from beginning until the end, they are Lucille and Ted Ambroise. Whether it was the humiliation that Lucille suffered when her husband left her for a former girlfriend (a painful but not unusual occurrence), or the rage that Lucille harbored to "get even" with Ted for leaving her, or an unfair judgment in favor of Lucille during the pendente lite hearing, theirs is a classic case of "how not to divorce."

When Lucille went to court for temporary support, she put together a list of her monthly needs, which included a clothing allowance of many thousands of dollars; cleaning needs; household staff; upkeep for her car; massage therapy; a trainer; allowances for makeup, hair, and nails; and liquor for entertaining. She also included on her list maintenance for her cooperative apartment, a weekly arrangement of flowers, and utilities. The judge awarded her a monthly stipend based on her presumed needs that totaled more than twenty thousand dollars a month. The irony was that Lucille, much to Ted's dismay, never spent any money on clothes; refused to hire a housekeeper; did not have a car; never used a masseur, a masseuse, or a personal trainer, or went to the hairdresser for manicures, pedicures, or her hair. She was a recovered alcoholic, so she obviously never kept liquor in the house. As for the maintenance for her cooperative apartment and utilities, much later during negotiations it was discovered that her small company paid all her phone and electric bills, which she deducted on her joint tax returns with Ted.

The supreme court judge who heard Lucille's request for pendente lite had awarded her the requested monthly maintenance but did not set a date for the litigants to return to court with a final settlement. The negotiations dragged on for nearly a year, during which time Ted was obliged to pay Lucille more than two hundred thousand dollars in temporary maintenance. When the final judgment was rendered, substantiated by financial records, certified by the forensic accountant, including bank statements and credit card bills, the court awarded Lucille twenty-five hundred a month for three years in addition to a cash settlement that Ted was ordered to pay, which represented half of Lucille's interest in his country house.

"One of the travesties of justice," Ted's lawyer admits, "is that emergency maintenance or temporary support is given without having to substantiate every expense. It wasn't unusual for the Lucille Ambroises of the divorce world to inflate the figures, notwithstanding the lawyer's best efforts to prevent it, and lie to the court. It happens all the time. When

Ted wanted money back after all the financial records were submitted, he was advised not to bother. It would have cost him as much or more in legal fees and many more months of anguish."

"It's a bad system," Lucille's lawyer agreed. "But it's a hard call. I signed off on Lucille's list of expenses because the law only calls for the lawyer at that particular stage of the case to take the client's word. After all was said and done, it was apparent she lied. The problem is that, try as we do to prevent it, almost everyone lies when it comes to temporary support. It's found money."

THE ARGUMENT FOR PENDENTE LITE (moving quickly so as not to inflict unnecessary hardship on those in dire need) is much like the argument against capital punishment. It is better for one guilty person to be spared the death penalty, even for a heinous crime, than to execute one innocent inmate. The similarity, of course, is that it is far better to give a woman or man emergency relief quickly, eliminating lengthy corroborating documents, than it is to make the process for emergency relief more complicated so that the needy suffer.

Often, women in dire straits who appear in family court receive an order for child support and maintenance, only to have their husbands or partners not comply. Those are the situations, however, where a judge can issue a bench warrant, and the delinquent spouse or partner can be arrested for nonpayment.

RICHARD F. IS A SUCCESSFUL economist who had been married for more than twenty years. He has three children, two of whom are in college. From the beginning of his marriage, Richard was a devoted father and husband who was the major wage earner. His wife was a social worker and earned much less than her husband, though she was responsible for running the home and caring for the children. When Richard was fifty years old, his father died, and when he was fifty-one, his mother died. Something snapped.

The first sign of change in Richard was physical. He let his hair grow, wore only jeans and T-shirts, began going to rock concerts, and spent hours viewing pornographic sites on his computer. He also stopped having sexual relations with his wife and where once he was a doting father, he took little interest in his children. During an interview, he claimed that Dorothy, his wife, "refused to keep up with him."

When asked to give precise examples, Richard said, "She turned into a middle-aged woman overnight. She hated rapper music, only cared about what I wanted for dinner, and made scenes about the way I looked. She was overly concerned with the children and resisted making new younger friends."

Predictably, Richard filed for divorce. Dorothy was shocked when she received a letter from the lawyer her husband had retained. She was even more shocked by the way her husband announced he was moving out of their home.

"Richard left a message on my voice mail," Dorothy explains. "The message was curt and to the point. He just said that he decided to leave me and the children because every time he looked at me, he saw his own death."

Given Richard's state of mind and his wife's shock over the impending divorce, the lawyers for both sides were prepared for a protracted fight over money and custody. To their surprise, Richard was amenable to providing for his wife and paying the college tuition for his two older children. From the moment the decree was signed, however, Richard simply stopped paying anything. In the beginning, Dorothy made repeated pleas to her lawyer, who went to court on her behalf. After six months of wasted court appearances, loss of time at work, and her inability to pay legal fees as well as her monthly household expenses, Dorothy went to family court on her own to make her ex-husband pay.

As expected, the court issued a summons. Richard appeared in family court and because he had no legitimate reason for not paying what the supreme court had ordered, he was given two weeks to come up with back maintenance and child support. Two weeks came and went and still Richard did not pay. Ordered back into family court again, he was given a week to pay his wife what was owed her. Finally, after six weeks, during which Dorothy had no money and was forced to borrow from friends and family, the court issued a warrant for Richard's arrest. He was picked up and incarcerated. Richard languished in jail for over a month before he ultimately paid Dorothy what was owed. When asked why he put himself and his family through such unnecessary agony, his answer was "I just wanted her to know what it's like to live in misery and I was willing to sacrifice myself so she would give up and get on with her life."

AS STATED EARLIER, the formula for who pays what to whom is based on income rather than assets.

In supreme court, many upper-middle-class women who have been in short-term marriages with no children, despite the fact that they have their own money and independent income, will present their immediate needs for temporary support. As explained, these women can do that without having to furnish precise proof. A judge will award these women temporary luxuries as well as necessities under the same guidelines as those women who can't pay rent or buy food.

One of the few judges who decided that assets and income should not be the sole criteria in a divorce case as it concerned temporary maintenance was Judge Rosalyn Richter, who now sits in a New York State appellate court. The case involved Barbara W. Hearst, who was divorcing William Randolph Hearst Jr.

Mrs. Hearst had been awarded $26,000 a month tax-free as maintenance by another judge, Justice Laura Visitacion-Lewis, as well as insurance premiums and medical expenses.

When Mrs. Hearst went to the New York Supreme Court to ask that that sum be augmented to $90,000 a month, she found herself before a new judge. Judge Richter, hearing the case for the first time, heard the petition and instead reduced the monthly amount to $20,000 because she suggested that the wife was "looting" her husband's estate. According to papers filed in the New York Supreme Court, the judge's decision was based on her findings that Mrs. Hearst had transferred most of her disabled husband's assets to her own name in a "highly questionable manner." Further, Judge Richter ruled that Mrs. Hearst's "standard of living" claim was not significant as "the husband was sick and confined to a wheelchair for the last ten years of their marriage," and could not share in his wife's lavish lifestyle.

The couple married June 21, 1990, several months after William Hearst, then fifty-six and heir to part of his family's huge fortune, had suffered a debilitating stroke. Judge Richter wrote in her twenty-four-page decision that at the time of their marriage, Barbara Hearst, then fifty, lived in a rental house on a farm, had recently filed for bankruptcy, and owed the Internal Revenue Service $50,000.

In her decision, Richter also wrote that, "over the course of the marriage, nearly all of the husband's cash and investment accounts, which were funded by millions of dollars in distributions from the Hearst family trust, were transferred into accounts held solely in the wife's name. With those funds, Barbara Hearst bought six pieces of real estate, three in New York—Sag Harbor, Bridgehampton, and Manhattan—and three in North and South Carolina, all of which are solely in her name as well. Mrs. Hearst also had partial title to two other properties and controlled a trust that owned a ninth property. The wife also had nearly $8 million in liquid investments in her sole name, whereas the husband had only approximately $400,000 in a joint account he shared with his daughter. It is clear to this court that the husband never intended for his wife to take all his money and place it in assets in her control."

Though it was apparent that Mr. Hearst had an income of between $5 and $6 million from the Hearst trust, and despite Mrs. Hearst's attorney arguing that Hearst should be forced to pay while he was alive since only his descendants could inherit from the trust, Judge Richter did not amend her decision. In this case, unlike the case of Lucille and Ted Ambroise and countless others, Mrs. Hearst lost because Judge Richter decided that assets counted more than income and at the time of the hearing, Mrs. Hearst's assets were far larger than her husband's.

It was a courageous decision and proof that some judges can make precedent by examining each case on its own merits or demerits.

Though Richter's decision was unique, other judges believe that obliging women to use their assets to support themselves falls into a gray area of the law and can be potentially unfair.

Judge Tommy Zampino of New Jersey believes that judging the financials in a divorce on income rather than assets is often unfair, especially when it comes to temporary maintenance. He maintains, however, that there are problems when it comes to deciding at what point a judge can fairly make that decision.

"Assuming there is a disparity in income between the husband and wife," Judge Zambino explains, "it is the spouse, usually the wife, who receives maintenance and will never earn what the husband earns. How many millions in assets does the wife have to have before a judge can fairly say, no maintenance? What's the minimum or maximum a woman has to have to base the case solely on assets—fifty million, twenty-five million, ten million, five million? Suppose the guy makes twenty-five million a year. Is that fair? Now the wife is forced to use her assets to live, which means she can't save them for later when she is old or infirm. She has to keep her assets liquid and live off the interest. In the 'wonderful' case when one party has tremendous income and the other has no potential for earning that fantastic salary, there are no automatics."

In those cases where there are many millions of dollars at stake, even before litigants appear in court for temporary support forensic accountants may have already begun the process of sifting and tracing assets. The assets they focus on are bank statements, credit card bills, stock portfolios, real-estate holdings, pension plans, trust funds, jewelry, artwork, antiques, cars, and any other material property belonging to both or one or the other litigant.

Throughout the settlement process, including the motion for pendente lite, the job of the forensic accountant, hired by lawyers for each side, is to decipher and analyze the material in order to determine which assets are part of the "marital pot," or commingled, and which are separate. The situation becomes more complicated in that often funds are commingled. In most marriages if one of the parties inherits some money (which in many states would be considered separate property and, therefore, not part of the marital property to be divided), they do the almost automatic thing: they put the money in a joint account to be utilized for the couple's bills. The problem is, in some jurisdictions, this has the effect of the property losing its identity as being "separate" and makes it part of the marital mass that is to be divided between the parties. This is why lawyers frequently advise clients who are about to inherit money or receive gifts of money to establish a separate bank account and not intermingle it with marital funds.

Depending on the worth of the case, and how complicated the records are (often there are boxes and boxes of bank statements, credit card records, and all other relevant material), this will or should reveal the net worth of each litigant. Included in these documents are expenditures over the course of the marriage, as well as the weekly or monthly budget to run the household and support the children. This is when the forensic accountant enters the case.

Mark Gottlieb, a forensic accountant, says, "Usually after more than twenty hours of work on these papers, and in some cases far more— weeks and months—they are presented to the court. Most of the time the court doesn't read them in all their detail. Judges and/or their clerks are glossing over the documents before they casually put a number on the amount either the wife or husband is demanding as temporary sup- port. It is also far easier to lie on credit card bills that show expenditures since there is no absolute proof that those credit card statements have been paid. It is far more difficult to lie when presenting a bank state- ment, which clearly enumerates what was paid, deposited, and spent. It is all tedious work for the court. Bear in mind, the judges are so overloaded. If they really read the mounds of paperwork that comprise these reports, people would be waiting years instead of months to have their cases heard. It is precisely rude justice that keeps people alive until the trial or until a decision is rendered and there is final settlement of the case. True, there are some states that put people on the stand and require testimony before temporary award is given, but most of the time, in the majority of cases, that doesn't happen."

When there are limited assets, such as only the marital home and car, or if there are no assets other than the salary of one or the other litigant, often a forensic accountant will not be involved. It is likely, if there is a family residence, that only an appraiser for real estate would be required. Instead, the lawyers for each side, or a mediator, will request a list of assets before beginning negotiations. In these sorts of cases, the couple has some general—and usually specific—sense of the nature and size of the assets.

Whether the divorce is expensive or modest, after there is an award of temporary support or maintenance, a predictable game often ensues. If the award is beneficial to one party, he or she will prolong and delay a final trial when proof of expenses is required. The same is true for men or women who get away with paying far less than what they know will be eventually awarded. They too delay and prolong a final settlement. As a result, absurdities occur.

It is not rare that in a short marriage, a temporary award goes on longer than the length of the marriage itself. For instance, if there is a marriage of six months and a temporary award is made (since in most jurisdictions the length of the marriage is only one factor out of many that the court considers), that temporary award may last for two years until the case is eventually tried.

In the most opulent circumstances, special attention is paid to "lifestyle." Invariably, lifestyle cannot be maintained for both the husband and wife comparable to the one they enjoyed before the divorce case. "Two can live as cheaply as one" is an old lie. The truth is that there is never adequate money or a settlement considered by both sides to keep both partners in the "style" to which he or she was accustomed. By definition, divorce, whatever the financial level, rarely allows two people to end up in the same position as they were before the divorce. A perfect example of that truth is the divorce of Alex and Jocelyn Wildenstein.

9

THE WILDENSTEIN CASE

"Sir, if you were my husband, I'd poison your drink."
"Madame, if I were your husband, I'd drink it."
—CONVERSATION BETWEEN SIR WINSTON
CHURCHILL AND LADY ASTOR

THE WILDENSTEIN FAMILY had the distinction of being the most famous art dealers in the world. In addition to owning paintings by such masters as Renoir, Van Gogh, Cezanne, Gauguin, Rembrandt, Picasso, and El Greco, they also owned a 66,000-acre ranch in Kenya. The property, Ol Jogi, was five times the size of Manhattan, and included hundreds of buildings, a hospital, school, many varieties of animals, and about four hundred employees. The Wildenstein family also owned the largest private residence in Paris, a compound in the Virgin Islands, an apartment in Switzerland, and three adjacent townhouses located on East Sixty-fourth Street between Madison and Fifth avenues. One building was the actual gallery, its interior copied from the Wildenstein Gallery in Paris. Another building was utilized for living purposes, where Alex Wildenstein, his wife, Jocelyn, and other members of the family lived on the third, fifth, and sixth floors.

Besides the fact that the family was notoriously wealthy beyond the average person's comprehension, Jocelyn Wildenstein garnered a great deal of press as a result of her physical appearance. Though she started off as a quietly pretty woman with even features and a sweet face, she disfigured herself drastically after a series of plastic surgeries which altered her face. Each feature was pumped up or distorted. Her cheekbones were enlarged, shiny and bulbous; her lips, fattened and fleshy, were spread over the space above her upper lip and below toward her chin; and her eyes were artificially widened to make the outer corners of her eyelids curl upward to give them a feline aspect. Her scalp line was set back on her forehead—the result of numerous operations—which made her hair jut straight out like wheatgrass and surround her head like a halo. The image that comes to mind is Arcimboldo's vegetable heads, especially as a respectable body of criticism suggests that they were born of the painter's lunacy.

Jocelyn Wildenstein was the stuff of nightmares, and not without justification did the *New York Post* feature a photograph declaring her "The Bride of Wildenstein."

The family drama—as played out in the press—began innocuously. Jocelyn told her husband, Alex, that she was leaving for Kenya for a prolonged stay at their ranch. Instead, she showed up at the couple's townhouse accompanied by two private detectives and found Alex in bed with a woman. Facing two strange men in his bedroom, Alex quickly wrapped himself in a dressing gown and picked up his Smith & Wesson 9mm automatic pistol and pointed it at the detectives and his wife. The detectives called the police and Alex was arrested and charged with three counts of second-degree menacing. Though he had a license for the gun, the charge, if he was found guilty, could have sent him to jail for a year.

Alex was released from jail on bail, and immediately canceled his wife's credit cards and telephones, and locked many rooms in the townhouse with the exception of her bedroom. He also shut off her access to bank accounts, instructed his chauffeurs not to drive her, discharged her accountant and, in a final act of retribution, told the household staff to stop preparing her meals.

The next move was predictable. Jocelyn moved for exclusive occupancy of the townhouse and temporary support. According to England's newspaper *The Mail on Sunday,* Jocelyn said, "The truth is we spent a million dollars a month, what with the many homes, and legions of servants."

Enumerating her annual expenses, Jocelyn Wildenstein claimed that the telephone bills were $60,000; food and wine was $547,000; laundry and dry cleaning were $36,000; flowers were $60,000; massages and pedicures were $42,000; insurance for her jewelry and furs was $82,000; veterinarian bills and pet food was $60,000; her dermatologist cost $24,000; pharmaceuticals were $36,000; and payment of her American Express and Visa bills were approximately $494,000 based on the previous year.

In addition, Jocelyn's annual payroll for the townhouse included $48,000 for a chambermaid; $48,000 for a maid to attend to the dogs; $60,000 each for two butlers; $60,000 for a chauffeur; $84,000 each for two chefs; $102,000 for an assistant; and $102,000 for a secretary. Wherever she traveled, she explained, she flew in a private jet and was always accompanied by the "pet monkey and five Italian greyhounds."

As stated previously, according to several experienced lawyers and judges, the first offer a woman receives is usually the best and she should take it. In the case of Alex and Jocelyn Wildenstein, this was true.

Jocelyn demanded temporary support of $200,000 monthly for living allowance, payment of her personal staff's salaries and expenses, and a $50,000,000 security deposit pending permanent distribution of the marital property.

Alex claimed he had "less than $75,000 in his bank accounts." His only earnings were approximately $175,000 a year (supported by multiple affidavits), as "unpaid personal assistant to father Daniel Wildenstein." Alex also pointed out that he continued to pay Jocelyn $50,000 a month. His offer to his wife was to divide in half on-the-spot the marital property, the total of which was $10,000,000—the worth of her personal jewelry. As stated, in any divorce case, both parties have to submit a net worth statement as to their assets.

As for the exorbitant bills that Jocelyn claimed "maintained their lifestyle," they were all paid either by Alex's father, through "other bank accounts in New York, Paris, and Switzerland," or by "The Wildenstein & Company account, the Wildenstein & Company Special Account, and their family businesses." Alex was not a citizen of the United States, nor was his money earned here, nor did he even have a green card. Legally, he was a tourist.

In the end, the judge awarded temporary support of $140,000 a month and denied Jocelyn's application for experts' fees, such as accountants, valuation experts, a security deposit, and separate payments to her personal staff. When Jocelyn complained that she did not know how to operate a stove, the judge suggested she invest in a microwave oven.

The interesting aspect of the Wildenstein case was that the lifestyle portrayed of the family was accurate, which is usually not the case. Exaggeration is endemic in partisan court papers. The problem was that the money that supported their extravagant lifestyle did not come from Alex, but rather through the generosity of his father. When the case went up on appeal, the appellate court acknowledged that the money flowed from "imputed" income. The court determined that all funds were gifts from Alex's father and from payments made through various companies owned by his father, and ". . . the extraordinarily lavish marital lifestyle provided a basis for the court to conclude that the husband's actual income and financial resources were substantially greater than he reported."

This decision had broad-reaching consequences in other cases, particularly to fathers who had been underwriting their adult children's lifestyle. It demonstrated that a temporary support award could be made based on a grandfather's largesse.

The next problem was Jocelyn's right to remain in the townhouse while the case was ongoing. This is also a common situation. Parents allow their married children to live in a home which they own or provide. In her decision, the judge stated, "During their marriage the parties and their children shared a townhouse and the law is clear. When a matrimonial action is pending, regardless of whether the husband or wife is the owner of the marital premises, the other may not be evicted."

Admittedly, Alex did not own the house, as ownership traveled through a number of other entities which never ended with Alex, but that did not change the judge's decision.

Though Jocelyn and Alex Wildenstein were unusual people in many respects, and their separation and divorce were anything but ordinary, both suffered from the same emotions that any average couple experiences when they face the rupture of their marriage.

The most prevalent motivating force that prevents people from facing their own complicity in a failed marriage is fear. Fear is the one emotion that transmogrifies into irrational and uncontrollable behavior. Just as fear becomes rage on the road to recovery, it usually makes a brief stop at blame.

10

Fear, Rage, Blame—How to Ruin a Good Divorce

Marriage is a three-ring circus. An engagement ring, a wedding ring, and suffer-ing.

—Anonymous

EVEN UNDER THE MOST terrifying situations when women and men fear for their physical and emotional survival in a marriage, the fear of living alone and even dying alone is often so strong that it can cloud judgment, preventing a person from seeing the wisdom of seeking divorce. At the beginning of a divorce, most people are stymied by their fear and, as a result, are incapable of behaving rationally.

Adele Hammerstein is an eighty-year-old woman who recently filed for divorce. The question her attorney raised, as well as her friends and family, was "Why now?" Her response was both tragic and telling.

"As I aged, death became a reality. The thought of having a stroke or heart attack alone and dying on the floor with no one there to discover my body was my greatest fear. Then I began thinking about that final ambulance ride. I was afraid of being alone, heading to the hospital for what would probably be my last stay. When I turned eighty, I suddenly realized that perhaps I had several more years. The thought of living in an unhappy marriage for the rest of my life was more frightening than my fear about dying alone."

Judge Jacqueline Silbermann served as New York's statewide administrative judge for matrimonial matters from January 1997 until December 31, 2008. During that time, from March 2001 until December 31, 2008, she also served as the administrative judge of the Supreme Court, Civil Term, New York County. Additionally, she is certified by the International Institute of Conflict Prevention and Resolution as a mediator and arbitrator. When Judge Silbermann resigned from the bench on December 31, 2008, she joined the firm of Blank Rome to serve "of counsel" in the matrimonial department. Based on her years of experience, Silbermann concurs that fear is the one emotion that drives both men and women to do irrational things.

"Fear plays a big part and that fear is based on different things when it comes to men and women. It is not just women who cry or who are afraid of facing life alone. We all know about women who are afraid of the unknown when they are no longer Mrs. So-and-So and are suddenly without a husband. We also understand the financial fears that women have, whether they are rich, middle class, or poor. Men also have fears. They're afraid of losing their children since they are usually the ones who are forced to leave the family home and become the visiting parent rather than the custodial parent. I had a case where a man came into the courtroom crying. He had been served with divorce papers, hadn't retained counsel, and was fearful of being put on a schedule when it came to seeing his children. Both parties know the lifestyle they've known is about to change drastically, and fear of that change causes them to do all kinds of terrible things."

Judge Rosalyn Richter, who until recently was a matrimonial judge in the supreme court of New York, and who now sits in a New York State appellate court, has seen all the emotions expressed by litigants when they came before her in divorce cases.

"Fear is what makes it so difficult to settle cases," Judge Richter says. "People are afraid of living their lives without the other person. They're afraid of not having enough money. Most of the time, they're simply afraid of how they will manage their emotional lives as divorced people rather than having some kind of security by being married, even unhappily married. What I've heard so many times in matrimonial cases is 'it's not fair.' I always asked what is the 'it' they're talking about? What's not fair? The responses are always the same. 'We can't afford the same standard of living.' Or, 'It's not fair that he or she is having a child with another person.' Before sitting in matrimonial court, I sat in criminal court for twelve years and that's hard or even harder when you're sending someone to jail for a long time on a victimless crime—such as drug use. I found it actually helped me to understand how people felt facing divorce. Judges ultimately make the decision to take these peoples' lives away. I saw so much crying in matrimonial court—grandparents cried, children cried, defendants and plaintiffs cried. It's not rational but it happens all the time."

Men often combat fear by aggression.

Women are often empowered by fear.

Women facing divorce have burned down vacation homes, poisoned family pets, cut up their husband's clothes, called their husband's customers or clients, and turned in their husbands to the Internal Revenue Service. Without thought as to how their actions might affect them, women are often blinded by a false sense of power or being in control.

The future ex-wife of a famous plastic surgeon would periodically show up at her estranged husband's office and make violent scenes in front of a waiting room filled with patients, some preoperative, most postoperative. On one occasion, the irate wife accused a patient of sleeping with her husband and, despite the latter's bandages, broke her nose postsurgery.

Anita Brandon admits, "The terror of not being his wife, or of another woman carrying his name or children, drove me crazy. I didn't care if he would lose patients and income, though I knew that it would directly affect me and our children, I just wanted to punish him."

Another woman filed abuse charges against her husband, an internationally renowned architect, and had him arrested and dragged out of his office by the police. Whether or not the charge was true, she insisted her estranged husband be removed in handcuffs.

The embittered future former wife of a major real-estate figure sabotaged her husband by constantly canceling his credit cards, phone, and electricity, and generally subverted every aspect of his life.

One spurned woman, Jane S., an inmate at Bedford Hills prison, attempted to murder her husband and his girlfriend rather than suffer the indignities of a divorce. "I thought about the consequences and going to jail, but frankly," Jane S. says, "the thought of being out there on my own was more frightening."

Women aren't the only ones who resort to violence or destructive behavior. There are men who lack the courage or strength to go through the agony, humiliation, or financial trauma of a divorce without causing horrific consequences. Some are habitually delinquent on child support or maintenance, forcing their wives to take time from work to make desperate pleas to the court to feed their children or pay their rent. Some, like Scott Peterson, kill their wives and their unborn children. Who will ever forget Laci Peterson's mother yelling out in court, "Divorce was always an option," after the guilty verdict was brought down against Scott Peterson.

Malicious or deadly behavior stemming from fear during a divorce is gender neutral. Men are also on the receiving end of unthinkable acts at the hands of their wives.

The story of Linda Calbi is but one example of an egregious miscarriage of justice where a man suffered the inequities of the legal system, which more than terrified or enraged him.

In 2001, Mr. and Mrs. Calbi were divorced after fifteen years of marriage. A year later, Linda Calbi was sentenced to three years in prison for beating her son to death during a violent argument at their home. The boy died from internal injuries. Originally, Linda was charged with murder, but the charges were downgraded to aggravated assault based on expert reports that medical error at the emergency room contributed significantly to the boy's death.

A few months after his son's murder, Mr. Calbi fell behind in his alimony payments to his wife and filed papers in court seeking a reduction or termination of his payment obligations. Until she was convicted and incarcerated, he had been paying his wife $3,183 a month. In papers submitted to the court, Mr. Calbi claimed that his wife had "taken his oldest son from him, scarred his younger son for life, and tore the fabric of his soul." He asked for relief from paying his wife alimony at least while she was in jail as he did not want to "reward this evil and violent woman by allowing her to deserve financial benefit from the family she destroyed." He told the court that to make him continue paying alimony could only be described as a "perversion of our justice system." The court denied his appeal. Mr. Calbi was ordered to pay the full amount of alimony to his wife while she was in prison.

Linda Calbi was released from jail in 2008. She still receives alimony from her husband.

That description of one man's shock seems banal when describing the irrational actions of one spouse toward another. Otherwise rational people do irrational things indeed when they decide that the love affair or marriage is over. In one case, the husband was handicapped. When his wife left him alone in the house stripped of everything that was familiar to him, including a recliner chair into which he was able to maneuver himself from his wheelchair, his whole world fell apart. Fortunately, this was one case where justice was served.

Another example of a man who was terrorized by his wife is Nunzio Bagliere.

"My wife drove me home and told me she would be right back," Bagliere says. "When I entered the house my golden retrievers were gone, along with most of the household furniture and all her clothes."

The couple had been married for ten years and had no children. Both had good jobs and similar salaries. A one-car accident, however, had left the husband paralyzed from the waist down and in a wheelchair. He was unable to work. Ordinarily, he might have sued the driver of the car, but he chose not to. The driver was his wife. Life went on for the next few years as normally as possible. The wife still had a good job and health insurance and the means to provide home care for her husband. Until one day she decided that she'd had enough. She no longer wanted to care for a handicapped husband.

The state supreme court, in conjunction with the American Disability Act, saved him, along with a good lawyer. When the case was heard, the judge awarded the husband alimony for life from his wife, along with half her pension.

Though fear impedes rational thinking in divorce, it is also an intricate part of the process. Fear that turns to rage is also part of the recovery, if it is contained. These two emotions—fear and rage—are predictable and prevalent when people experience the disappointment of lost dreams. Regardless of the reasons people marry, once they do marry, they tend to create the idea of how wonderful the union is or could be. When that idea of "marriage is perfection" crumbles, the fear of divorce turns to rage. Some psychiatrists believe that anger, if it is controlled, can help alleviate the frustration of failure and self-loathing.

Elisabeth Kübler-Ross, in her 1969 book *On Death and Dying*, described a process by which people deal with grief and tragedy, especially when diagnosed with a terminal illness or after experiencing catastrophic loss.

The stages she listed are denial, anger, bargaining, depression, and acceptance. Divorce, though not a terminal illness, is certainly a catastrophic loss that results in people being forced to change their lives, often dramatically. Those who are embarking on a divorce might feel the same emotions Kübler-Ross described in her five stages.

In the beginning, the first stage is denial that anything is wrong in the marriage, followed by anger when they become aware that something is indeed wrong. Bargaining comes next when they ask their spouse for another chance or they try to convince themselves that if they lose weight, get a facelift, stop drinking, get a better job, control their temper, be a better parent, give up the girlfriend or the golf or tennis pro, that the marriage has a chance to survive. Depression is the next stage when they realize that divorce is inevitable and no amount of bargaining or pleading will restore the marriage. Finally, there is acceptance. If people are disciplined and rational at that point, they will realize that divorce is not, in fact, a terminal illness but rather a life-changing experience that could give them a new and positive beginning. Those who are unable to accept the finality of divorce, viewing it as the only way to have a chance at a better life, become flooded with fear. These are the people who have difficulty adjusting. They fear living alone, dying alone, going to the store alone, taking trips alone, and even going out with friends as a single man or woman. Regardless of how much they end up with after the divorce, they still fear the notion that they are on their own to face all the potential problems that could arise. Jocelyn Wildenstein put it simply when she said, "The idea of not having someone to talk to when there were problems put me in a state that vacillated between terror, rage, and ultimately back to terror. I needed a partner."

Several psychiatrists we interviewed believe that most people approaching the decision to divorce experience depression, fear, and anxiety. According to one of the psychiatrists, "Most people find themselves suffering from all the classic symptoms of depression caused by fear. They combat this hopelessness or avoid sinking even further into depression by venting their anger toward their spouse. Not only does it protect them and enable them to function when it comes to holding down a job or caring for children, but it is also an avoidance tactic where they refuse to accept any blame for the breakup of their marriage."

Blame is a sure sign the divorce will be filled with acrimony, and the

ideal way to guarantee anguish in the months and years following divorce. It is rare to find a case where there is mutual agreement and the
desire to remain friends after a divorce. If that ever happens, it usually
takes years, when the acrimony, financial devastation, humiliation, and
resentment are not forgotten but buried somewhere. Usually, détente occurs when both partners have moved on to new and fulfilling lives, either
with other partners, or because they found diverse interests emanating
from resources they found within themselves.

Eleanor Alter, a prominent matrimonial attorney in New York City,
has had years of experience dealing with clients who are in full "blame
mode" when they retain her to represent them in a divorce. According to
her, she has had clients—both men and women—who are unwilling and
unable to accept responsibility for a failed marriage.

"No divorce ever happened, or almost never happens, because one
party was a saint and the other was the devil," Alter says. "The cause of
the divorce, why a marriage went wrong, has to do with all the stuff you
bring from your childhood. More than often people pick their spouse for
all the wrong neurotic reasons. Women pick men who treat them badly
perhaps because they like that, maybe because their fathers treated them
badly and it's just so familiar. Many women come in and tell me that
their husband has a twenty-five-year-old girlfriend," Alter says, "which
entitles them to more than sixty percent of his assets." She shakes her
head. "I try to explain that there is no such thing as reparation money in
divorce. There is no formula that states the younger the girlfriend, the
bigger the settlement. The usual reaction from these wounded women
who blame their husbands for ruining their lives is that because he committed adultery, he can't see his children. The biggest problem lawyers
have is convincing clients that divorce should not be about revenge or
blame, but rather about doing a deal that is fair for both parties. The
bottom line is that a settlement can be fifty-fifty, sixty-forty, or even
seventy-thirty, but rarely hundred-zero. Legally, blame has nothing to do
with money."

Blame, or rather, proving wrongdoing, is not grounds for divorce. In
most states, people do not receive reparations because they were less
than perfect husbands or wives. Even in cases when one side or the other
can prove adultery, there is no difference in the financial resolution. Those
people who believe that the settlement goes up if there has been more

than one lover are in for a surprise when they appear before a judge. Whether someone has had one lover or ten, no marriage ever ended because of adultery. There are always other reasons.

The way men approach their spouse's adultery is much different from the reaction of their wives. A wife will usually get upset once if a husband commits adultery and then is prepared to move on. Whether there are multiple women or men, for that matter, she does not dwell on the transgression but instead focuses on the children, money, and keeping the home together. A husband could be maintaining a harem, and will justify it for one reason or another, but as soon as he learns that his wife is involved with another man, he loses all sense of sanity. He keeps repeating the details to his lawyer, giving graphic descriptions of who did what to whom and how many times and basically sees it as something tantamount to genocide.

Admittedly, Lester T. hired prostitutes almost every night while he was in the middle stages of a divorce. When one of Lester's friends told him that his soon-to-be ex was dating a variety of men, he became irrational.

"I told my lawyer to get a detective so I could catch her in the act," Lester says. "My lawyer told me it was pointless, that it was a waste of my money. Then he moralized with me when I said I wanted to fight her every inch of the way when it came to giving her any money. What really got me angry was that my lawyer actually asked me what difference it made since I was spending money on hookers."

According to Lester T.'s attorney, he was finally able to convince Lester that the best course of action was for each of them to go on with their lives and not get embroiled with detectives, which would only cause more animosity and bitterness.

"It was the old story," the lawyer says, "give it to her, not to me, and get the divorce over with as quickly as possible. It would be so much easier not to become focused on a contest of wills in any divorce."

Lester T. was lucky. He had a rational attorney who convinced him that bad legal advice would only cost him time and money.

Adultery is a symptom, not the disease.

New Jersey Supreme Court Judge Tommy Zampino lauds the fact that there is never punitive alimony in his state, and especially in his courtroom. "I remember one particular situation," Judge Zampino says, "where there was an intact marriage with children. At some point, the husband found out that his wife, the mother of his children, had sex with a friend of their sixteen-year-old son. During the divorce proceedings that followed, the fact that the wife had sex with a minor obviously impacted on custodial arrangements and parenting access. But it had nothing to do with the financial outcome of the case though the husband tried to get all the assets and get away with paying no alimony or maintenance. A good judge in a no-fault state has to narrow the basis or look at the balance of things in each individual case. In New Jersey we never let money play a part in punishing one spouse or the other. There is no place for fear, rage, or blame in our court. Our motto is to tell people to get on with their lives, fault is not a factor in equitable distribution and revenge is the last in the line of factors on which alimony is based. In the end I will decide, according to need, disposable income, length of marriage, and other concrete factors, how much one or the other gets, so why do I want to hear about the bitterness? It's irrelevant to my judicial decision. That's not to say that as a human being, I'm not sympathetic when one or the other litigant has clearly contributed to the demise of the marriage. That is also not to say that when one litigant expresses fear about their futures, it doesn't move me to feel their pain. But it never influences my decision in the financial aspect of a case."

To prove his point, Zampino refers to a case in New Jersey which indeed set a precedent in the law when it came to punitive alimony.

"This happened back in the seventies," Zampino says. "The case was *Greenberg versus Greenberg* and the couple were already in divorce court. The wife was in the hospital and the husband brought his girlfriend to the marital home to have sexual relations with her. The judge in the case immediately increased the wife's alimony from fifty to one hundred dollars a week. When the husband appealed, the appellate court reversed the decision, stating that alimony cannot be punitive."

There are exceptions that propel a judge to order punitive alimony, and that occurs only when there is egregious fault. In those cases, fear of physical harm, or rage that can manifest in violence, can cause a judge to place blame on the offending spouse. Several cases are clear examples of one spouse having committed acts of violence that result in the victim receiving the major share of assets during a divorce.

"Obviously," Ken Burrows, an attorney in Connecticut and New York, says, "if it's a matter of egregious fault, such as someone putting a contract on a wife or husband's life, that's enough to influence the court when it comes to a distribution of assets."

One case like that did occur in New Jersey, but given the circumstances, the husband was not only financially penalized but also convicted in criminal court.

The case was *Blickstein v. Blickstein.* The husband had offered $50,000 to an individual to murder his wife. The Blickstein case tested the limit of the law when it came to egregious fault. The decision brought down by the New Jersey Court stated, "where a spouse has committed an act so evil and outrageous that it must shock the conscience of everyone . . . it is inconceivable that this court should not consider his conduct when distributing the marital assets equitably."

During testimony, Mrs. Blickstein stated, "At first, my fear was free-floating. I was afraid of being alone and not having a life. After my husband began threatening to harm me and later on, to have me killed, my fear became very substantial and rational."

There is another well-known case where the husband attempted to prove egregious fault in order to claim the major portion of his and his wife's real estate assets, as well as retroactive child support. Though that case did not entail attempted murder, the lawyer cited the *Blickstein v. Blickstein* decision as precedent to prove his case to the wife's advantage.

In May 1997, Jennifer S. and Bill S. married and subsequently had four children. On or about February 2004, Jennifer S., the defendant in the case, began an affair, became pregnant, and had a son. The infant, named Charles, was born in December 2004 and was welcomed into the family as Jennifer and Bill's fifth child.

Things went along without incident until, in the spring of 2007, Jennifer began another affair, but on that occasion, suggested to her husband that they have a trial separation. For whatever reason, when the idea of separation was raised, Bill became suspicious that Charles was not his biological son. According to Bill, for years he had been hearing jokes from friends and family how Charles "looked nothing like him."

In February 2008, without telling Jennifer, Bill arranged for a DNA test and learned that, in fact, he was not Charles's biological father. When he confronted his wife, she finally admitted that the boy was not his son but rather the issue of an affair. At that point, Bill was the one who instituted divorce proceedings and charged Jennifer with both adultery and cruel and inhuman treatment. He also filed a separate claim of fraud. As damages for the fraud, Bill wanted to recover all the expenses he had paid for raising Charles as his own son, his attorney's fees, and profits from their investments "from the time of Charles's conception until the beginning of his action for divorce." In response, Jennifer countersued for divorce on the grounds of abandonment. By then, the acrimony had become almost untenable and by May 2008, Jennifer, through her lawyer, made a motion to the court to dismiss the claim of fraud to which Bill cross-moved to prove his wife's "egregious fault."

Though the court denied Jennifer's motion to dismiss the claim of fraud, it also judged that the "defendant's alleged misconduct did not constitute egregious fault and had no bearing on spousal maintenance and equitable distribution." In lay terms, while the court ruled that the wife had been unfaithful and had concealed the truth about Charles's parentage, it had no bearing on the equitable distribution of marital property. When it comes to egregious fault in a divorce case, there has to be behavior that is "so egregious or uncivilized as to bespeak of a blatant disregard of the marital relationship—misconduct that shocks the conscience of the court, thereby compelling it to invoke its equitable power to do justice between the parties."

There are other examples of behavior that fit the definition of egregious fault which *does* make fear, rage, and blame part of a judge's decision and *does* have an impact on equitable distribution. For instance, a husband who raped his stepdaughter is one example. In another instance, there was a mother who took her children, against a court order, to Lebanon, which the court ruled was a "war zone." Another case involved a man who beat his wife with a barbell and a piece of pipe, breaking her nose, jaw, and some of her teeth, causing multiple contusions and lacerations, as well as permanent neurological damage and other serious injuries. In that case, the court found the husband guilty of attempted murder.

Domestic violence often begins as emotional and verbal abuse, and escalates into egregious physical abuse which is clearly rage and which absolutely causes fear, and which puts blame squarely on the spouse who batters. That said, even in those cases of egregious behavior brought before a court during divorce proceedings, it usually does not condemn or blame the abuser financially or criminally until the abuse reaches unspeakable levels. For example, verbal harassment of minor children, or several acts of "minor violence" against the wife does not automatically, according to the court, constitute blame or the legal term, egregious fault.

In one particular case, *Kellerman v. Kellerman* in 1992, the court ruled that the defendant (the husband), though he verbally harassed his mentally challenged son and pushed his wife on several occasions, neither "endangered nor deliberately embarked on a course designed to inflict extreme emotional or physical abuse upon them."

Fear, rage, and blame, which can lead to egregious fault, can be the usual components in any divorce. Whether or not there is violence or egregious fault in a divorce, however, the decisions regarding maintenance, alimony, child support, and financial settlements are not always equal. In fact, emotions aside, the goal in most divorces is to reach an agreement which would represent equitable distribution. The problem is that most people do not understand that equitable does not mean equal. Equitable in the eyes of the law and in the minds of judges means fair. Obviously, what is considered fair to one side is not always fair to the other.

Part Two

The Equality Myth

11

Family Court and Supreme Court

Criminal court is where bad people are on their best behavior. It's much more dangerous for lawyers and judges in family court, where good people are at their worst.
—RICHARD DOOLING, AUTHOR OF
WHITE MAN'S GRAVE AND PROFESSOR OF LAW
AT THE UNIVERSITY OF NEBRASKA

THERE IS THE BELIEF, and not without merit, that women suffer more than men after a divorce. It is true that single men are more of a commodity than single women. People are less fearful about inviting divorced or widowed men to a dinner party than they are about the presence of divorcées or widows. Though it is statistically a fact that divorced men are as eager to find a new mate as are divorced women, or more so, women without husbands or lovers are often viewed as predators who are bent on threatening other women's marriages.

From experience, matrimonial lawyers understand that women are far more equipped emotionally and psychologically to leave a marriage without having a new mate on the horizon than men are. Instinctively, many women have far more access to their inner lives than men. Women will walk out even if they have children and strike out on their own without the guarantee of ever becoming one half of a couple again. Their immediate objective is frequently safety and serenity. Those priorities at the moment they make the decision to leave take precedence over their fears of long-term repercussions. Women are adept at creating homes that are cozy, comforting, and secure for themselves and their children. They are able to care for themselves, as they are programmed to nurture. They also have the benefit of more attentive and accessible support systems, whether that means other single women, family, or groups that discuss the perils and advantages of being divorced. Women are more prepared to juggle jobs and children, as they usually were functioning in dual roles even when their marriages were intact. Generally, women have less pride about voicing their fears, anger, depression, or loneliness. Consider the reaction of people who know single mothers who manage jobs, grocery shopping, picking up children from playdates or school, and who rarely exhibit the slightest surprise that women can juggle everything alone.

Men are far more fearful of living alone and caring for themselves. Men are more apt to leave a marriage when they have another woman waiting to step into the role of mate, caregiver, and steady sexual partner. Many men believe that to express hurt and fear is a sign of weakness. Men often do not have the advantage of a solid support system since confiding in friends and family is not the usual behavior between male friends or their extended families. Those men who end up as the custodial parent are often overwhelmed with the tasks of caring for children and functioning at work. Consider the admiring and surprised reactions when people know of single men who are managing jobs and children.

In addition to certain legal issues that should be changed to make divorce easier, society should adapt its mind-set when it comes to the aftermath of divorce and what constitutes success. Financially, there are no winners in divorce unless the litigants are among the small percentage of people who have millions or billions with which to maintain two high standards of living. If society did not judge coupling as the measure of victory and success for divorced men and women, the playing field would tilt in favor of women. Coupling should not be the ultimate litmus test of adjustment. In reality, many people marry the same type of person the second, third, and even fourth time they walk down the aisle, whether out of habit, comfort, or some form of self-inflicted punishment. Divorce does not change the people involved but rather offers an opportunity for them to create lives that are not filled with apathy, bitterness, or boredom. A neurotic person will remain neurotic, just as a jealous spouse will still be jealous of any new partner. Men usually end up with a younger version of the wife they divorced and women frequently find men who are psychological carbon copies of their former husbands.

LEGAL DECISIONS IN MOST divorce courts happen too slowly or too quickly. When rulings are made too quickly, it is because a judge has limited time to go over detailed legal briefs and other forensic financial material. Not only is there a dearth of matrimonial judges, who are over-worked and underpaid, but there is also an overload of cases. In some instances, a judge has more than three hundred cases to study at the same time. In far too many situations, a clerk will review documents for a judge and make recommendations based on a broad interpretation of the law. There is simply not enough time to take into consideration ex-tenuating circumstances or nuances that make each and every divorce different. Because of the volumes of documents that must be studied, judges, though they try, are not always able to set a date that requires litigants to appear before them to announce that they have reached a fi-nancial settlement. Nor do they have the ability even to set a date when the parties and lawyers should appear in court to discuss a settlement. In those cases when an appearance is set, there is often little time to oversee negotiations to reach a final settlement. As a result, cases can drag on for months.

Rethinking domestic relations law is a potentially lengthy and conten-tious process. In order to achieve change that will not take decades, soci-ety must alter social and cultural judgments about marriage, which, in turn, will influence the legal system concerning divorce. Even more critical is that those going through divorce need advice and encouragement to view the process, though painful, as an opportunity for another chance. An astute lawyer knows instinctively that deep down people who have decided to divorce have harbored resentment or held on to unrealistic expectations dating back to the beginning of the marriage. Rich or poor, educated or illiterate, young or old, most divorcing couples understand somewhere in their psyche that either they should never have married their spouse in the first place, or that love had died long before they faced the decision to divorce. Many people who have been unhappy for years have spent those years dreaming, fantasizing, imagining, and creating dif-ferent scenarios to find the nerve to break up their marriages.

A North Dakota divorce attorney with more than thirty years of experience believes that even the people involved really don't know why they have decided to end their marriage at any particular moment in time.

"Only the two people involved and maybe not even both of them know," he says. "They'll tell you things—like he ran around or she spent too much money or a slew of other rational or irrational reasons. At the end of the day, the emotional dynamic between two people remains a mystery even to them."

Presiding over a matrimonial case is complicated, as it includes many facets of the law, which is one reason why judges do not remain indefinitely in parts of the court devoted to marital matters. According to Judge Jacqueline Silbermann, it has always been difficult to get good judges who are willing to serve in this area largely because the cases are complicated and time-consuming. Added to that, matrimonial cases are usually decided by a judge rather than by a jury, meaning that everything involves motion practice, which accounts for the inordinate amount of time required.

"In a matrimonial, the judge is never right," Judge Silbermann says. "Everyone complains about the decision. Unfortunately, matrimonial judges don't often get the same respect as those judges who sit on medical malpractice cases or in surrogate court. Add to that reality, matrimonial judges earn about half to two-thirds of what a lawyer gets at a law firm fresh out of law school. There are no shortages of people who want to be judges, but matrimonial court is a very sensitive and difficult position. While judges in surrogate court will get rational people before them, in matrimonial court, you get people bursting into hotel rooms with cameras trying to catch someone committing adultery. This lower opinion of matrimonial judges isn't fair, since in a matrimonial case, the judge has to know the law when it comes to complex financial issues, similar to dissolving a business partnership or dividing assets. There is also a great deal of commercial, real estate, and corporate law involved, plus all the issues about children and the family."

Not only are matrimonial judges often given less respect, but also matrimonial attorneys are generally not as revered as even those trying white-collar crime or criminal cases. One of the problems that confronts matrimonial lawyers is the emotion involved. The difficulty that some attorneys have when it comes to persuading litigants to be rational and calm is that they themselves become emotionally attached to the case and, as a result, are not always able to advise objectively. Issues of support for minor children, inability for the wife or husband to pay for rent, heat, and food, or other dire concerns make some lawyers as indignant and irate as their clients. The fact that there are many inequities in matrimonial law does not make things easier.

Family court is perhaps the one legal venue that is unimpressed by celebrity. Those judges who sit in family court tend not to get emotionally involved in cases, as the turnover is quick and the caseload is tremendous. It is a situation of "Move the merchandise." Unlike the supreme court, family court hears cases whose urgency requires swift decisions, as family situations are far more crucial than requests for money for personal trainers or clothes.

When Brazilian model Luciana Morad sued Mick Jagger for child support for her infant son, the celebrated rocker was forced to appear in New York City's family court since the couple was not married. Only married couples, regardless of their financial status, who are in the process of divorce are obliged by law to be heard in a supreme court or its equivalent. The law usually states that in all cases where couples are unmarried, even if the father has established paternity, any action for support must be heard in family court. The prevalent explanation throughout the legal profession is "Cases involving unmarried couples are not worthy of being heard in supreme court." That even includes celebrities, which was why Jagger and Morad were forced to appear in family court even after paternity tests confirmed that Jagger was indeed the father of Morad's baby.

The family court ordered that Jagger provide a net-worth statement that would be used as a guide for the amount of support he would pay to Morad for their child. Though ordered to appear in person, Jagger was able, on March 15, 1997, to testify by telephone from England. Jagger's lawyer, John Vassallo, appealed the ruling that would have surely meant that Jagger's net worth would be published by the international media. At the same time, Vassallo assured David Kirshblum, the family court examiner, that his client would be willing to pay any "legal and reasonable child support amount the court ordered." It was an odd venue for someone like Jagger to be heard, even by telephone from England.

Morad asked for $35,000 a month until the infant was twenty-one. The court was not buying, and ultimately, Jagger was ordered to produce his financial information despite his demand for privacy. Eventually the case was settled.

Another celebrity matter that was relegated to family court involved the singer Tom Jones. In that case, there was a humorous aspect.

One of the last times that Judge Judith Sheindlin sat in court before becoming Judge Judy on television, she heard a paternity case involving Tom Jones and a woman named Katherine Berkery. According to testimony, the singer met the woman at Regine's in New York, which at the time was a popular bistro and discotheque. Seduced and charmed by the singer's attention, Ms. Berkery went back to his hotel suite at the Essex House and spent the weekend with him in bed. Several months later, she found that she was pregnant with his child.

The trial began with the results of the DNA test as 99.66 percent certain that Tom Jones was indeed the father of Berkery's child. Because paternity is based on percentages, the singer decided to fight the results and hold firm that he was not the infant's father.

In court papers, Katherine Berkery had listed her occupation as model, which predictably, and unfairly, got transformed in the press as prostitute, later to be amended as mistress of John Gotti, the late Mafia boss. Neither alleged occupation or relationship was true.

One of Tom Jones's lawyers was Barry Scheck, an expert in DNA, who made his name years later when he was one of O. J. Simpson's lawyers during the football star's trial for double murder. At the Jones/Berkery trial, Scheck produced a professor of genetics who testified that although the DNA was 99.66 percent positive as a paternity match, it did not preclude 74,000 white males in the metropolitan area from being the father. During cross-examination, Berkery's lawyer, the coauthor of this book, asked the professor only one question:

"Do you know whether any of these seventy-four thousand white males was in Room 816 of the Essex House on the evening of February fourteenth?"

It is not often that a family court judge has the opportunity to laugh given all the misery presented before the court. On that particular occasion, however, Judge Judy did laugh. In the end, because of the DNA test, and the mother's testimony, the singer lost his case and was obliged to pay Berkery child support until the infant was twenty-one.

FAMILY COURT IS KNOWN as the "poor man's," or everyman's, court.

Judge Jacqueline Silbermann explains the real differences between supreme court and family court: "The main difference is not just that a divorce can only be granted in supreme court, but that the rich or upper middle class can't expect family court judges to rule on equitable distribution. They can only give a woman or man emergency maintenance and child support, whether the person who appears is married or single. The people who come to family court are not asking for personal trainers, hairdressers, clothes allowance, nannies, or restaurant expenses. They are in real need. In other words, rich people don't go to family court. Rich people have lawyers who take them to supreme court, and that costs money. In family court, the person files a petition and the judge will give a temporary order of support come hell or high water. You walk in and boom, you get it, but that never includes frivolities. The question you might ask is, If it's so easy, why doesn't everyone go to family court? The answer is obvious. Rich people have far bigger numbers, which they will never get in family court. A family court judge will not be sympathetic to a woman who is demanding luxuries. They hear too many cases where women are in need of food for their children."

Those who don't have the means to engage lawyers to negotiate their divorces or who do not have the funds to make repeated appearances in state supreme court or the equivalent state trial courts risk being at a distinct disadvantage. The system is not set up so that less fortunate couples can use family court to entertain status lawsuits, for instance those for divorce or separation. It can only grant support and custody, and address related problems. They can only achieve what the supreme court can provide for the upper middle class and rich. In addition, the family court can and does deal with problems affecting unmarried couples where custody, paternity, domestic violence, unpaid child support, and maintenance are the issues.

Many lawyers believe that support standards should not differ in the supreme or high-level trial courts, from family court venues. Unfortunately, as a practical proposition, those who are married and use family court to settle financial disputes often cannot expect to receive the same level of financial awards granted in supreme court.

The other problem with family court is that it is not used to dealing with convoluted or complex economic issues. The villain that makes family court less equipped to deal with more complicated subjects is the sheer volume of cases coming before judges who sit there, and the number of those matters that need instant attention.

There should be a better system.

There *could* be a better system if rules were changed to make divorce for all economic classes of people more equitable. One possible solution is to relegate couples involved in a divorce, whether they are rich, middle class, or poor, to separate courts according to the potential worth of the divorce. Presently, small-claims courts or local informal courts that are at the bottom end of the food chain have a cut-off point, which is anywhere from $500 to $25,000, depending on the state. That is true for all cases with the exception of landlord-tenant disputes, which are unlimited in most states and can be the province of a separate, dedicated court.

The system that deals with divorce does not set a monetary limit where the financials of a case are heard in different courts, as happens with commercial or tort cases. Actually, in many states such a system is in effect in another area of law. In estate matters, for example, there are larger filing fees involved for larger estates than for lesser ones. In probate matters heard in surrogate court, when the initial forms are filled out, the value of the estate must be included, usually for the purpose of informing the state estate tax authorities to determine the categorization of the estate to be probated. Similarly, when a divorce case is commenced, the parties should have to state the potential amount of monies involved.

It would seem more equitable if lawyers were required to file papers to make a disclosure of the amount of the potential dispute. Fees and costs should also be set utilizing that figure.

In many jurisdictions, family court or its judicial equivalent is designed for accessibility of the less financially fortunate. But it is also, as explained, a court that does not often have the authority to grant a divorce or, unless specifically allowed in a judgment, agreement, or statute, to uphold or enforce a settlement already made in supreme or higher trial courts.

The situations in which the courts involve professionals, those who comprise the "cottage industry" associated with divorce, varies from state to state. Each state has its own guidelines. A dreary economy unquestionably makes it more difficult to have forensic help available. In one state, until the late 1990s, the mental health unit of the family court had a staff to deal with custody and visitation disputes for lower-income people. The mental health unit would also conduct forensic evaluations on abuse and neglect cases. Currently, those who use the family court do not have an on-staff unit to help them but instead, in order to get a forensic evaluation, they must qualify under certain sections of the local law. This qualification allows them to get a forensic evaluation paid through a voucher system to the state. The rates are far lower than those a professional therapist or mental health expert receives by the hour, which means it is often difficult to get "good" people to do the work. A psychiatrist who does work in the supreme court will receive four hundred dollars an hour, while the equivalent professional appointed by the family court will only receive between seventy-five to ninety dollars an hour. In a poor economy, there are fewer funds available to hire professionals, regardless of hourly fees.

In supreme court, when the custody case involving the billionaire head of Revlon, Ron Perelman, and his former wife, Patricia Duff, was assigned to a forensic psychologist, they were obviously in a position to pay him or her the higher rate, which should have assured them of an excellent evaluation. Those who suffer the most from this system are those people who fall somewhere in the middle, where they are not rich enough to pay for their own experts, and not poor enough to qualify for court-appointed professionals. Some of these cases involve abuse or neglect of children. These families have no option except to try to work it out on their own.

An example of a case where the parents did not have the money to engage a competent forensic expert, but did not qualify for the funds or vouchers which would have at least given them access to an expert appointed by the family court, is especially tragic. In those cases, everyone suffers.

The parents were both artists, a struggling young couple who were educated but clearly too young and without adequate emotional and financial resources to begin a family. By the time the case came to family court, the couple had two young children, aged four and six. The mother suffered from significant bipolar disorder. She was hospitalized repeatedly. She was also accused of behaving badly toward her children. Despite her history of illness, she managed to get the husband evicted from the marital home by alleging abusive behavior on his part. When she was finally alone with the children, she discovered they had contracted head lice at school. She boarded up the windows and threw out all the furniture for fear that the lice eggs were in the house or could come in through the windows. Eventually, the father managed to get custody of the children. An attorney for the children was appointed to figure out how to provide the children with safe contact with their mother, who had always been the primary caregiver. Unfortunately, the family did not have the resources to seek professional help to prevent them from being totally torn apart. In the end, the mother moved back to Florida, where she had family, and that was the end of her relationship with the children. Though the children missed her terribly and despite the husband's willingness to allow her telephone contact with them, the mother was financially unable to seek psychiatric care and, as a result, could not maintain regular contact or visits with her children. Though she acknowledged that she needed help, the resources were unavailable and so the family was torn apart. As of this writing, the mother is still isolated from her children and untreated by doctors. Family court and the system failed these people.

IN ALL JURISDICTIONS, family court is perceived as an easier venue for those who can't afford to hire a lawyer.

In family court it is quite possible to proceed without an attorney.

In supreme court, the process is, in most cases, impenetrable for a person without legal representation.

To file a motion in family court, there is a fee required, but if the litigant is unable to pay, family court judges will often waive the fee altogether.

A fee is also required in supreme court or its equivalent.

If the system were changed, even slightly, psychiatric and other relevant services to help the poor and middle class could be put back in place.

The way marital case law is written today, each case is treated in the same way except for the diverse dollar amounts and other details pertaining to each divorce. Not all people have multiple dwellings, retirement plans, children, or trust funds, for example.

Rich or poor, in divorce court, people worth millions or hundreds of millions pay the same nominal fee to have their case heard as someone who earns minimum wage. It is usually a given that the more money involved in a divorce, the longer the litigants will tie up the court's time and usually the more expensive lawyers involved, the more legal thrusting and counter-thrusting, and more time in court, all becoming a dance to the sound of a frenzied cash register.

Instead of charging everyone the same fee to be heard in court, there should be a sliding scale based on the monetary worth of the divorce. A cabdriver or a factory worker, or a litigant who earns a set modest salary in a corporation or company, should pay far less than someone like Ron Perelman to appear in divorce court. The way the system is today, however, whether the litigant is Ron Perelman or a cabdriver, everyone, regardless of their financial worth and the potential monetary worth of their divorce, pays the same fee—usually around two hundred dollars—to have their case heard in supreme court.

The extra money received from those whose cases are worth seven to nine figures could pay those involved in the "cottage industry," in family court as well as in supreme court. Only then could everyone—rich, middle class, or poor—benefit from experts so that families are not torn apart.

Obviously, not everyone will need a forensic accountant, but many could use a parenting coordinator or even a visitation supervisor to help them work out custody and visitation issues. Also, therapists, social workers, and psychiatrists could be in place to work with people to limit the level of acrimony and pain.

Charging according to the value of a divorce would also unblock the courts to hear more cases. As there are an insufficient number of judges hearing cases in supreme court, presiding over a high-profile hugely complicated divorce where assets are in the seven- to nine-figure range renders judges unable to move modest cases along at a reasonably rapid rate. Judges and lawyers know that a divorce involving millions or billions will tie up the court far longer than an uncomplicated case where the litigant files a simple W-2 form or has few or no assets other than his or her salary.

Ironically, though family court is a crucial venue for emergency hearings throughout the country, it remains a court where there is the common perception that judges are not as knowledgeable about family law as are sitting judges in supreme court.

Herbert Glickman, a former New Jersey Supreme Court judge, maintains that new judges are sent to family court regardless of their experience, often resulting in "terrible decisions."

"Most lawyers dread going before a family court judge," Judge Glickman says, "because they know the judge has limited background in family law. Most are sitting in that court to put in time before they are transferred out after a year or two. The goal of most judges is to get out as quickly as possible. Another problem with family court is that the volume is so big that judges are unable to intervene early on, in the beginning stages of a divorce."

Former New York Supreme Court Judge Thomas Beeler agrees, and adds that all judges, not just family court judges, need emotional intelligence to handle cases that involve so much emotion.

"It is the substance of a case and not the mechanics," Judge Beeler says. "Judges who sit in family court or in supreme court need emotional intelligence more than just a brilliant grasp of the law. The majority of judges I know have that component built in, and that comes out with an absence of a jury. Judges make a tremendous impact on a case and a difference in people's lives. If we ask the right questions and are proactive, things tend to work out better. Male judges, like female judges, do come with their own baggage or life experience. But with experience, good judges learn not to consider their own feelings in a case even if we hear things that are shocking. For instance, if someone can't tell you the name of her baby's father, or we hear that a man is a serial philanderer or a woman abuses her children. Some things are crucial and will influence a judge. Other things are sociological and we need to understand the basis in culture that drives a man to beat his wife because that's what's done in certain religions. It's not acceptable, but it's important to understand the genesis of the behavior. Because judges hear more than the average lawyer hears from clients, our shock and disbelief at certain situations cause less of an emotional reaction. It's also easier for us to be more impartial than lawyers. Don't forget that lawyers are living on a daily basis with the client and the evolution of the case—blow by blow and step by step."

Transparency would be a remedy for many inequities in court. Officially, from the United States Supreme Court on down, the emphasis is that under our American system, courts are open to the public. Many cases, however, involve minor children. Judges feel in extreme cases involving children that there is enough reason to ignore the requirement of an open courtroom. Though divorce hearings in supreme court are open to the public, in family court, it is difficult to sit in on a hearing. In family court, which deals frequently with minor children and their abuse or delinquency, the court protects the rights of the minor from the press or those who have no direct involvement in a case. Commissions that sit in judgment of judges (one of the authors was chairman of one such state commission) frequently hear complaints about judges who close their courtrooms.

Family court is even more closed, as there are many cases that concern child abuse, adoption, intrafamilial criminality. In those cases, judges are justified to close their courtrooms. Many other cases not involving children do not legally warrant closing the courtroom. However, the architects who designed these courts often left no room for a spectator section.

Family courts, while user-friendly, are decidedly not observer friendly. It is far easier for judges sitting in those courts to claim that due to the high and rapid turnover of cases, many of which suggest a closed courtroom, it is advisable simply to shut the doors to the public.

There is no doubt that the most influential person in every divorce is the judge who hears the case. While clients can change lawyers and lawyers can refuse to represent clients, lawyers cannot, with one exception, ask for the dismissal of a judge in any case.

California has a very interesting and virtually cost-free mechanism regarding judges. In any single case, either lawyer, for any reason they see fit or for no particular reason at all except instinct, can ask for the judge who has been assigned to the case to be removed and another assigned. This mechanism is only allowed once in every case. This is a simple process that helps divorce matters move forward. Every lawyer simply wants a judge who knows the law, is fair, and proceeds expeditiously in the matter. Under the California system, judges do not want to have a record of being knocked out of the box repeatedly by numerous lawyers since it reflects on their reputations. The system works and many lawyers throughout the country have written to chief judges to suggest that the law be put in place in other states. The response has not been positive. The problem is that the judges themselves disapprove of the law and, statistically, in most trials, motions to remove judges are seldom granted.

One of the most prevalent reasons that lawyers ask for the removal of a judge is because of a judge's reputation to be biased toward either the husband or the wife, or because the judge is known to be bitter because of his or her own personal experience with divorce.

Some lawyers believe that male judges, especially African-American and Jewish judges, are predisposed toward women, even those without minor children, or those who have been in short-term marriages. The reasoning is that coming from a traditional matriarchal society those particular male judges may feel more protective toward women. According to several prominent matrimonial judges, it doesn't help certain male litigants that many judges assume that a large percentage of those men will ultimately default on alimony, maintenance, or child support. In cases where a man has left his wife for another woman, it is even a greater impetus to feel that women need protection and a guarantee that they will be cared for financially.

When it comes to female judges who have been working all their lives, lawyers believe that, perhaps on an unconscious level, they are offended when women appear before them expecting to be supported forever.

Whatever the parties' gender, race, or religion, judicial opinions based on personal history or family background do not always make for equitable or fair decisions.

12

VOICES FROM THE BENCH

Judge: "Miss West, are you trying to show contempt for this court?"
Mae West: "On the contrary, Your Honor, I was doin' my best to conceal it."

THOUGH LAWYERS ARE THE FRONT LINE in every divorce, and clients experience a myriad of emotions that they, with the help of their lawyers, often can overcome without making things worse than they already are, judges also play a critical role in bringing the litigants and their attorneys toward a sane settlement.

Judges see and hear everything, from comic to tragic, from shocking to mundane. They are the people who, if they are knowledgeable about the law, fair, and willing to put every effort into settling a case, litigants and lawyers are fortunate to have in the courtroom.

The big difference between lawyers and judges is that litigants can choose their attorneys, while judges are appointed to hear cases. Often it is a matter of luck to be heard before a judge who is sensitive, experienced, and knows how to avoid conflict in the courtroom. Judges, however, are people too. It is human nature that they bring their own history with them when they hear a case.

Judge Jacqueline Silbermann admits that she would not have made some of the same decisions she made at the beginning of her career had she considered all the variables and had more experience.

"When I first got on the bench," Silbermann says, "my feelings about giving big maintenance awards to women was based on the fact that I've been a working woman all my life. I used to think the woman could go out and work. Of course that isn't always possible if someone hasn't been in the workforce for twenty years, even if she has a college education. Who's going to hire a fifty-year-old woman? She would need retraining at best. But then, it's no different for a man who hasn't worked in twenty years. No one is going to hire a fifty-year-old man who hasn't been in the workforce for years. The difference, of course, is that more women have been out of it than men because they have chosen to raise children."

In retrospect, Judge Silbermann admits that on one case, she had a negative first impression of a litigant before she really became deeply involved in the specifics of the divorce.

"I remember hearing a custody case. I thought the woman involved was despicable and cold, and saw that she was alienating everyone. The case went on for a long time. The husband in the case was a lawyer and at some point he fired his own lawyer. Since a lawyer is always a buffer for the litigant and usually presents his or her client in the best light, it was a really bad move. As soon as the husband began representing himself, I realized that he was the culprit in the case, and while the wife came across as unpleasant, her case was clearly stronger when it came to getting custody of the children. In the end, I ruled that the husband could only have supervised visitation with his children. I realized then I had been wrong in my initial judgment of the wife without having heard the entire story, and after getting to know and understand the psycho dynamic of the husband."

Silbermann has realized some mistakes she had made while on the bench. It is unfortunate that despite her own self-criticism, several decisions on high-profile cases were highly criticized throughout the legal profession as well as in the media. That they might have been criticized does not necessarily mean that they were wrong. Indeed, unpopular decisions might well reflect that a judge was courageous.

SANDRA JENNINGS WAS A FORMER DANCER with the New York City Ballet when she met the actor William Hurt. They began a relationship, lived together, and eventually had a son. In the winter of 1982–1983, when Hurt was filming *The Big Chill* in Beaufort, South Carolina, Jennings claimed that Hurt told her they were married "in the eyes of God." Jennings further claimed that because South Carolina recognizes common-law marriage, Hurt had turned their live-in relationship into a legal union.

When the couple broke up, Jennings sued Hurt for half his net worth, claiming that they were common-law husband and wife. The couple appeared in New York State Civil Court in Manhattan before Judge Jacqueline Silbermann. After hearing testimony from both sides, Silbermann ruled that Jennings was never the common-law wife of William Hurt and was, therefore, not entitled to a share of the actor's income or net worth.

"The parties were not generally viewed as husband and wife while in South Carolina," Judge Silbermann wrote in her decision. "They did not list themselves in any directories in South Carolina or in New York as married. Employment records or insurance policies do not designate Jennings as Hurt's wife. The parties never filed joint tax returns or had a single joint bank account."

Silberman added that "none of the testimony by friends and acquaintances of Mr. Hurt and Ms. Jennings showed that the couple ever held themselves out as married or thought of themselves as married. The couple never characterized themselves as spouses on other legal forms.

"New York State does not recognize common-law marriages," Judge Silbermann went on. "And because I don't know the credibility of the statement by Mr. Hurt when they were in South Carolina, I can only construe it to mean that Mr. Hurt only expressed his desire to continue their live-in relationship, which began in 1981. He did not intend for them to be considered as a married couple."

The judge's ruling was assailed by Ms. Jennings's lawyer, Richard Golub, who said he was "disgusted" by the decision. He said Judge Silbermann's decision was biased because she fell in love with Mr. Hurt during the six-day trial in June.

"The decision is a love letter from the judge to Bill Hurt," Mr. Golub said, adding that the judge was "not just infatuated with Bill Hurt but was in love with Bill Hurt."

Judge Silbermann declined to comment on the accusation.

Madeleine Kesselman, a lawyer who represented Ms. Jennings before the trial began, also stated in a pretrial hearing that the judge "seemed starstruck."

"The judge's first words," Kesselman reported, "were that *The Big Chill* was her favorite movie and that he was her favorite actor."

After Judge Silbermann's decision, Mr. Hurt said he felt vindicated. "I felt that I simply could not continually give in to the pressures that have been constantly put on me for more and more money and other accommodations from Sandra Jennings and others," he said.

Judge Silbermann's ruling did not deal with financial support for the couple's six-year-old son. Mr. Hurt, however, had already agreed to pay Ms. Jennings up to $65,000 a year for their son's support.

Anything can happen in court. Suppose William Hurt had been Angelina Jolie and the judge had been a man, or another woman, who happened to have a crush on the actress. According to media reports, the judge's decision might have favored Jolie. Then again, crush or no crush, based on the merits of the case, Judge Silbermann ruled according to the law, which clearly states that New York State does not recognize common-law marriage. Nor did the couple ever do anything legally that would substantiate Ms. Jennings's claim that they were, in fact, either married "in the eyes of God," or under the laws of South Carolina.

In the case of William Hurt and Sandra Jennings, it was clearly a case of *res ipsa loquitur,* or "the thing speaks for itself." The facts were overwhelmingly in favor of William Hurt. According to the laws of New York State, where the case was heard, there is no common-law marriage, nor does New York recognize common-law marriage from another state. Additionally, the couple did nothing legally to indicate that they both considered themselves to be married under common law in South Carolina. Unfortunately for Judge Silbermann, the accusations that she favored Mr. Hurt or was impressed by his star status affected the reaction, both by the media and within the legal profession, to a later decision she made. In that case, the facts were far more egregious and damaging than the Jennings/Hurt case, and in the end, Judge Silbermann's decision was overturned on appeal.

Silbermann's record throughout her career on the bench has been highly respected and lauded by her colleagues. Almost every judge has had decisions challenged or has made errors in judgment. In the case of Judge Silbermann, in 2007, shortly before she retired, she was criticized a second time in her career for her ruling on a case that surprised even some of her more staunch supporters.

In August 2007, after a three-year battle, Susan Gass won a ruling in the New York Court of Appeals to overturn the uncontested divorce that gave her husband 100 percent of their assets. In their ruling, the court of appeals went further when they criticized Judge Silbermann for awarding the husband everything without the wife even knowing that she had been sued for divorce. Apparently, Susan Gass had been told repeatedly that she could not fight the decision that Judge Silbermann had brought down concerning her 2004 divorce from her husband, Thomas Gass. In her brief to the court of appeals, Susan Gass claimed that politics influenced the judge's decision, as her husband was the former president of the Village Reform Democratic Club in Manhattan. In its decision, the appeals court said Silbermann "abused her discretion" when she ignored Gass's repeated attempts to fight the divorce, which awarded child custody and the house to her husband.

"There was a complete lack of due diligence on the part of all the judges," Susan Gass claimed. Mrs. Gass went on to explain that her husband had filed for an "uncontested divorce" without ever serving her, though he counterclaimed that he had served her with divorce papers.

"I couldn't go to my grave letting them do this to me and get away with it," Susan Gass added.

In fairness, it should be noted that appellate courts can do things trial courts cannot. Trial court judges must follow precedent. Appellate courts make precedent. The reality is that lawyers initiate precedent in the law. That happens when a lawyer "pushes the envelope" in a case and then, on appeal, his argument is sustained. That creates precedent.

THERE ARE MORE EGREGIOUS examples of judges who allow themselves to form opinions about litigants rather than the case the litigant presents. One example was Judge W. A. Waltemade, who died in 1985.

Waltemade was a Supreme Court judge and former assistant district attorney who was forced to retire after a highly criticized remark he made to two lawyers in a divorce case. In fact, he was censured for the remark by a special court and he ultimately retired after the Democratic Judicial Convention for the First District denied his renomination in 1975.

After the husband in the divorce case finished his testimony, answering simple questions posed by his lawyer, Judge Waltemade stared at the man for several seconds before calling both lawyers up to the bench. According to the lawyer who represented the husband, the judge said, "He looks like a fag to me." Instead of granting the divorce, he deferred the matter to the court's Social Services Department. Though the man eventually got his divorce, the newspapers got hold of the incident and printed the story. After the media reported Waltemade's remark, the man in question claimed that there was sufficient information in the press so that his friends and colleagues at the advertising agency where he worked recognized him as the subject of the articles. It was because of the man's complaint about the judge that Waltemade was removed from office.

IN EVERY DIVORCE, judges understand that sex, lies, or lunacy are part of the process and are inextricably linked to money. Even those cases which justify going to the appellate court are directly associated with financial support.

Alimony is more than just money. It is a lightning rod or measurement for society's conflicted feelings about the sanctity of marriage, the anguish and consequences of divorce, as well as the feelings that both husband and wife harbor as to who bears the greater responsibility for the breakdown of the marriage. The aggrieved spouse, the one who perceives that he or she has been abandoned without cause, will feel a sense of entitlement. Financial compensation is often the only way to assuage their sense of anger, humiliation, abuse, or failure. The spouse who wants out may see alimony as the ticket to start a new life. When dirty dealings on the part of one spouse incite the other to retaliate, the tempest escalates, keeping the family embroiled in controversy that often continues long after the divorce is finalized. That kind of behavior falls under the heading of irrational behavior or lunacy that should be avoided at all costs.

Herbert Glickman, formerly the chief judge in New Jersey Supreme Court, has had experience with what he terms as "serial filers," people who keep coming back to court to amend an agreement.

"It's amazing," Judge Glickman says, "but some cases last so long that people actually forget they were ever married. People have come back before me because they think the courtroom is their kitchen table. They believe the way to communicate with each other is in front of a judge. Most of what I did in my career as a judge was common sense. Most cases are not that esoteric in nature, at least not on the surface. They become so because people create long-term financial issues that keep changing. I had one case where the people had been divorced for five years and every few months they kept coming back. One morning, on the docket, a name looked familiar. It turned out it was this couple's son, who was divorcing his wife. When their case was called, I actually asked them if their parents told them who their judge was. I felt like part of the family, at least because I became the family divorce judge."

According to many judges throughout the country, one of the major problems in any divorce is that both parties, because of an inability to reason, miss the point when a settlement is reached. Both litigants are systematically asked by their lawyers and the judge if the amount agreed upon for maintenance and child support allows each to live a comparably decent lifestyle, relative to what they both had before divorce.

In almost all cases, the parties respond that the outcome is acceptable and all is fine. In reality, the answer to that question should be a resounding *no*. People always struggle to say yes because they are so afraid to sabotage the agreement and delay the divorce.

When judges inquire about lifestyle, it is not a question that is limited to the lifestyle of one person, but rather the lifestyle of both who are living on diminished income. People often don't want to consider the possibility of remarriage in the future or of having more children. Their response is both hopeful that they *can* make it financially, and unrealistic that they *can* make it financially. When circumstances do change and one or the other is forced to come to court to ask for an increase or decrease in payments, it is often more complicated to amend an agreement than it is to formulate one in the beginning. Over the last two decades, the term "marital lifestyle" has become a pivotal issue in divorce cases. On May 31, 2000, the New Jersey Supreme Court decided in the case of *Crews v. Crews,* that marital lifestyle must be given special attention, both in the preparatory phase when lawyers gather information from the client as well as in the preparation of temporary support. Though people will define "marital lifestyle" by describing their expenditures, it is often difficult to determine what is relevant to the eventual outcome of support. The following facts are taken into consideration by the court—marital residence, vacation homes, other real estate, and improvements to real estate; savings; automobiles, boats, planes, motorcycles, and other recreational vehicles; extent of vacations; furs and jewelry; stores frequented; country clubs; entertainment including, but not limited to: gambling, sports and hobbies, restaurants, theater, movies; gifts; household help; household furnishings; children's expenses; available cash; free time; personal expenses that are charged off to a business, and pets.

According to an Arizona judge, "Those who appear in court for a modification of an agreement have several excuses or reasons why they are there. Either they challenge the way it was done because it is no longer working, or they forgot something, like sleep-away camp for a child who, at the time of the divorce, was too young to leave home, or a dramatic, unanticipated change in circumstances. There are other cases where provisions were not made for a child or children to visit one set of grandparents who live out of state. Other cases focus on the husband who is habitually late with his support payments. In most cases, the wife comes back before the same judge in supreme court who heard the case, or if that judge is either retired or expired, she finds herself in front of a new judge who has to begin at the beginning to understand the nuances of the case. The nature of the work for judges is a repetitive process that does not always end with a signed agreement or a decree."

Judge Glickman has heard post-decree cases on numerous occasions. "Let's be clear," Judge Glickman begins, "two people can live together in a certain way when there is a combined income. Once they separate, each has only one-half of that income, which makes that lifestyle tougher to maintain. Add to that the possibility that one or the other spouse wants to remarry and start a family and things really become untenable. The point is that all of that should be carefully considered before an agreement is signed because life is never static. The unfortunate part is that people in the throes of a settlement and before they are divorced are just not themselves. Even calm people become crazy."

One attorney reports that he represented a school principal whose wife was also a principal. Each earned $125,000 a year so that together they had a combined income of a quarter of a million dollars. The husband fell in love with a teacher and during the course of negotiations he and his wife agreed that there would be no alimony but rather an equal division of pension plans and other assets with the wife keeping sole ownership of the house. When the court asked the woman if she was comfortable that she could maintain the same standard of living, her response was unusually lucid.

"Are you kidding me?" the woman replied. "Even though he gave me the house, how am I supposed to maintain the payments when my income is suddenly cut in half? It's a mathematical impossibility."

Other circumstances are not technically covered under the law. Judge Rosalyn Richter describes an uncommon occurrence.

"Take the case of the couple where one set of grandparents is subsidizing the family," Judge Richter says, "including European vacations and private school and camp for the children, live-in nanny, and a generous monthly allowance so the couple can enjoy certain luxuries they ordinarily wouldn't be able to afford. Now there is a divorce. There are no legal grounds to come back to the grandparents to continue that support, as it was given out of generous choice rather than familial responsibility. There are some judges, however, who might rule that there should be a consideration of how the family lived given the largesse of the grandparents when fixing support for the wife and children. If the husband's parents were subsidizing the family, the judge may award the wife maintenance and child support higher than what would be the usual percentage of the husband's income, given that his parents could and probably would continue to subsidize him. If it was the wife's parents, the support payments might be lower in anticipation of her parents continuing to subsidize her."

An exaggerated example of a judge taking into consideration the generosity of the parents of one spouse or the other to contribute to support is the Wildenstein case. Jocelyn Wildenstein would never have received maintenance of $140,000 a month, since her husband, Alex, had virtually no money or income and depended solely on the largesse of his father.

A good judge will consider each case individually without necessarily using strict mathematical formulas to set support. There are extenuating circumstances in every divorce. Though lawyers can influence clients as to what is productive and reasonable, even more important is a conscientious judge who will set a date for the litigants to come back to court with an agreement. The longer the negotiations drag out, the more costly the divorce. The more costly the divorce, the more time it will take to settle the case. The longer it takes to settle a case, the crazier the litigants get.

Judge Tommy Zampino believes that it is the responsibility of all judges to be "hands-on" when hearing divorce cases.

"I try to listen to every person who comes before me. Each one has a different story and each case is different. After I ascertain how I can waver from set formulas or rules, the next step is for me to convince the litigants that after a while there isn't enough money to pay everyone," Judge Zampino says. "If lawyers hate each other, that's one ingredient for a case to go on forever. One might ask, what's in it for the lawyers? Ego, money, of course, and winning. In most cases, people are manageable but timing is essential and judges must give direction to bring resolve by a certain date. Lawyers will advise me in chambers where not to walk if there are extremely sensitive issues or land mines, and I listen to them in order that the case has a chance of reaching conclusion in a reasonable way and in a reasonable amount of time. Part of any judge's job is to help lawyers get their clients to listen because frequently clients don't listen to their lawyers unless they have a good reason. If the judge gives them a rational and unbiased reason, they will listen. I usually tell the litigants— both of them—that you have good attorneys and you should listen to them because you're paying them for their expertise and advice."

Good and sound advice from judges is valuable and, if followed, can simplify the legal aspect of divorce. So, what makes people crazy? What makes them lie? What makes them lose their sense of propriety and dignity and use graphic descriptions to recount their sex lives? The answer is fear, rage, humiliation, loss of control, or simply that they were crazy before the divorce.

Judge Jacqueline Silbermann wonders why anyone "in their right mind," especially high-profile couples, would opt to go to court rather than settle, either with a mediator or around a negotiating table in a lawyer's conference room. "I suppose the words 'in their right minds' is key," Judge Silberman says. "As a former matrimonial judge, I can say that the best thing for any couple facing divorce is to stay out of court. The real question is why people can't settle things out of the courtroom. And, the reason gets back to the rancor, and rage they can't get rid of. How can they make it easier on themselves? Take a Valium. The truth is at some point in the court, there's a rushing of the time line. Judges are pressed by standards and goals to push and move a case. Rage is normal in the beginning, when two people hate each other so much, they want to beat each other over the head. Most rational people pull away from that rage. Granted that women who've been left need time to work with a lawyer or a therapist and then confront what's really important. At the end of the day, either they'll kill their husbands or get a standard of living and move on. Any sane person doesn't want to take that rage with them for the rest of their lives."

It is hard to control rage, especially if one or the other spouse has been broadsided by a process server, or shocked by the way he or she is apprised of a spouse's intention to divorce. Though Judge Silbermann's advice about doing everything not to appear in court is sound and sane, frequently the decision to divorce is not a mutual decision. Even when a divorce is not mutual, however, there are decent and indecent ways to bring people to the negotiating table. The ideal is when the couple agrees to the financial terms, custody, and a division of property. That is a judge's dream.

In most jurisdictions, simple, uncontested divorces are done by a submission of papers to the court. There are still many occasions where a judge will grant the divorce from the bench. In those cases, with the plaintiff on the stand, the lawyer usually asks a preprinted list of questions that are already prepared. After the plaintiff answers them, the judge will say "divorce granted." In some courts throughout the United States, there are fifteen or twenty of these uncontested divorces heard and granted in one day. The usual scenario is that the plaintiff is sworn in, takes the stand, and goes through the testimony, which has been rehearsed. After the judge grants the divorce, the next customer is called. It is virtually no different from a bakery where people "take a number," stand in line, and wait to be served. There are exceptions, unexpected situations that can arise where the automatic questions and answers of a prearranged divorce don't go smoothly.

One case in particular would have reached a conclusion without complications had the husband, the defendant in the matter, not behaved in an inappropriate, though not illegal, manner. In supreme court, though much more open to the public than family court as related above, there remains a certain unspoken etiquette which judges try to enforce. For instance, it is considered inappropriate for a litigant to bring a girlfriend or lover to court during preliminary divorce hearings or during a trial. A lawyer from Oregon describes the pain and anguish his client experienced during every appearance in court when her spouse brought his girlfriend.

"My client had suffered the heartache of knowing that her husband was seeing another woman for about a year before they finally split up. But when she was forced to look at her in the courtroom during hearings, it was just too much."

The judge in the matter had no idea who the woman was who accompanied the defendant. The judge was aware, however, of the distress evident in the plaintiff's face each and every time her husband entered the courtroom during the first week of hearings. At first the judge thought it was just the emotion of the proceedings. On Friday, at the end of the week, the judge called the two lawyers for each side into chambers.

"My first question was, who exactly is the woman who accompanies the defendant and why are they holding hands?" the judge explains. "Obviously, by then, I realized the woman in question was more than someone connected professionally to the case. When the husband's lawyer explained she was the guy's significant other, I was furious at the insensitivity of the husband to subject his wife to that kind of humiliation. I banned the woman from the courtroom. Imagine my surprise when she showed up again arm in arm with the husband on Monday."

The husband's lawyer ignored the judge's order because, in his words, "There is no law which states the courtroom should be closed to spectators unless it is a matter that involves minor children." During an interview the judge had with the lawyer "off the record," he explained that his client refused to obey the judge's order. "There was nothing I could do except cite the law. My client was mad as hell at his wife and wanted to do anything he could to make her miserable. At the end of the case, he succeeded in torturing her."

The attorney for the wife was unable to do anything either. He advised his client to try not to react. "I told her that the judge was obviously not favorably disposed toward her husband and all we had to do is get through the facts and hope for a good outcome, which we got. My client got support and custody of the children. After the divorce was final, the husband would pick his children up from my client's house and the girlfriend would be sitting in the car. By that time, my client was beyond being hurt, and after a while, just ignored him. There was nothing she could do since the divorce was final and apparently the girlfriend was not abusive or nasty to the kids."

In a family court in Des Moines, there was another case where the husband also systematically had his girlfriend in the car when he picked up his children. In that case, the judge ordered that the lawyers for each side discuss the situation to work out a remedy that was acceptable to both litigants. Unfortunately, once again, the lawyers were unable to reach an agreement and the husband persisted in bringing his girlfriend along when he took his children for his weekend visits.

Judge Nancy E. Gordon, a district court judge in Durham County, North Carolina, has a particularly realistic outlook concerning the demand on the part of litigants that girlfriends or lovers should be banned from contact with children until they make their relationship legal.

"Eventually, everyone understands that after the divorce," Judge Gordon has said, "if the husband is living with the girlfriend or in the event they marry, it is hardly realistic to demand that the woman leave the home when the children visit their father, or not be present when he picks up his children. The problem judges have is that before the divorce is final, there isn't much we can do except try and reason with both sides."

In response, Judge Thomas Beeler, a former matrimonial judge, says, "Suppose the couple doesn't plan on getting married, but instead, intends to live together as a couple? What's the time period before the man or woman is accepted as the de facto partner who doesn't have to leave the home or not be in the car when the children visit? Is it a year, five years, ten years? It's totally unrealistic to put a time limit on cohabitation or to insist from a moral point of view that the couple is legally bound as husband and wife. Naturally, if there are issues of abuse or addiction, that's another story and should be brought before the court whether or not the couple is living together or is married."

There is a good argument for observing how a relationship develops between children and a girlfriend or lover of one parent or another. Common sense dictates that the children should be introduced to the prospective spouse and a relationship be allowed to flourish or fall apart. The problem, as one family court judge explained to an ex-husband, is that relationships end. There are no guarantees.

"I really believe that you believe you are going to marry this young woman," the judge said during divorce proceedings, "but what happens if you don't? There may be another, then another, and then another person who you believe you are going to marry, and it is for this reason that on your visitation no unmarried female should accompany you."

The reality about judges, whether they are men or women, is that they are human, and have their own preconceived moral judgments, family history, and even religious convictions. There is no way to predict if any of their feelings, opinions, or reactions will work for or against one litigant or another. In fact, litigants are not the only ones who are confronted with bizarre and often unfair rulings by sitting judges. New York attorney Ken Burrows once got an odd piece of advice from a sitting judge on a case he was trying in Nassau County.

"At the time, it was essential to prove not one but two incidents of physical cruelty in order to use that as grounds for divorce in New York State," Burrows explains. "I was representing the woman. I was about to lose the case because I could only prove that the husband assaulted my client once. The judge was Catholic and for obvious religious reasons was basically against divorce. He advised me in private to wait to try the case, as the rotation of judges meant that the next one to hear my case was Jewish and not Catholic and had no particular opposition to divorce in general."

Judges are human. Litigants are human. Matrimonial lawyers are human. Any one at any time who finds himself or herself in divorce court will experience some form of discrimination. The pursuit of equality is often not more than a slogan professed by all sides, used when it is convenient to win an argument. The reality in court is that gender discrimination is probably one of the most prevalent examples of a miscarriage of justice.

13

THE GENDER EQUALITY MYTH

*Never underestimate a man's ability to underestimate
a woman.*
                    —KATHLEEN TURNER IN THE MOVIE
                                V. I. WARSHAWSKI

THIRTY YEARS AGO, the United States Supreme Court ruled against
gender discrimination as it concerned alimony. Though the law stated
that men as well as women had the right to receive maintenance, alimony, and child support, few men were willing to admit that they were
beneficiaries of that law. When they did talk about it, many requested
using first names only, or pseudonyms.

According to Alan Feigenbaum, coauthor of *The Complete Guide to Protecting Your Financial Security When Getting a Divorce,* men were not on the
receiving end of monthly support during the 1950s and 1960s when most
wives were homemakers. In the 1970s, however, society and divorce laws
shifted. Women entered the workforce in larger numbers, and family
laws—courtesy of the United States Supreme Court—regarding marital
support were made gender neutral.

With the rising incomes of women, and as the women's movement
gathered momentum in the 1970s, there was a backlash against alimony. "If they want to be independent, let them be independent" was
the unspoken and unwritten attitude of a segment of the then male-
dominated judiciary and legal profession. As time went on, the pendulum

shifted and the courts understood that some women had been economically disadvantaged by their marriages and therefore needed alimony or maintenance to survive. According to statistics gathered from the United States Department of Labor in 2005, women who have been out of the workforce for a decade or more lose 3 percent of their earning abilities per year. A woman in her forties who has stayed at home since having children in her thirties would have difficulty supporting herself, according to her past experience and education level, in the event of a divorce.

Women have made great strides from the early part of the twentieth century until the mid sixties and seventies, beginning with obtaining the right to vote and ending with a partial breaking of the glass ceiling, helping to create professional, academic, and business equality. In many cases, the protests for equal rights as it concerned couples' relationships alienated men and caused the divorce rate to soar more than it has during the last fifty years.

Year	Divorces per 1,000 population[1]
1950	2.6
1955	2.3
1957	2.2
1960	2.2
1965	2.5
1970	3.5
1971	3.7
1972	4.0
1973	4.3
1974	4.6
1975	4.8
1976	5.0
1977	5.0
1978	5.1

Year	Divorces per 1,000 population[1]
1979	5.3
1980	5.2
1981	5.3
1982	5.1
1983	5.0
1984	5.0
1985	5.0
1986	4.9
1987	4.8
1988	4.8
1989	4.7
1990	4.7
1991	4.7
1992	4.8
1993	4.6
1994	4.6
1995	4.4
1996	4.3
1997	4.3
1998 [2]	4.2
1999 [2]	4.1
2000 [2]	4.2
2001 [2]	4.0

[1] Includes reported annulments and some estimated state figures for all years.
[2] Divorce rate excludes data for California, Colorado, Indiana, and Louisiana; population for this rate also excludes these states.

Source: U.S. National Center for Health Statistics, *Vital Statistics of the United States,* annual; and *National Vital Statistics Reports (NVSR)* (formerly *Monthly Vital Statistics Report*); and unpublished data. See also http://www.cdc.gov/nchs. Courtesy of the American Bar Association.

The feminist movement during the 1970s revered women who chose to stay at home and care for their children, recognizing that motherhood and running the home were jobs as or more important than working in a large corporation. If and when divorce occurred, the time women spent as mothers, wives, lovers, nurses, psychologists, chauffeurs, cooks, and housekeepers was taken into consideration and compensated financially during settlement negotiations. In many jurisdictions, when the financial aspect of a case is tried, a wife/mother will put an economic expert on the witness stand to testify what the husband/father would have had to pay for a housekeeper, cook, messenger, etc., all of which had been done by the wife without pay.

The feminist movement recognized the importance of those women who chose to work at home and so they were not penalized for not supporting the family financially but were instead rewarded to continue (if they were fortunate) to live in an appropriate style to raise their children. One problem, however, is that divorce frequently reduces the lifestyle of both litigants, regardless of who is paying how much to whom. The first exhibit to support that argument is just a glance at rent, food costs, and other bills.

Currently, one problem that affects some women is the attitude of men toward stay-at-home wives. One of the most important issues to understand when it comes to divorce is that the law is filled with contradictions and exceptions in each state, which have different formulas and rules concerning divorce.

According to Ken Burrows, in Connecticut, a judge has the authority to decide which litigant is responsible for the breakdown of the marriage. The court can assess an uneven distribution of assets.

In some states, the abandoned wife or husband may still seek fault as justification to get a larger settlement or maintenance award. When love is gone and one or the other has run off with someone else, notwithstanding the law, the core of the case in the minds of the litigants is always about "fault."

"I've seen it all," attorney Eleanor Alter says. "I've seen men who are the Bernie Madoffs of divorce. They have no guilt. They come in and tell me their wife is a bitch, she's lousy in bed, can't cook, that they hate her mother. This is a guy who has no mercy and no guilt. He's filled with rage that he didn't do this twenty years or five years earlier instead of wasting his life with a woman he hates. This is the kind of person who'll tell me that his wife made him find someone else, that it's all her fault. Then there's the other side of the story. I've seen fifty- or sixty-year-old women come into my office and tell me their husbands never let them do their own thing. They were going to be president of General Motors, and blame the husbands for impeding their success. I ask them what business school they went to and they say none. I ask them if they ever worked and they say no, but it's still all the fault of the husbands who stopped them from achieving tremendous success in business. Some of these women actually tell me how lucky I am to have a career, and I want to jump over my desk and strangle them. Like someone gave it to me. These are women who tell me they had one child and then another and I want to say to them, What about the women who had babies in law school or college or who are single mothers, slaving away at menial jobs? The truth is that the more money available in a marriage, the less the woman did because there was a night nanny, a day nanny, a weekend nanny, a maid, a cook, a laundress, and a driver. That's not to say I don't feel bad for these women even if they weren't making dinner every night, because that wasn't their deal for twenty some odd years. I'm not critical. But then the deal suddenly changes. The husband walks off with a twenty-five-year old and he says his wife should work so he doesn't have to maintain her in the style she is used to. That's not fair. But then I see younger women who left their husbands because they fell in love with their personal trainer or golf pro. They make excuses that they were vulnerable because their husbands are boring—all they do is work. Those husbands don't have it so good either. I think most men are in jobs they don't love but they don't have a choice if they're the sole bread-winner. These are the same women who tell me how their husbands have this great life and all they have is a Jaguar, a country club, furs, and jewelry. On the other hand, I had a woman client who was an in-vestment banker and the sole support of her family. Her husband didn't work and she traveled all the time and had little time to see her kids, so it goes both ways."

Alimony or maintenance is an issue that often mirrors the disagree-ments that occurred between couples during their marriages. In some cases, there were power struggles over money, demands by husbands that their wives go back to work outside the home to supplement the family income, and economic pressures caused by too much spending—all emotional conflicts that contributed to the demise of the marriage. When women go to court and ask for maintenance to keep up their previous style of living, many men view those demands as a repetition of the problems that destroyed the marriage.

Gender equality is a cloudy issue.

There are certain givens that society accepts and demands when it comes to gender equality—equal pay, job opportunity, and respect.

When it comes to divorce, society and the courts are tilted too much to one side or the other depending on preconceived notions and circumstances.

The general consensus is that women suffer more than men after divorce. Contrarily, the other side of the coin is that society often judges that men, obliged to assume the financial responsibility for wives and children, suffer more than women. The reality is that everyone suffers after a divorce, though there are certain assumptions, often erroneous, about the impossibility for women to find a partner as easily as men can.

The historic axiom is that men are the providers, while women are the caregivers. In reality, a vast cultural inequality exists between men and women that has more to do with social judgments than the law. For instance, women who date, love, or marry younger men are often unfairly ridiculed. The cultural and social inequality has much to do with reproduction and the subtle awareness that women over a certain age can no longer have children. It is an absolute fact that a man who weighs three hundred pounds and has millions of dollars can date just about any gorgeous twentysomething woman he wants. A woman of equal girth and worth would have trouble dating or even paying for a male companion.

Think about a restaurant like Le Cirque or '21' in New York City, or consider a diner in a small rural town. Imagine a man with a much younger woman on his arm who walks in to be seated for a meal. At worst, there are envious stares, and perhaps whispered comments about who the couple is, if the woman is his daughter or paramour, or how much money the man must have to have seduced a much younger companion. Regardless of the reactions, men with younger women are envied and the women are assumed to be trophy wives or girlfriends who are able to guarantee the older man, at least as he convinces himself, immortality. According to more than fifty men interviewed for this book, 80 percent claimed that their former wives, who were age appropriate, reminded them of "death, impotency, and their mothers."

Those same men—80 percent—also maintained that after going through the misery of divorce, they were entitled to "begin again" with a younger woman who would give them "far more pleasure" than one who was the same age as their wives. Curiously, only 35 percent of those men interviewed claimed that their wives had "let themselves go physically." Those men cited numerous other reasons for divorce and yet stated that, if pushed to make a hypothetical decision, they would absolutely "date, live with, or marry younger women."

Add to that cultural scenario drugs like Viagra, Cialis, and others that temporarily cure erectile dysfunction, and the world sees middle-aged women, and women of a "certain age," marginalized even more. Forget their limited reproductive years, aging body, and wrinkles, and focus on the fact that their husbands are capable of sustaining a sexual relationship with a much younger woman.

Women with much younger men are not only the focus of much harsher criticism, but the men are instantly judged to have ulterior motives. People assume they are gay, gigolos, or have some psychological problem that attracts them to a woman old enough to be their mother.

According to a geriatric psychiatrist from Iowa, "It is common belief that [relationships between] older women and younger men go against nature. Though it is often true that some men do need an older woman as a replacement for their mother, or they're sexually unsure with younger women, basically, it's dangerous to generalize and not take into consideration all the inexplicable reasons why people fall in love. What makes the object of their affections attractive? There are a variety of reasons, some of which are inexplicable but have to do with comfort, intellectual compatibility, and shared interests."

Because youth is revered, firm skin is envied, smooth complexions are bought and paid for, well-toned bodies are desired, and single heterosexual men are a sought-after commodity on the dinner party and divorce circuit, certain realities exist.

Women in the process of divorce know that demanding and getting large financial awards will reduce their former spouse's financial conditions to problematic levels, resulting in an inability to support and maintain a second family.

The courts will award women who have been out of the workforce for a certain number of years adequate means—paid by their husbands—to support them and their children.

Many of the laws in place for support were tailored to protect minor children. The problem is that there are not two or three sets of criteria to separate the emergency situation where children have to be fed, from the bitter wife without children who simply wants to settle the score—money to assuage the humiliation and loneliness.

Revenge is a full-time job.

Equality in divorce or family court can frequently mean that either men or women—equally—find themselves at a disadvantage or become targets of social criticism. This inequality is largely grounded in the social and cultural history of love, courtship, marriage, and divorce.

The laws, and the social stigma that goes along with some laws, can and often do affect men as well as women. For example, when the husband earns little or no money and the wife earns a big salary, are men entitled to spousal maintenance? The answer is obviously in the affirmative. Yet, many men feel uncomfortable taking alimony from their wives. Not surprisingly, there are just as many wives who find it "unnatural" for a man to seek support. Those men who are uncomfortable taking support have been inculcated into believing that they are the ones who have to provide for their families. One man who was interviewed for this book put it this way, "Getting alimony from my wife wouldn't play out well at the job or at the bowling alley."

Based on one hundred interviews with a cross section of men, 65 percent felt uncomfortable asking for money from their wives. These men were low- to middle-income blue-collar workers who had been laid off, fired from their jobs, or had suffered some kind of disability where they were unable to work.

Of those men interviewed who had once earned upward of $250,000 and who had a college education, or celebrities who earned far more but did not have college degrees, 70 percent maintained that they had no problem asking for support from their wives. For example, Parker Stevenson sought $18,000 a month from Kirstie Alley when they divorced. Singer Nick Lachey sought support from Jessica Simpson. Madonna paid Guy Ritchie millions to end their marriage and retain custody of their children.

Kim Shamsky is a forty-seven-year-old successful businesswoman who pays her sixty-five-year-old ex-husband thousands of dollars a month in alimony. He was once a major league baseball player who has since retired. The couple has no children. Shamsky resents supporting her husband. She said that it is not as if he is taking care of the children while she is out earning a living, since they have no children. The basic reason why Shamsky is angry is that she is aghast that women should be obliged to pay men alimony.

"They are supposed to be the breadwinners and not the bread takers," she claims.

Despite society's preconceived notions about men who ask for and receive maintenance or alimony, divorce experts claim that fewer men are rejecting the notion of taking alimony. According to the United States Census Bureau, the percentage of men who are awarded alimony rose to 3.6 percent during the five-year period ending in 2006, up from 2.4 percent in the previous five-year period. The Census Bureau also predicts that the figures are likely to rise given that more women are becoming the primary wage earners. In fact, as of 2008, wives earned more than their husbands in 33 percent of all families, up from 28.2 percent a decade earlier. In any recession, the economics of employment dictate that savings are garnered by employers by firing the highest-salaried employees. As a result, often women/wives will continue to work while their husbands, who have earned more income, are laid off or fired.

Men are standing up and demanding compensation for years lost as well as putting their wives' careers before their own.

One man stood up in Los Angeles Superior Court, claiming that if it had not been for the joint decision to support his wife's career advancement to the "detriment" of his own, he would be earning considerably more money than he currently was, and much more than his wife. He further maintained that when he agreed to move to Los Angeles because his wife was offered a job for $1.5 million a year, he was forced to give up his job, for which he earned more than $500,000 a year. In the dismal job market, it was impossible for him to find another job that would pay him what he had been earning. In his petition filed in Los Angeles, he also claimed that because of his professional sacrifice, he could no longer maintain the standard of living he had during their marriage.

According to a *Wall Street Journal* article in September 2008, not all men are loath to admit they receive alimony, and some, in fact, feel entitled based on what they consider was the point of the feminist movement.

John Castellanos is an actor best known for his longtime role in *The Young and the Restless,* a daily soap opera. Castellanos claimed in court during his divorce that he had acted in and produced only five movies since the demise of his marriage. He also claimed that if any of those projects actually were produced, he would be the first to relinquish the monthly payments he receives from his former wife, Rhonda Friedman. Friedman, however, does not feel comforted by her former husband's claim.

It's been reported that Friedman said, "I feel financially raped."

In fact, Friedman admitted that she found the monthly payments so distasteful that after writing the check, she would spit on it before sealing it in an envelope. Even more incendiary to Friedman are the enormous legal fees she was forced to pay when Castellanos prolonged the trial until he got the amount of money he felt he needed and deserved.

In defense of Castellanos, he believes that he deserves support from his ex-wife for the same reasons that she (Friedman) says he doesn't. During six of the nine years they were married, he was the major wage earner. Only after he lost his role in *The Young and the Restless* did she begin earning more money. For years his hefty paychecks supported their lavish lifestyle. In response, Friedman, who earns more than $500,000 a year as the supervising producer of the soap opera *The Bold and the Beautiful,* says, "I don't understand why someone becomes your financial responsibility just because you married him, especially if there were no children."

Not all women share this philosophy about having to pay their husbands alimony. In 1992, television personality Joan Lunden was ordered to pay her former husband $18,000 a month. At the time she made the following statement to the press: "Why the courts don't tell a husband who has been living off his wife to go out and get a job is beyond my comprehension."

Lunden was criticized for her statement both by men who felt they were entitled to the same rights as women in a divorce, and even by women's groups who felt that paying alimony to husbands was the natural evolution of gender equality. Through her publicist, Lunden amended the statement she had made in 1992 by saying, "That was a statement I made in haste many years ago. I regret having said it."

Gloria Allred, who represented Nicole Brown Simpson's family during the civil trial against O. J. Simpson for murder, believes that awarding men alimony shows progress. "We can't assert rights for women and say that men aren't entitled to the same rights."

Other scenarios are presented to the courts that oblige women and men to take on the financial responsibility or burden of supporting their wives and husbands. Serena is yet another example.

It never occurred to Serena that she would end up as a single mother paying her ex-husband, Alex, maintenance. When the couple first married, Serena put her husband through a Ph.D. program with the understanding that he would go into research medicine and, with his Ph.D. in biochemistry, have an interesting and fulfilling career. That never happened. The job market was partially to blame for Alex's inability to get a job, as well as his unwillingness to take a position as a science teacher at a prestigious private school.

After the birth of their two children, Serena went back to her job as an executive at a major credit card company, earning a salary in the high six figures. Though Alex had no job, he nonetheless refused to care for their children. As a result, Serena not only had to support the family, but also was obliged to hire a nanny so she could work. It was unclear what Alex did all day, though he assured her he was looking for work, a quest that never materialized into a concrete job.

Eventually Serena decided she wanted a divorce. Imagine her surprise when she discovered that as the primary breadwinner, she was advised by her lawyer that Alex would be considered the dependent spouse. When Serena realized that she would be financially responsible for her husband, as well as for herself and their children, she decided not to prolong the negotiations, as lawyers' fees for both sides would just cost her additional money. Serena's lawyer agreed to mediate the settlement and, with little resistance, she agreed to give her husband half of their assets— which were basically her assets—the family car, and a monthly stipend of two thousand dollars until he was able to get a job. Five years later, Serena is still paying Alex maintenance and Alex is still not working.

"I stopped myself from walking around being angry and bitter and just chalked it up to a mistake I made when I believed Alex was my partner as well as my husband. The only thing I promised myself was that if I ever married again, I would have an ironclad prenuptial agreement. Frankly, the notion of remarriage is still one of the most frightening thoughts I have, and when I meet someone, I usually tell them right away that marriage is not something I envision in the future."

A woman doesn't have to be Britney Spears or Reese Witherspoon to be sued for alimony by their husbands. According to the Bureau of Labor Statistics, in one-third of all marriages, wives are the primary wage earners. Call it the "dark side of the liberation coin."

Another inequity in the law concerns unmarried women who have been cohabitating with men for years and who suddenly find themselves abandoned without support. Currently, in order to obtain any money, the burden of proof is on the woman even if the man has supported the household for all the years they were living together. The court demands that the woman prove that the man had made an express promise in writing to support her, or the commitment has to be made explicitly in a manner amenable to proof. What that means in its most simplistic terms is that there must be evidence to back up the story, such as someone having overheard the conversation or the ability to have testimony that deals with the issue with a great degree of specification.

The man's defense is usually that if he intended to care for her financially to the point where she would have been entitled to all benefits of a married woman, he would have "legalized" their living arrangement. The fact that he did *not* marry her, so goes the man's thinking, is the best proof he never intended to have a relationship with all the obligations and responsibilities attached to a conventional marriage.

If the law kept up with the times and the ways people choose to form family units, the presumption would be that there was indeed an intention and responsibility on the part of the man to support the woman when they had been living together for a specific number of years. The burden of proof should be on the man to demonstrate that there was an intention *not* to accept these responsibilities.

Yet another inequity in the law happens when a divorced woman or man who has been awarded alimony from a former spouse remarries. Upon the remarriage, the law states that the man or woman loses the maintenance. If this subsequent marriage fails, whether after a brief number of weeks, months, or years, and the individual isn't entitled to support given the short duration of the legal union, the result is that the person now finds he or she has no means of support, having already relinquished alimony awarded from the previous marriage.

In some jurisdictions, there was an acceptance of a "reversion back" doctrine. It makes much more sense and fills a societal need better than the present state of this law. For instance, if a woman or man divorces his or her spouse and receives alimony, in most cases that alimony stops upon remarriage. In some cases, it even stops if the individual cohabits with someone without marriage.

The coauthors of this book disagree on a just solution to this problem.

Raoul Felder says, "Another way, perhaps less acceptable philosophically, would be to allow specific time imposed which would oblige the husband or wife, who suddenly has no further financial responsibility, to continue paying the former spouse alimony even if there is a remarriage. Financial support from a former spouse should stop when and if the remarriage lasts more than a modestly stated period of years. Five years could be the point when the courts would award support that the new spouse must pay. Marriages of a shorter duration, unless there are children, are usually dissolved without a court awarding maintenance. In other words, alimony or maintenance should not automatically stop upon a remarriage. It should stop after several years to make certain that the remarriage 'takes' so the women or man is not left without any income."

Barbara Victor says, "To oblige individuals to continue paying alimony or maintenance after the remarriage of their ex-spouse puts the burden of the new marriage on the financial shoulders of the former spouse. Though it is correct that the courts don't usually award alimony or maintenance in short-term marriages where there are no children, there are always exceptions. To put into law that a remarriage must last a certain number of years before the former spouse is relieved of support is a contradiction of the point of maintenance or alimony. The court rarely awards maintenance or alimony for an infinite number of years, but rather limits the award to give the recipient enough time to make a new life, or get back into the workforce. The emotional ability of people and their new partners to make a marriage work should be carefully considered before the marriage takes place. Part of that consideration should include the reality of losing support from a former husband or wife. Divorce is and should be the end of any emotional connection that is detrimental to either party. Hoping that a remarriage works out, and being that involved in that aspect of an ex's life prevents the ex-spouse from 'moving on.' It is tantamount to using abortion as a means of birth control."

THERE HAVE BEEN CASES where an unmarried couple has lived together for more than two decades and then married. When the marriage ended after a brief period (marriage in some cases ruins rather than builds a relationship), the court does not take into consideration the number of years the couple lived together prior to legalizing the union. Though it is rare, the court will award alimony or maintenance based on need rather than the length of the marriage. Had the couple not married, however, the spouse in financial need might have received more had he or she brought an action for palimony.

Palimony, or support provided after the breakup of a live-in relationship that did not involve marriage, is a term that was coined in 1977 by divorce lawyer Marvin Mitchelson, and made famous during the trial of Lee Marvin and Michelle Triola when she sued the actor for palimony. Triola claimed that the actor had promised to support her for the rest of her life despite the fact that Marvin was married for the entire time that the couple lived together. The California Supreme Court noted that "social norms had changed as more adults were living together without entering into marriage." Keeping the evolving social mores of its citizens in mind, the Marvin court held that "nonmarital partners may lawfully contract concerning the ownership of property acquired during the relationship [and] equity will protect the interests of each in such property." The court also ruled that express agreements could be enforced unless they "rest on an unlawful meretricious consideration and in the absence of an express agreement, the courts may look to a variety of other remedies in order to protect the parties' lawful expectations." Though Michelle Triola received only $104,000 (for what was called "retraining," as she had been a singer before living with Lee Marvin in his home in Malibu for seven years) upon appeal, Triola lost even that paltry sum. Marvin Mitchelson, however, made headlines. He saw no reason why a lack of marriage should be an obstacle to a financial settlement when a couple parted ways. His statement "palimony was a commitment with no rings attached" sent chills through the Hollywood community, especially since California was and is a community property state, in which property acquired by a married couple is owned, and divided, jointly. It was certainly a shock when the California Supreme Court agreed with Mitchelson that live-in lovers could sue for financial support. The ruling, Mitchelson declared, was "the biggest setback for show business since John Wilkes Booth." Even more surprising was that the case itself and the publicity it garnered paved the way for many other palimony suits against celebrities such as Liberace, Rock Hudson, Martina Navratilova, and Bill Maher, among other ordinary couples who had been living as common-law husband and wife.

The most spectacular case—other than Lee Marvin and Michelle Triola, given that it was the first—was the case that Marc Christian brought against the estate of Rock Hudson. In October 1985, at the age of fifty-nine, Rock Hudson died in a private clinic in Paris, France, where he had gone for innovative treatment for AIDS. Christian's case for palimony had a component that was not present in the other palimony cases. His case was a landmark inasmuch as he was awarded $22 million by a California court, later reduced on appeal to $5 million, and subsequently settled for a figure somewhere in between those two figures..

The Hudson/Christian case was less about remuneration based on palimony or common-law marriage than it was about Christian's claim that Hudson did not tell him he had AIDS while continuing to have sexual relations with him despite his diagnosis.

"This case was a landmark not because it involved a gay couple," Christian said, "but because Hudson did not disclose his illness to me. When people are involved, gay or straight, you have to tell each other about any medical problems or any other problems you have. That's an honest relationship, married or unmarried, gay or straight." He was only partially correct. When married there is a duty to tell your wife of a communicable disease, but in casual hookups, or even those that violate the law, there may not be such a duty.

The further irony is that common-law marriage is recognized in certain states but never applied to same-sex couples. It only applies to opposite-sex couples who have lived together for a certain length of time. The exact laws that apply and the time necessary to qualify for common-law status vary from state to state. The usual stipulations are that a couple must live together for a significant period of time, though that time is not defined in any state; they must hold themselves out as a married couple by using the same last name, and referring to each other as "husband" or "wife";

and they must voice their intention to marry eventually. One of the considerations in awarding money in a common-law union is that the court takes into consideration the value of "housekeeping services" of one or the other partner while living in a "meretricious relationship." What the court will not take into consideration is any services having to do with "sexual relationships or bearing children."

As our country developed westward, the pioneer couples often paired without benefit of marriage, though commitment was the basis for the coupling. Because there was an unfortunately limited number of chapels, parsons, priests, rabbis, or ministers on the prairie, a commitment ceremony was developed where the parties would join together under the eyes of God as husband and wife.

As the county industrialized, states stopped recognizing these kinds of unions, and as a result, only twelve states still recognize common-law marriage today. Those states that do not themselves recognize common-law marriage do generally, however, accept and acknowledge common-law unions if they took place in those states where it was legal.

STATES WHERE COMMON-LAW MARRIAGE IS RECOGNIZED

Alabama	New Hampshire[3]
Colorado	Ohio[4]
District of Columbia	Oklahoma[5] (Okla. Stat. Ann. tit. 43, § 1)
Georgia[1]	Pennsylvania[9] (23 Penn. Cons. Stat. § 1103)
Idaho[2]	Rhode Island
Iowa (Iowa Code Ann. §. 595.11)	South Carolina
Kansas[8]	Texas[6] (Tex. Fam. Code Ann. § 2.401)
Montana (Mont. Code Ann. § 26-1-602, 40-1-403)	Utah[7] (Utah Code Ann.§ 30-1-4.5)

1. Only for common-law marriages formed before January 1, 1997 (1996 Georgia Act 1021).
2. Only for common-law marriages formed before January 1, 1996 (Idaho Code § 32-201).
3. Common-law marriages effective only at death (N.H. Rev. Stat. Ann § 457:39).
4. Only for common-law marriages formed before October 10, 1991 (*Lyons v. Lyons* 621 N.E. 2d 718, Ohio App. 1993).
5. Only for common-law marriage formed before November 1, 1998 (1998 Okla. SB 1076).
6. Texas calls it an "informal marriage" rather than a common-law marriage. Under § 2.401 of the Texas Family Code, an informal marriage can be established either by declaration (registering at the county courthouse without having a ceremony), or by meeting a three-prong test showing evidence of (1) an agreement to be married; (2) cohabitation in Texas; and (3) representation to

others that the parties are married. A 1995 update adds an evidentiary presumption that there was no marriage if no suit for proof of marriage is filed within two years of the date the parties separated and ceased living together.

7. Administrative order establishes that it arises out of a contract between two consenting parties who: (a) are capable of giving consent; (b) are legally capable of entering a solemnized marriage; (c) have cohabited; (d) mutually assume marital rights, duties, and obligations; and (e) who hold themselves out as and have acquired a uniform and general reputation as husband and wife. The determination or establishment of such a marriage must occur during the relationship or within one year following the termination of that relationship.

8. Kansas law prohibits recognition of common-law marriage if either party is under eighteen years of age (2002 Kan. Sess. Laws, SB 486, §23-101).

9. Pennsylvania law was amended to read "No common-law marriage contracted after January 1, 2005 shall be valid" (Pennsylvania Statutes, Section 1103).

Source: National Conference of State Legislatures (http://www.ncsl.org/default.aspx?tabid=4265)

Then there are wives who were in brief marriages without children and had more assets than their husbands. But because of the law that stipulates income and not assets decides who pays alimony, maintenance, or child support, many women are able to keep their nest egg and also have their husbands support them. When there is a divorce, the spouse with higher income is responsible for supporting the other spouse.

An astute lawyer will ascertain the weak points in every case. Weakness does not necessarily mean adultery, violence, or addiction. Weakness can be a possession—children, a weekend house, art—anything that one litigant feels fiercely about and that the other will use to his or her advantage.

14

Separate and Commingled Funds

Marriage is give-and-take. You'd better give it to her or she'll take it anyway.

—Joey Adams

SUSIE AND SAMUEL O. had a divorce that was unfair, for many reasons, to both sides. In the end, when it was all over and signed, even their lawyers admitted that it was one of the most glaring examples of a miscarriage of justice.

Susie was sixty years old and her husband, Samuel, was fifty-nine when they married. They had been living together for two years prior to their marriage, which lasted for three years. Each had grown children from previous unions. Each also had several million dollars in assets. Susie owned her own cooperative apartment, while Samuel owned a country house. Though Susie only earned approximately $35,000 a year, Samuel pulled in a high six-figure income and paid for all the expenses to maintain the country house as well as Susie's cooperative apartment, where they both lived. Putting aside the emotional issues and rancor, the divorce could have been simple, with legal fees in the five figures rather than in the high sixes.

Before they married, Susie and Samuel agreed to put their respective properties in joint names. When they said their vows, Samuel fulfilled his promise and gave Susie half ownership in his country house. Susie promised to do the same with her cooperative.

From Samuel's point of view, he had been "duped" by Susie from the beginning. According to him, she gave the appearance of a woman who was responsible about her work and their home, and was the kind of wife who would be an asset when he needed to go to social functions related to his job.

"Every promise she made, she never kept," Samuel explains, "including the one about putting her coop apartment in joint names after I put my country house in both our names. When she was arrested twice for shoplifting, I stood by her, but she retreated and would have nothing to do with me. I was at a loss. I was never unfaithful to her until the end. I didn't want to live a lie so I told Susie I wanted a divorce."

Susie knew that Samuel's country house was something he loved. He had built it himself and found solace there on holidays and weekends. Away from the stress of the city and his job, he loved to ride his tractor through the fields, plant flowers, and cut trees.

When negotiations began, all Susie wanted was to take the house away from Samuel.

Forensic accountant Mark Gottlieb does his job without emotion. According to Gottlieb, it is rare that he gets involved or upset when dealing with numbers in any divorce. There are exceptions, however, when he will realize that the opposition has focused on an issue that is important to his client, or the "weak point" in the case.

"Don't think poorly of me," Gottlieb says, "but I don't form personal feelings for the litigant. I'm an advocate for the approach I take in finding net worth, assets, and income of my client, as well as my conclusion, which is based on proper due diligence and professional judgment. Unlike some lawyers who are known to represent mostly men or mostly women, I'm not for one gender or another. My practice is unique as I represent the husband as frequently as I represent the wife. The good part about my job is that I can and do detach myself from the personality of the case. Lawyers get involved with the children and other family-related matters. That's not my responsibility. Obviously in meetings with clients when they start talking about the family or the pressure and strain of going through a divorce, it's sad. It's always sad to see a family break up. There was one case, that of Samuel and Susie O., that really got me, and maybe because I understood what his wife was trying to do and perhaps I related to my own feelings about a country house that I own and love. Samuel was willing to give his wife a fair share of his assets. She focused on his country house, which he built and designed and gave him enormous pleasure. The wife had no particular interest in the property except to punish Samuel by trying to take it away."

During negotiations, Susie would go up to the house during the week and break things, or remove certain items that Samuel had bought only to replace them with discarded ones that had been retired to the garage. She would rearrange the furniture and leave dirty pots and pans in the sink.

The judge did not seem to take into consideration that the couple had agreed to put their respective properties into joint names. The fact that the marriage was so brief and without children also did not sway the court. The judge focused on the fact that Samuel had given his wife ownership of half his country house, and that Susie owned her cooperative apartment alone. The judge ruled that while the divorce was in the stage of pendente lite or temporary maintenance, Samuel would either have to "share" his weekend house with his wife, or pay her so that she could rent a comparable property for the summer months. Through their lawyers, Samuel agreed to give Susie the money to rent a house with the understanding that as part of the final settlement, he would have the country house appraised and "buy out" his wife in a sum that was equal to her share. In addition, when Samuel offered Susie a car, she refused unless he agreed to pay to garage it in the city. Instead, the judge ordered Samuel to pay for a rental car every weekend so that his wife could drive to and from her rental house.

When interviewed long after Susie and Samuel's divorce was final, Mark Gottlieb, the forensic accountant, remarked, "No doubt I was emotionally involved in that case. The only other time I found myself emotionally involved in a case was once again a matter of the husband falling in love with another woman. As it happened, in that case, my client was the wife," Gottlieb says. "In the middle of preparing the discovery papers, she went on a spending spree. She bought a car for $100,000, jewelry for $75,000, clothes, and even charged hundreds of lightbulbs, which she claimed were necessities. I thought it was despicable but I kept it to myself. It wasn't my role to judge."

The dynamic between a lawyer and his or her client who has been left and one who has done the leaving is delicate and entails thought and consideration to the needs of each client, rather than responding in a punitive way that fuels the animosity. The yin and yang of divorce is that the spouse who leaves feels angry and guilty. The one left feels bitter. That said, it is not always the spouse who walks out the door who actually is responsible for the breakdown of the marriage. Often, the spouse who, on the surface, appears to have been abandoned has done nothing to make the marriage work, or to keep up his or her end of the bargain. Indeed, as a matter of law, it is possible that the spouse who leaves is not the spouse found guilty of abandonment. Sometimes, by word or deed, a spouse can be driven from the marital home.

Increasingly under the law, guilt or innocence, as well as contributions to a business or lack of such contributions, play less and less of a role in the division of marital assets. A wife who spent her days consuming bonbons or lunches with friends may be given the same financial consideration as that of a wife who has toiled in the family business. There is no automatic in this kind of situation. Often it doesn't matter if the wife worked outside the home or if the arrangement was that she stayed home and did whatever she pleased.

There are many cases that are even more glaring examples of a miscarriage of justice. One is the case of *Fields v. Fields*. Mr. Fields purchased a townhouse in 1978 for $130,000 with a $30,000 down payment and additionally by taking out two separate mortgages. The house was purchased eight years after Mr. Fields married his wife. According to Mr. Fields, the funds he used for the down payment came from an inheritance from his grandparents. Half of that down payment of $30,000 came directly to him from a bequest and the other half he borrowed from his mother with a written agreement to repay her when he had secured the two mortgages. None of Mrs. Fields's money was used either to purchase the building, for expenses, or for capital improvement.

One week after Mr. Fields bought the building, he transferred one-half interest to his mother. From that point on and for the next five years, Mr. and Mrs. Fields lived together in an apartment in the building along with their five-year-old son. One year later, Mrs. Fields became ill, ostensibly from the mildew and moisture in their basement apartment. She moved into another apartment in the building on a higher floor. Four years later, after a burglary, she moved again into yet another apartment in the building. For the entire time Mrs. Fields was living in those two different upstairs apartments, she continued to use the original duplex apartment where her husband and son resided. Eventually she moved back into the duplex but avoided the basement area of the apartment.

When the couple was in the process of divorce negotiations, the husband claimed that the building was entirely his, as it had been purchased with money left to him by his grandmother and borrowed from his mother. In July 2006, an appraiser valued the building at $2.6 million. Deducting the $30,000 down payment and the outstanding debt on the building, the referee hearing the case concluded that Mr. Fields owned half interest in the building (with his mother owning the other half). The referee also decided that Mr. Fields's interest in the building was indeed marital property and awarded Mrs. Fields 35 percent of $1.2 million, or 35 percent of her husband's 50 percent.

The Fields case seems to contradict the point of hiring a forensic accountant to sift through the assets and liabilities of couples going through a divorce—deciding what is marital and individual property. After hearing the referee's recommendations, Judge Jacqueline Silbermann upheld the decision based on the fact that "all property acquired by either or both spouses during the marriage without regard to the form in which title is held" defines marital property. In addition, Judge Acosta, representing the majority vote on the appellate court, also wrote, ". . . that the husband used separate property for the down payment and that the property was titled in his and his mother's name does not change the fact that his half interest in the property is a marital asset." Further, Judge Acosta concluded that the bottom line for the couple was that "Mr. Fields was entitled to a credit for the separate property—the $30,000 down payment—but the remaining $2.5 million increase in its [the building's] value since the 1978 purchase had to be shared with his wife."

Once again, the statutes of domestic law are not always clear or certain. As Harriet N. Cohen, a matrimonial specialist who was not involved in the case, explained, "There is uncertainty and unpredictability in the law because of the tension between the definitions of marital and separate property in the statute."

In the case of *Fields v. Fields,* as in numerous other cases of deciphering marital from personal property, because of lack of clarity and vagueness in the law the final judgment also depends largely on a judge's life experiences concerning the specific needs and rights of each litigant.

Though there is no "automatic," there are cases where women are the ones who suffer financial inequality in certain instances more frequently than men.

Mr. and Mrs. Fleischman were married for thirty years. From the beginning of their marriage, the husband put himself through law school and became the sole support of the family. During that period, the wife worked in the anesthesiology department at New York University Medical Center while earning a master's degree in allied health at Rutgers University. When she had her first child, she quit her job and subsequently gave birth to two more children. For the duration of the marriage, the wife stayed home, cared for the children, attended her husband's business events, and hosted clients and coworkers at their home.

On January 23, 2006, Mrs. Fleischman filed for divorce. She requested a fifty-fifty split of both the value of her husband's law license and partnership interests in his law firm. In 2007, the couple agreed that it was Mr. Fleischman who had constructively abandoned his wife. They decided to share custody of the couple's three children and to sell the marital home. The couple also agreed to live near each other in separate residences for the sake of the children. Despite the agreement concerning grounds for divorce and joint custody of the couple's children, there was no agreement when it came to the financial settlement of the divorce.

During the ten-day trial, Justice Lewis J. Lubell stated that because Mrs. Fleischman had only contributed "minimally" to her husband's law license, she was only entitled to 10 percent of its value. He further stated that Mrs. Fleischman had not only not contributed to her husband's education but had devoted most of her time to her own studies, which resulted in modest and unspecified contributions to the "marital pot." When it came to equitable distribution of her husband's partnership earnings, the judge ruled that though Mrs. Fleischman stayed at home to care for their three children, and attended and hosted business functions, and notwithstanding that that the marriage had lasted for thirty years, she was only entitled to 25 percent of his partnership interest.

In a brief statement by Mr. Fleischman's attorney, Ronald Bavero, he saw this decision as a "continuation of the recent trend of the appellate division which is to limit the equitable share for licenses and practices of law partners and other professions."

The question that arises concerns the wife who has toiled at a menial job, forsaking her own education, to put her husband through law school or medical school. How does the court differentiate between a woman actually working outside the home to subsidize the family income while her husband pursues a degree with a woman who facilitates the husband to pursue that degree by staying home and caring for his children and his physical needs?

15

GROUNDS FOR DIVORCE

In every marriage more than a week old, there are
grounds for divorce. The trick is to find, and continue
to find, grounds for marriage.
— ROBERT ANDERSON, ECONOMIST
(1861–1939)

IN 1967, MORE THAN THIRTY STATES adopted a divorce reform law, nearly two centuries after the original divorce laws were passed in 1787. More than anything else, this demonstrates how the law reflects the slow evolution of public morality. In 1977, nine more states had adopted no-fault divorce laws. By late 1983, every state but South Dakota and New York had adopted some form of no-fault divorce. South Dakota finally adopted it in 1985. New York did not have a no-fault provision in its divorce laws until October 12, 2010. Under New York State law, it used to be that only if both parties agreed or if they notarized a separation agreement and lived separately for one year could a judge issue a divorce without citing fault or grounds. After Governor David Paterson signed into law the new amended no-fault provision in New York State, couples could divorce based on the following ground in addition to the other grounds that had been in effect.

The amendment states that "if the relationship between husband and wife has broken down irretrievably for a period of at least six months, provided that one party has so stated under oath, divorce can be granted." The amendment also states that "no judgment of divorce shall be granted under this subdivision unless and until the economic issues of equitable distribution of marital property, the payment or waiver of spousal support, the payment of child support, the payment of counsel and experts' fees and expenses as well as the custody and visitation with the infant children of the marriage have been resolved by the parties, or determined by the court and incorporated into the judgment of divorce."

This new amendment is not retroactive. It was put into law on the sixteenth day after signature by the governor, or sixteen days after October 12, 2010, and applies "only to matrimonial actions commenced on or after such effective date." To appreciate the trajectory of the change in divorce law in the United States, it is interesting to cast a glance at what the grounds were in New York before the new amendment. As the last "holdout state," New York had only five grounds for divorce. They were adultery; abandonment for a year or more, which includes constructive abandonment (refusal to have sex); cruel and inhuman treatment; incarceration in prison of one party or the other for three consecutive years; and if the husband and wife lived apart pursuant to a decree or judgment of separation for a period of one or more years. The last of these was naturally the most antiseptic and sane, but emotions often preclude sane and rational people from recognizing that if they waited a year, it was unnecessary to hurl accusations, defamation, and cause general trauma. Then there were those who simply could not wait the year to embark on a new life or could not reach an agreement that would start the year running.

The changes in divorce law in the United States signified a departure from traditional American values, yet the legislation of these changes was enacted for a far more cynical reason. Lawyers, judges, and litigants understood that when seeking divorce where fault was necessary, couples manufactured evidence of guilt while judges and lawyers simply looked the other way. The majority of litigants were virtually given a license to lie so the divorce could be granted.

Judge Rosalyn Richter was a matrimonial judge in the New York Supreme Court, and now sits in New York State Appellate Court. She believes that no-fault divorce in New York remained in effect at the "behest of the Archdiocese, upheld because of the strong axis between Albany, the state capital, and the subservience of Albany to Cardinal [Francis] Spellman and his successors in New York."

Attorney Ken Burrows adds, "Nothing could get done in New York politically without the cooperation of the Catholic Church, starting from Tammany Hall days and continuing through Roosevelt, Wagner, and Dinkins, though Mayor Lindsay was somewhat more independent. Al Smith was the first Catholic governor and he obviously left a lasting imprint on the way things worked. Politicians all bent their knee to the Archdiocese because that's how they got reelected."

New York is a curious case. Not just the Catholic Church but also the feminists, including the National Organization for Women, were influential in preventing New York from becoming a no-fault state until 2010.

The Roman Catholic bishops in Albany took the position that "it shouldn't be easier to get out of a marriage than a car lease." Opposition from the Catholic hierarchy to no-fault divorce was certainly not a surprise, except for the fact that they were joined by the National Organization of Women, the state's leading feminist group. Leaders of NOW expressed their resistance to no-fault by stating, "We see it not as no-fault but as divorce on demand—unilateral divorce. We believe that the push for no-fault is coming from wealthy husbands who want to dump wives who are less able to afford the costs of lawyers." Feminists also stated that judges—women and men—are "career people who have no respect for housewives."

The feminists, in concert with the Catholic Church, took the position that fault was good for women as they could "sell" their husbands a divorce when the husband in question took the "best years of their lives" and then moved on to a younger woman. Their position came under the heading of "woman power," as women "charged for men's freedom."

Back then, before no-fault became a law, the only way to get unmarried was to prove misconduct (in New York it had to be adultery). Proving adultery was not easy. When adultery had to be proved, one or the other litigants, usually the woman, hired a detective, a photographer, a girl, and a hotel room, often with the complicity and consent of the husband (in instance, where both parties were eager to establish a basis for divorce). The other way to get unmarried was to have the marriage annulled. Usually in those cases, the mother of the bride would swear in court that her daughter wanted children and that her son-in-law refused to have them, and additionally this was revealed in front of her in an argument between the husband and wife in question, or some similar fantasy.

Once again, this was frequently done with the consent and complicity of the husband. Apparently, the Archdiocese thought it was better to lie to get unmarried than to simply tell the truth and say the couple was incompatible or unhappy.

In 1976, times were changing and even in "fault" states the grounds for divorce were extended to allow for abandonment, both actual and sexual, lesser standards of cruelty, and some version of consensual divorce. In 1979, states began playing around with mandatory counseling before a judge would grant a divorce.

Recently, the Women's Bar Association in New York, which had been opposed to making New-York a no-fault state, changed its position. According to Elaine Avery, the former president of the group, "a woman who was a victim of domestic violence would no longer be forced to waste time, money, and emotional energy on proving who did what in the breakup of a marriage. Instead, they would be free to focus on what really matters—the custody of their children, child support, and the fair and equitable division of the parties' financial affairs."

Alton L. Abramowitz, a matrimonial lawyer who chairs the Committee on Matrimonial Law at the Association of the Bar of the City of New York, which supported the change to no-fault, said that because of the state's budgetary process, "a lot of major issues get lost in Albany." He said that as a safeguard in this process, they support "provisions requiring all issues involving equitable distribution and child custody be resolved before the judgment of divorce."

Adultery in New York State is technically against the law, though it is rarely ever enforced in a criminal context. The law against adultery took effect on September 1, 1907, and remains in force under Section 255.17 of the state penal law, which states: "A person is guilty of adultery when he or she engages in sexual intercourse with another person at a time when he or she has a living spouse." Considered a Class B misdemeanor, it is punishable by up to ninety days in jail or a five-hundred-dollar fine. It is interesting to note that under the law, even an unmarried person may be guilty of adultery. For example, when a married man seduces an unmarried woman, she is also guilty of adultery.

When Governor David Paterson held a news conference in Albany in March 2008 to disclose that he had had several extramarital affairs several years before, he said, at one point, "I didn't break the law." He lied!

Actually, the governor did break the law. The problem with adultery, however, or at least convicting those guilty of adultery, is that in hundreds of thousands of hotel rooms throughout New York State, ordinary citizens are hard at work breaking the law. A criminal ban on adultery has no practical significance. It is a celebration of hypocrisy: a triumph of religion over reality. Reality only comes into play when a spurned litigant wants to humiliate a spouse in the eyes of the church, synagogue, mosque, or his or her children, family, and friends.

Even Bernie Madoff isn't exempt from accusations of adultery. After his sentencing to 150 years in prison for rendering thousands of people penniless because of his Ponzi scheme, including close friends and family members, he was finally branded an adulterer. Sheryl Weinstein, the former chief financial officer of Hadassah, was herself bilked by Madoff, as was her family and Hadassah, admitted to having had an affair with the disgraced and reviled swindler.

In 1938, Frank Sinatra was actually arrested by police in Bergen County, New Jersey, for "carrying on with a married woman." The charge was later changed to adultery, a more serious charge, which implicated both Sinatra and the woman. In the end, the charge worked in Sinatra's favor, as the judge eventually dismissed the case so as not to implicate the woman.

A public divorce with a movie star is a perfect example of how reckless philandering can embarrass and humiliate the *aggrieved* party in a failed marriage.

Iolanda Quinn had been married to Anthony Quinn for thirty-one years. During their marriage, she had devoted her life to her husband and their three children. Quinn, however, at the age of eighty-two, fathered two children by his thirty-five-year-old secretary, Kathy Benvin, who later married Quinn and became his widow. Apparently he had always been a serial philanderer—in fact, during the investigation it was revealed that the actor had actually fathered thirteen children with two wives and three girlfriends. Not surprisingly, the media had a field day with the story and wrote countless articles about the octogenarian who kept fathering children. At the annual televised Academy Awards ceremony, watched by an international audience of many millions, Billy Crystal, the host, made the following remark: "Women who win tonight receive an Oscar. The losers can have a baby by Anthony Quinn."

When Iolanda fled to her family home in Italy, she was faced with a barrage of paparazzi and inundated with embarrassing questions about her husband's affair that produced two babies. When the case came to trial, the media was in breathless attendance. Iolanda's lawyer, one of the coauthors of this book, represented her and proceeded on the grounds of egregious fault. As explained, while fault does not generally affect equitable distribution, it does if the lawyer can prove that actions during the course of the marriage produced horrifying results. If proved, the court will award a kind of punitive damage to the settlement.

Anthony Quinn was represented by Barry Slotnick, who made his name as the lawyer for Bernard Goetz, who shot four teenagers on a New York City subway in 1984. In court, Slotnick accused Iolanda of abusing Quinn and also lying to him to win more than 90 percent of his multimillion-dollar estate. In reality, the truth was quite different.

When Iolanda's lawyer called their thirty-three-year-old son, Danny Quinn, to the stand, he admitted that though he loved his father, he accused him of abusing his mother by hitting her and shouting obscenities at her. Not surprisingly it was apparent to everyone in court, including the judge, that Iolanda had been an abused woman who had suffered years of cruelty inflicted upon her by her husband. Anthony Quinn settled the case before the trial went any further and more witnesses could be called to testify.

THE JOKE THAT CALIFORNIA lawyers and judges like to make is that unlike New York, where adultery is grounds for divorce, in California, adultery is grounds for marriage. In California, "married and having an affair" is considered the courtship that leads to remarriage.

In 1970, California was the first state to implement the concept of "no-fault divorce." Usually, divorce is granted on the grounds of "irreconcilable difference" or incurable insanity. Yet in California as well as in New York and throughout the country, there is a new form of adultery that has become the trend.

New York divorce attorney Eleanor Alter maintains that she is hearing more accusations from women that their husbands are watching pornography on television and on the Internet, a charge that some believe is tantamount to adultery.

"If I have another porn case," Alter says, "I'll scream. But this is the trend now. Women are accusing their husbands of watching porn and are claiming that the children can see it, especially if there is a divorce and kids are visiting their fathers. Statistics now show that more people watch porn than [I] ever believed possible. However, even these statistics are inaccurate because of the obvious: people don't admit to doing it (similar to Viagra. One would be hard put—pardon the phrase—to find a man who admits to using it, but it is the bestselling drug in the world). But now they don't have to sneak into a porn theater because they can view it privately at home on their computer. I suspect that when women get upset about this, it is less about the children seeing the porn than it is because they disapprove of their spouse's expression of their sexuality."

It is always difficult to prove someone was watching pornography on-line, unless their browsing history is still stored. Most hotel rooms do not label X-rated movies as "adult entertainment," but rather simply put "movie" on the bill. It is far easier to prove drug or alcohol use—that can be tested—than it is to prove that someone is watching pornography while he or she should be watching children. Proven or unproven, the accusation is harmful and attracts media attention when it concerns the rich and famous.

When Christie Brinkley and Peter Cook divorced in February 2006, Cook had already admitted to an affair with his eighteen-year-old assistant. In that case, adultery the good old-fashioned way was not enough for the prurient press. The age of the Internet captured audiences when it was revealed during the divorce trial that Cook was a habitual watcher of pornography. His monthly bill for accessing adult Web sites was about three thousand dollars. Not only did Cook post nude photos of himself, including several where he posed masturbating for the Web cam, but he also used an array of false names to attract other porn watchers.

A 2002 survey of the American Academy of Matrimonial Lawyers suggests that Internet porn plays a part in an increasing number of divorce cases. Brinkley and Cook weren't the first celebrity couple to cite pornography in their divorce. In 2005, Denise Richards accused Charlie Sheen of posting pictures of his genitalia online as well as frequenting "barely legal" porn sites. A year after the Brinkley/Cook breakup, in 2007, Anne Heche, formerly the partner of Ellen DeGeneres, accused her husband of watching pornography on his computer when he was meant to be watching their five-year-old son.

Masturbating while looking at a *Sports Illustrated* swimsuit model or at a *Playboy* centerfold is a one-way street: the images are intended to provoke fantasies, not to embody reality, since the women pictured aren't having sex for the viewer's gratification. Even strippers, for all their flesh-and-blood appeal, are essentially fantasy objects—depending on how you respond to a lap dance, of course. Hard-core pornography is real sex by definition, and the two sexual acts involved—the on-camera copulation, and the masturbation that results—are interdependent. Neither would happen without the other. The whole point of a centerfold is that she titillates while being unattainable. With hard-core porn, it's precisely the reverse. The porn star isn't just attainable, she's already being attained, and the user gets to be in on the action.

There is an obvious line between a suburban husband looking at *Playboy* magazine and one who pays thirty dollars a month to access hard-core pornography on his computer. The gray area arises when you compare that suburban husband masturbating to real sex, even though his computer is providing the stimulus, and a man who hires a prostitute to have sex. Neither is supposed to have any emotional connection. Morally, of course, there is a difference, and the distinction *does* matter in a court of law. But if infidelity is approached as a continuing act of betrayal, the conclusion might be that porn on the Internet is closer to the old definition of adultery than most porn users would care to admit. And there are many who maintain that watching pornography is tantamount to infidelity and ultimately adultery. They claim that pornography paves the way for more physical face-to-face betrayals, while still others say that one has no bearing on the other.

In a November 1978 interview with *Playboy* magazine, President Jimmy Carter quoted the Bible in answer to a question on adultery. "The Bible says," Carter explained, " 'Thou shalt not commit adultery.' Christ said, 'I tell you that anyone who looks on a woman with lust in his heart has already committed adultery.' I've looked on a lot of women with lust. I've committed adultery in my heart many times. . . ."

In Texas, as in other states, adultery is not a paramount consideration in most divorce cases. Texas is a community property state. If there is a standard "no-fault" divorce, assets are usually divided equally. If there is adultery, however, and it is properly asserted as grounds for divorce, a Texas judge always divides the property according to his or her discretion.

In addition to adultery, pornography, lewd photographs, and Internet sex, there is yet another ground for divorce that falls into a gray area of the law.

In 1982, the New York State Court of Appeals judged that the definition of abandonment should include a refusal by one party or the other to have sexual relations, also called constructive abandonment. The case that set the precedent for that ruling was *Diemer v. Diemer.*

In that case, the court of appeals held that the wife's religious scruples were not justification for her refusing to have sexual relations with her husband. The wife claimed that because they had been married in a civil ceremony and not according to the rules of the church, she had no obligation to have sexual relations with her husband. Her argument was rejected by the court, which judged that her refusal constituted abandonment.

One woman who appeared in a preliminary hearing for divorce was not in the courtroom five minutes when she blurted out for the benefit of the judge, "My husband and I had sex two months ago." When the time came to list grounds for her divorce from her husband, who had left her for another woman, any possibility of citing the more civilized "constructive abandonment" was impossible.

Once a judge hears such a comment, it brings down the curtain on a claim for constructive abandonment. A judge is the ultimate judicial officer and cannot be party to nor tolerate a lawyer's client testifying to one thing under oath and, at the same time, candidly advising the judge that the testimony was untruthful. In that particular case, when the woman wanted to list adultery as grounds for divorce, however, the judge asked her lawyer to reduce the charge to cruel and inhuman treatment— the best she could do given that constructive abandonment had been eliminated by the woman's outburst.

There are other cases where both parties have agreed to live together without having sexual relations for a long period of time until either the husband or the wife decides to divorce, and eventually they use that as grounds.

Jason H. and his wife, Sylvia, lived together for thirty-five years, and for thirty of those years, did not have sexual relations. When Jason fell in love with another woman, he was advised by his attorney to sue for "constructive abandonment," claiming that he and his wife had no physical contact for more than two decades.

The judge asked one question of Jason H. "During that time, did you make repeated demands of your wife that she engage in sexual intercourse with you?"

The word "repeated" was the key that prevented Jason H. from being granted the divorce on those grounds.

"I asked her," Jason H. answered.

"How often?" the judge asked.

"From time to time," Jason H. replied.

The judge ruled that a "refusal or failure to engage in marital relations, to rise to the level of constructive abandonment, must be unjustified, willful, and continued despite repeated requests from the other spouse for resumption of cohabitation."

The problem, of course, is that standards such as "repeated" and "periodically" or "from time to time," are vague and make it difficult for an attorney to advise his or her client on the law.

Generally, constructive abandonment as it is listed under abandonment for a year or more is perhaps the most interesting and nuanced of all grounds for divorce. One party must swear that the claim of "constructive abandonment" is true, while the other simply remains silent. Domestic relations law requires four elements of proof for constructive abandonment: "a voluntary separation of one spouse from the other, with intent not to resume cohabitation, without the consent of the other spouse, without justification, as the law states that there are basic obligations arising from the marriage." What that means in lay terms is that each spouse has the right to have sexual relations with the other. To claim constructive abandonment, one party must refuse to have sexual relations with the other and that refusal must be "willful and continued, despite repeated requests from the other spouse for resumption of cohabitation."

If both parties decide to seek divorce based on constructive abandonment, as long as they are willing to corroborate each other's claims—one claims he or she asked repeatedly for sex and the other chooses not to refute the allegation—it is impossible to prove. This is how it works, provided neither the judge nor lawyers know the charge to be untrue.

Judges usually do not require additional proof and, in fact, most judges understand that constructive abandonment, when not disputed, is usually used in "consensual" divorces after all the financial aspects of a case are settled. Put yet another way, constructive abandonment is almost always unable to be unproved—a sometimes lie that is accepted by the court (having no proof or evidence to suggest otherwise) to make a divorce quick, painless, and without trauma. The irony is that if one party accuses the other of constructive abandonment, even if it is true, it is impossible to prove, as it is a "he said, she said," accusation and defense. Lawyers are not private detectives nor are they obliged to have clients take a lie detector test. If clients are prepared to testify to constructive abandonment and indicate to their lawyers that the testimony is accurate, and the lawyer has no reason to believe otherwise, they become part of the drama.

New York attorney Barry Abbott explains how in acrimonious divorces, sometimes one litigant or the other will threaten to use more castigatory grounds if they are trying to block a divorce or if they are trying to embarrass or punish their future ex-spouse in the eyes of their religious group, children, family, colleagues, and friends.

"In one case where the man was blocking his wife from getting a divorce, he actually brought a bottle of Viagra into court," Abbott says. "He rebuffed his wife's claims of constructive abandonment and showed the judge that he had been trying to have sex, but even with Viagra, it didn't work."

There have been many "Viagra cases," including several where women have sued husbands and partners, citing the erectile dysfunction drug for what would be tantamount to "alienation of affections." One case involved an older couple who were not married. Dominic Barbara, a Long Island lawyer, represented the woman in this particular case. Barbara's claim was that the husband "strayed" because he had taken Viagra. One coauthor of this book represented the wife, who sued her partner for $2 million in palimony. When the newspapers became aware of the case, they labeled the husband the "Viagra man," and though the case was ultimately thrown out of court and resolved, it caused both plaintiff and defendant great embarrassment.

Though the Viagra defense, both in constructive abandonment and adultery, has been ridiculed in court, sex therapists and the media have long predicted that along with Viagra, the rate of infidelity would naturally increase. Even Dr. Ruth Westheimer weighed in with the cautionary statement "I don't want to sound like a Jewish grandmother who said I told you so, but I've said that unless the pill is coupled with education and sexual literacy, I predict a lot of troubles."

Other sex researchers have warned that many couples, without sufficient education and knowledge of the drug, may not be prepared for the changes that result from taking it. Older women in particular will not be able to match their partner's heightened sexual prowess.

Dr. Domeena Renshaw, director of Loyola University's Sexual Dysfunction clinic, said, "I had a couple come in where he's demanding sex since he went on Viagra, and she's not up to it."

CRUEL AND INHUMAN TREATMENT is far more serious than most people realize. For some, it might be misconstrued to mean that a litigant has had his or her charge cards canceled, or that one or the other spouse refuses to interact verbally or emotionally, or humiliates one or the other parent in front of the children, family, or friends. The legal definition of cruel and inhuman treatment, however, is a variation of "the conduct of the defendant so endangers the physical and mental well-being of the plaintiff as renders it unsafe or improper for the plaintiff to cohabit with the defendant." "Improper" is the key word.

There are certain exceptions that are steeped in laws that have been technically in effect in some states throughout the United States for centuries.

In the case of George M. and Mary Ann M., she refused to have sexual relations with her husband. Her refusal was found to be legitimate and justified as, according to Mary Ann, her husband demanded anal and oral sex, as well as demanded that she wear erotic undergarments. The court found that the husband's "unconventional sexual demands were responsible for the wife's general lack of desire for conventional sex."

Though she accommodated her husband's demands on occasion, she claimed she found that his "favored forms of sex were either painful or unpleasant." Despite her admitted revulsion to her husband's sexual preferences, Mary Ann expressed her desire to remain in a loving marriage with him, but only if he would agree to have "normal sexual relations."

"Normal" is an impossible word to define when it comes to consensual sex between two adults. However, when charging a spouse with what might be considered "abnormal" sexual demands, it should be noted that the following states still hold sodomy and fellatio for both heterosexual and same-sex couples to be a crime.

Florida—misdemeanor punishable by up to sixty days imprisonment or a five-hundred-dollar fine.

Idaho—felony punishable by imprisonment for five years to life.

Kansas—same sex only, misdemeanor punishable by up to six months in prison and a one-thousand-dollar fine.

Louisiana—all sexes, felony punishable by up to five years in prison and a two-thousand-dollar fine.

Mississippi—all sexes, felony punishable by up to ten years of imprisonment.

North Carolina—all sexes, felony punishable by up to ten years of imprisonment and discretionary fine.

Oklahoma—same sex only, felony punishable by up to ten years of imprisonment.

South Carolina—all sexes, felony punishable by up to five years of imprisonment and a five-hundred-dollar fine.

Texas—same sex only, misdemeanor, punishable by up to a five-hundred-dollar fine.

Utah—all sexes, misdemeanor punishable by up to six months of imprisonment and a thousand-dollar fine.

Virginia—all sexes, felony punishable by one to five years in prison.

The following states have "invalidated" the laws concerning fellatio and sodomy, which means they are still "on the books" but cannot be enforced: Arkansas, Georgia, Maryland, New York, Pennsylvania, and Tennessee.

CURIOUSLY, NOT EVERYONE understands the definition of sodomy, as opposed to fellatio. One textbook case recounts the story of a man who, accused of sodomy, pled guilty and went to jail. Because he entered a guilty plea, there was no testimony taken or cross-examination. After languishing in jail for several months, he read up on the two words and to his chagrin, determined that though he had engaged in oral sex, he had not engaged in sodomy. He simply did not know the correct dictionary definition of sodomy. Eventually, the man got a new trial. The problem, however, is that the law, at least in states like New York, is very vague, and in fact, oral sex may fall under the category of sodomy.

There are countless nuances and technicalities in the law that often, at best, force people to live a lie or lie outright, or at worst, put their lives at risk. Other laws are influenced by social judgments that are not in step with life in the twenty-first century.

16

"Fair" Is a Four-Letter Word

Equitable does not mean equal. Equitable means fair.
Fair is not always equal.

—Barbara Victor

IN A PERFECT WORLD, a divorce lawyer's first instinct would be to ascertain whether there was a chance to save the marriage. New Jersey attorney Gary Skoloff, who has had thirty years' experience handling divorce, tries to give his clients a pragmatic yet optimistic approach to divorce. According to Skoloff, he has never had a client who isn't either racked with pain or filled with guilt.

"As much as I'd like to believe that reconciliation is always an option, most of the time it isn't. Even if there isn't another man or woman waiting in the wings, most people who reach that point of retaining counsel have no intention of ever going back into the marriage. It happens but it's very, very rare. I try to start off by giving my clients the harsh reality—that once they enter my office, divorce is inevitable in most instances," Skoloff explains. "Once they can accept that and once the litigant understands that punitive measures—whether blocking access to children or stripping their spouse of every penny—won't change that reality, they somehow begin to realize that the more they fight, the more costly it will be and the longer it will take them to begin the healing process. If the litigants can also admit that they've been unhappy or have suffered humiliation, they're better off ending the marriage. My advice is always get it done and get it done fast. Until it's over, most people are in a chaotic mood. Either I have clients who tell me to throw another million in the pot just to get rid of it or they tell me that every nickel matters."

Other lawyers see clients who have no particular problem, nothing draconian happened in the marriage, and the union was relatively uneventful. In those marriages, in particular, lawyers would like to stop before the wheels of litigation begin to grind.

Many lawyers understand that the step before divorce would be to try to convince these couples to talk to a marriage counselor. One divorce lawyer explains it like this: "The couple has a decent life. The kids are fine. The couple is functioning as a unit. They're socializing with friends, going to the club, taking vacations, planning graduation parties, and then suddenly, the guy wakes up one morning and says he wants a divorce. Why? Because he feels old and impotent, not just physically or sexually, but emotionally as well."

Joel and Loretta S. are typical examples of what he described. Joel and Loretta were married for twenty years when things began to unravel. Theirs was a traditional marriage. He worked while she stayed home to care for the children. Joel was a successful executive, and they were able to live an upper-middle-class life, which included vacations, private school, and camp for their two children, membership to a country club, two luxury cars, and household help. On the surface, they had everything: a beautiful home, money, friends, trips, and two wonderful children whom they both adored. When the younger child left for college, the couple suddenly realized that they no longer had anything to discuss except each other. His involvement with his business bored her, while her interests in theater and travel did not appeal to him. Even their tastes in movies, plays, and other leisure activities were incompatible. Though both admitted they were unhappy and unfulfilled, they had never contemplated an affair nor were they angry or seeking revenge. The one thing they had in common was that both were miserable and had reached a point in their lives, especially since their children were out of the house, when they knew they had nothing in common. They wanted a divorce. Both expected to make new and better lives.

When interviewed as to why she chose divorce instead of simply living her life while her husband lived his, she replied, "We decided to bail out. We were both discouraged, disheartened, and disappointed. Maybe we were just bored. The real question is why we stayed together so long. I've thought about that and maybe Joel was bored or I was bored and each assumed that the other was as well. Perhaps we were just putting up with an inferior state of life instead of acting on what we knew to be true. We had grown apart and didn't love each other anymore. I looked around and saw that the brave ones were escaping over a wall to get out of a lifeless marriage. Divorce is a fabulous option. In my opinion, having lived married and now divorced, I truly believe that there could never be a promise of an emotionally fulfilling marriage without divorce. If there was no such thing as ending a marriage, or knowing there was the possibility of ending a marriage, there would be more spousal murders or less marriages in the first place."

Joel, Loretta's husband, had yet another opinion on divorce and why, in the beginning, he resisted getting married. "I was in love with Loretta, that wasn't the problem, but I was afraid of having to compromise. I also enjoyed my life. I had no responsibility except to get myself up every day and go to work, do my job properly so I wouldn't get fired, and achieve something. Marriage to me meant giving all that up, and her problems would become mine. Married, I'd have to consider another human being. Why did I get married? Because as I said, I loved her, and if I hadn't married her, she would have left me."

Another divorce lawyer who has heard the other side of the story said, "I've had cases where the marriage seems perfectly intact until one day the wife comes to my office and says she wants a divorce. When I ask her why, she'll tell me that she feels unappreciated and used up. She'll explain that having sex with her husband is like having sex with a 'relative.' If I had a magic wand, I'd wave it and hope that both of them would come to their senses."

According to this lawyer, he convinced the husband to give the marriage another chance. "Of course, it's the classic story," the lawyer says. "Unbeknownst to the wife, the husband wanted a divorce because he found a young girl who made him feel alive. When the guy told me that, I suggested he seek therapy and see if he can't do what he has to do without breaking up the home. Here's the problem. The guy was willing, as was his wife, and they went to therapy and decided not to divorce. I really felt uplifted, that I had some influence in keeping a home together. The nod and the wink, of course, was that the guy would still see the young girl without the wife knowing it and everyone would live happily ever after. Everything fell apart when the young girl started pressuring my client, telling him she wouldn't wait around, and if he didn't get divorced, she'd leave. So, since she's the only thing in his life that makes him feel alive, he's frightened of losing her and files for divorce."

There are yet other cases where lawyers will convince clients to postpone filing for divorce for reasons that have less to do with saving a marriage than with getting the best deal they can in court.

In the case of Lisa T., there were very practical reasons to discourage her from seeking divorce, and advising her that she would be better off remaining in the marriage for at least another five years.

Lisa T. was a beautiful twenty-six-year-old Russian woman who was married to a Greek billionaire for only two years. When she came into a lawyer's office seeking counsel to divorce her husband, the conversation began.

"Tell me a bit about your life," the lawyer began.

Lisa replied, "I have a son from another relationship and my husband treats my child as his own. We live in luxury. My husband travels a lot and every week he leaves about thirty thousand dollars on the dresser for me to use as I want. Our rent is about fifty thousand dollars a month, which he pays, and I have a nanny, maid, and a driver for our Rolls-Royce. I also have a black American Express card which my husband pays. I have no limits on what I can spend."

"Now tell me a bit about your husband and why you want a divorce. What are the grounds?"

"Grounds?" Lisa asked, bewildered.

"Is he unfaithful?"

"No, never," she answered.

"Does he beat you?"

Shocked, she replied, "Never. He would never hurt me."

"Does he make you do bad things?"

"He's a gentleman."

"Does he curse at you?"

"He never raises his voice to me."

"Is he nasty to you?"

"Never."

"Does he sleep with you?"

"Maybe once a month."

At the end of their meeting, Lisa was advised by her lawyer not to divorce, as the court would never agree that her husband keep her in the style to which she had been accustomed given the length of her marriage and the fact that she had no grounds that would cause her either emotional or physical harm. The lawyer emphasized that given the brief length of the marriage, there would be automatic restrictions on what she could expect as a financial settlement.

Lisa left the lawyer in a determined and defiant mode. Five years later, almost to the day, Lisa T. returned to the lawyer's office.

With a broad smile on her beautiful face, she asked, "Do you remember me?"

The lawyer nodded.

"Have things changed?" he asked.

"No," Lisa answered thoughtfully. "Except I listened to you and stayed with my husband for five years and now I want a divorce."

The lawyer who met with Lisa T. took her case. When she left his office five years earlier, it was less a matter of trying to keep a marriage intact than it was a determination to maximize financial results. She knew there was a good chance that a short-term marriage without children would yield little in the way of financial remuneration and, in cold-blooded response, went to a Plan B.

The problem is that not all short-term marriages yield minimal financial remuneration. After only a three-year marriage, Susie O. received a lucrative settlement from her husband, Samuel, which only proves that there are no ironclad rules when it comes to divorce. There are always extenuating factors, as well as judges who hold different views on what is important and what can be ignored in any matrimonial. In Lisa T.'s case, it was undoubtedly her young age, while in Susie's case, it was also her age and the fact that her husband was age appropriate. Lisa T.'s husband was more than thirty years older, which perhaps would not have made a favorable impression on the judge.

ONE OF THE MOST enlightened states in the country is also one of the most unfair when it comes to maintenance and alimony.

Massachusetts, where some of the country's most illustrious colleges and universities are located (venerable institutions of learning that have educated many of the world's most successful women), and the state that first recognized gay marriage, is also the place where divorce laws are patently unfair and archaic. In fact, the majority of lawyers in Massachusetts agree that the laws are so archaic that the act of marriage gives many sane people reason to fear taking that legal step. As for prenuptial agreements, they too give little guarantee that litigants won't be punished for life when it comes to paying alimony, as some Massachusetts judges routinely dismiss them on relatively flimsy grounds.

There is much discussion in Massachusetts over reforming the state's alimony laws to bring them up to date with the economic realities of the twenty-first century, instead of the year 1950. Two groups, Massachusetts Alimony Reform and The 2nd Wives Club, support a bill that would reform alimony laws in a fair and sane way.

The bill, HR 1567, was introduced in January 2008, and a day of hearings was held. The testimony was heartbreaking. The legislators on the judiciary committee were moved by the horror stories from men, women, and children. Yet the committee referred the bill for "further study." The bill was reintroduced in January 2010 and people were urged to write to their state senators and congressmen to urge them to support HR 1567, which would reform alimony laws, though not child support. The reform of this law would also take away some judicial discretion. As of this writing, the governor of Massachusetts has been silent on this issue. Surprisingly, the only opposition to reforming these laws comes from lawyers. The code words from lawyers are "judicial discretion." They are in favor of leaving everything up to "judicial discretion" because judges, therefore, would have all the power, and cynics claim lawyers would continue to get all the money by forcing people to court to amend agreements. If judges are called upon to decide every case over again, lawyers can bill the litigants ad infinitum.

According to an editorial from *The Boston Globe,* if the laws are clear and fair, which would happen if the alimony reform bill goes through, lawyers would lose all the money they stand to earn from repeated court appearances. Lifetime alimony means a lifetime of an individual being hauled into court to see "judicial discretion" in practice. Returning to court over and over to amend financial agreements has to do with the "sword and shield theory." A husband cannot use a remarriage as a *sword* to reduce a former wife's alimony, but a remarriage can be used as a *shield* to protect the ex-husband from his former wife seeking an increase in support. Predictably, neither works all the time.

Karen H., a teacher from Weston, Massachusetts, was ordered to pay her husband's former wife alimony because he had lost his job. The court held Karen responsible to contribute her earnings until such time as her husband could resume paying his ex-wife out of his own salary. Though the laws are gender neutral, the reality is that 95 percent of those who pay alimony are men, who are ordered to pay approximately 20 to 40 percent of their gross earnings to their wives. Alimony is usually in effect until the recipient either dies or remarries. The current trend is to pay alimony for a stated period of time—sometimes linked to the length of the marriage. However, this kind of decision is subject to review and can be overturned by the appellate courts. Even more incomprehensible is that sometimes alimony continues when a woman lives with rather than marries a boyfriend. Often, the salaries of new wives are considered when determining how much alimony a man must pay to his ex-wife, because a court *can* consider total household income.

One particularly egregious example of the results of this law is the case of Mary L., who, when her husband lost his job, was obliged to put their infant into day care to take a job as a waitress in order to help support her husband's former wife. When she appealed to the court for relief, her demand was rejected by the court.

Divorce in Massachusetts means repeated visits to divorce court if and when financial circumstances change due to job loss, illness, or retirement. Years after a divorce is granted, people can be summoned or summon their former spouses to court for post-divorce modifications to alimony, child support, and maintenance.

Under the present legal system throughout the country where each state has its own laws and peculiarities, there are often cases where women are unfairly penalized when it comes to alimony and maintenance.

GRETA L. HAD NO CHILDREN, was married for only six years, and earned six thousand dollars a month. Her husband, Richard, earned only two thousand a month. Greta claimed that Richard did not lack job skills but, rather, was lazy and refused to look for a job that would require more time and energy. During the first three years of their marriage, Greta was aware that Richard was often depressed. He felt himself a failure in the face of her increasing professional success. She avoided traveling on business, as she was concerned that, left alone, he would become even more despondent. After a while, not only did she grow resentful that she was working twelve- and fourteen-hour days when he was making no apparent effort to find a better job, but he began to take out his frustrations and sense of failure on her. In the beginning he was verbally abusive, which slowly turned into physical abuse. Greta moved out of their apartment and stayed with her sister. She continued to pay rent on what had been their marital home, knowing that Richard had nowhere to go and no money to pay rent. Within two weeks, Richard filed for divorce and cited abandonment as grounds (some jurisdictions require abandonment for longer periods of time). Though it was true that Greta was the one who actually left the marital home, there were extenuating circumstances that caused her to leave. After she retained counsel and told the story to her lawyer, she refused to countersue her husband for cruel and inhuman treatment.

"I was afraid it would be on the record and would hurt Richard in his quest for another job," Greta explains.

Richard, however, had no such concerns when he pressed his suit for abandonment and further claimed that Greta had refused to have sexual relations with him for more than two years. Still, Greta refused to defend herself by explaining to the court that Richard's verbal and physical abuse caused her to leave the marital bed. In the end, the judge hearing the divorce awarded Richard two thousand dollars a month in maintenance until he found a job which paid the same as his ex-wife's. Two years later and Greta is still paying Richard maintenance and still he has not looked for a higher-paying job. Greta is bitter. Her advice to women who are the primary wage earners and who are contemplating divorce is "Get fired or quit your job if you're about to divorce a husband who earns far less [advice no ethical lawyer would give]. For some reason, successful women who earn more than their husbands are penalized in a divorce court."

As for refusing to brand Richard as a victimizer, Greta adds, "I'm out of a bad marriage. My only penalty was money. If I had accused him of all sorts of things which happened to be true, I still believe I would have ruined his life. I suppose being considerate cost me."

AS THE RATE of divorce rises, those who are on the receiving end of divorce papers often describe the process and the laws that govern divorce as a shift of power which favors the self-interest of one spouse over the other. To many litigants, the issue of control has everything to do with which partner decides the marriage is over. The one who decides usually has to pay for his or her freedom. The one who decides, however, is often the first one to retain counsel. It is rare that couples decide to end their marriages at the same moment on mutually acceptable terms.

Regardless of the intensity of fault and violence, the financial settlement is not always equal. In fact, though the goal in any divorce is equitable distribution, equitable does not mean equal. Equitable means fair. These are the horror stories. Compared to what can and often does happen, divorce can be a happy and bright alternative. That doesn't say that there aren't gross inequities in the law, not as draconian perhaps as rape or murder, but nonetheless difficult.

The ideal of equality in the law is described in a quote by Anatole France: "The law, in its majestic equality, forbids rich and poor alike to sleep under bridges, to beg in the streets, and to steal their bread."

There are other serious ramifications of divorce, especially for children, who frequently experience inordinate mental anguish. Some of the most difficult cases a judge hears are those involving minor children. As supreme court judge Tommy Zampino says, "If the couple decides to break up and there aren't any children, it's high school all over again. Once children are part of the equation, my job as a judge becomes far more complicated and difficult."

PART THREE

CHILDREN

17

CUSTODY AND CHILD SUPPORT

You know what life can be like: See a guy and think
he's cute one minute, the next minute our brains have us
married with kids, the following minute we see him
having an extramarital affair. By the time someone
says, "I've got this cute guy for you," we shout, "You're
late again with the child support!"

—ANONYMOUS

WHEN OUT FOR REVENGE, some men and women will hide their anger under the guise of fighting for their children.

Attorney Ken Burrows believes that people will use their children as an excuse for "hanging on" or fighting their spouse to the end.

"How can you fault a mother who claims she is fighting for the sake of her children?" Burrows asks rhetorically. "Or, how can you fault a father who is trying to get custody of his kids because he says his wife is unfit? I know the truth in 99 percent of the cases I handle—that they are fighting to punish their future ex-spouse. Citing the kids makes their blood-bath look noble. It's also a way for people to get through the anger, and most people need that anger to get them through the divorce. When you convince yourself that you're angry on behalf of the kids or not having enough money to take care of your kids, you legitimize that anger. Basically, people fight over two things—money and children."

There are so many children, usually adolescents or preadolescents, who align themselves with one side or the other during their parents' divorce. One case comes to mind of a sixteen-year-old boy who refused to see his father. In that instance, the judge tried everything to determine if the refusal was because of abuse or because the mother poisoned the boy's mind against his father. After many meetings and intervention by a therapist, it was determined that there had been no abuse and no attempt by the mother to alienate the boy from his father. Try as he could, the judge could not fix the relationship. The boy considered his mother to be the victim. He lived with her and saw her tears and anguish as she went through the various legal steps toward divorce. The boy felt protective toward his mother and angry at his father.

The judge who heard the case maintains that he could identify with both parents, which made it difficult to render a decision. "You can't find a child in contempt," the judge says, "or put the child in jail for refusing to see a parent. But what I have done in certain cases is to penalize the parent if he or she turned the child against one or the other, or abused the child. And I've done that when it comes to maintenance and equitable distribution. In those cases, it is egregious fault as far as I'm concerned. But in this case, especially since the boy was sixteen, there was nothing I could do to convince the kid to see his father. I even had the parents in my chambers and they were willing to cooperate. Nothing worked."

There is now a name for a situation where a parent consciously and deliberately alienates the child from the other parent. It is called Parental Alienation syndrome, and it is more than a miscarriage of justice, it is a heartbreaking consequence of the bitterness and rage that couples experience when going through a divorce. It is also one of the most damaging fallouts, when judges faced with a custody decision are often unable to determine whether accusations against one parent by another are true or false.

There are many other custody cases, some far less serious, that judges hear on a daily basis.

Judge Herbert Glickman, former supreme court justice from New Jersey, remembers one case which was benign compared to some of the more serious ones he has heard. "The parents were getting a divorce," Judge Glickman explains, "and the wife was pregnant. There didn't seem to be any problem when it came to financial dealings or fault. Both sets of the couple's parents, all Italians, were in the courtroom and there was suddenly a tremendous ruckus. For the first time, there were allusions to a custody fight for a child yet to be born. I finally allowed the grandparents to approach the bench. It seemed the woman was carrying a male infant and the paternal grandparents wanted to name the baby Anthony after his father and grandfather. The maternal grandparents and the pregnant wife didn't want another Tony running around the house. Everyone was hysterical, so at one point, I said if everybody didn't calm down, I would order them to name the kid after me—Herbert. One lawyer knew I was joking but the other lawyer didn't. There was no way to settle this case. In the end, I called the lawyers into my chambers and told them that I had made a decision after reading all the papers. The boy will be called Robert Anthony after his paternal grandfather and his maternal grandfather. When I walked back into the courtroom, I gave the family a stern lecture. I told everyone that this child was not to be called Tony, just because that was his middle name. He is to be called Robert or any diminutive of that name. Ten years later, the mother came to see me with the boy and told me that everything worked out."

Cases involving children are obviously the most difficult. As New Jersey Supreme Court Justice Tommy Zampino says, "When you have litigants without children, it's only a relationship that's ending and that's like a Post-it. How people choose to end their marriage or relationship is up to them. There's obviously a good way and a bad way. The heartbreak happens only when there're kids."

A married woman from Cleveland, Ohio, was having an affair with the cantor from her synagogue. Ultimately, she left her husband and married the cantor. She had two daughters from her former marriage who lived with her but who visited their father on weekends. Three years into the marriage, the older girl was about to be bat mitvahed at the synagogue where both her parents were still members.

The Ohio judge who heard the post-decree case happened to be the same judge who had presided over the divorce when the woman divorced her husband to marry the cantor.

"During the bat mitzvah, the girl called everyone in her family to come up to the bema and light a candle, which is tradition," the judge says. "Fifteen people came up, including her parents, her sister, the cantor, grandparents, uncles, aunts, and even her stepsiblings. After each person lit the candle, the girl recited a brief poem about them and kissed them. That is, everyone with the exception of her father. To make matters even more painful, the girl talked about the most 'important' man in her life, whom she said was the cantor. Her father was embarrassed and humiliated."

One month later, the girl's mother appeared before the judge with an application to make the father pay for the bat mitzvah. The judge was livid.

"You want your ex-husband to pay for his own embarrassment?" he chided the woman before turning toward the cantor, who was with her. "And you, you were in a position to control the situation and to prevent this man from being humiliated and you did nothing."

The judge refused to award the woman money.

AT ONE TIME, the unwritten law called the "Tender Years Doctrine" was that children, particularly young children, were presumed to go with the mother in a divorce unless the mother was declared to be unfit. "Unfit" usually meant drinking, drugs, or physical abuse. In America, the test usually is whatever is "in the best interests of the child." However, the ghost of every judge's mother walks the corridors of courtrooms throughout the country, and men still do not as a rule obtain custody of children unless they can show something inappropriate that the wife does. It must be emphasized that this is not what the law says. In fact, the law says absolutely the opposite—that men have as much right as women to be the custodial parent—but many lawyers who specialize in this field have observed that this is one of those issues where law and reality don't always line up.

There is also the question of whether misconduct could be used to show that someone is unfit to parent. Let's take adultery. Divorce lawyers have a rude way of putting it: "Unless the adultery took place in Macy's window, it would not affect custody." If one looks at the kind of misconduct that does affect custody, you'll find horrendous cases that fall under the heading of egregious fault, such as the New Jersey husband who hired a hit man for $50,000 to kill his wife. Other kinds of misconduct can range across the spectrum from serious violence to incest.

One case is particularly shocking. The parents were separated, and both wanted custody of the children. Before the custody issue was settled, the children—all girls—lived with the mother. The father had visitation every other weekend and was allowed to come to dinner once a week at his estranged wife's apartment. Unbeknownst to the mother, the father had been regularly raping his two teenage daughters during their weekend visits. The youngest daughter was spared the abuse. The mother knew something was wrong and finally was able to get one of her daughters to tell her what was going on. The girl told her mother that her father had threatened to kill them all if she said anything. Eventually, the father learned that one of his victims had told and he attempted to kill the mother. She survived the attack but was too frightened to press charges against her husband. During that period of silence, the father was still seeing his children on weekends and still coming to his estranged wife's house for dinner once a week. According to the mother, she was living a "nightmare" but was still, for a time, too traumatized and terrified to address or report the abuse.

"When we had dinner together," the mother says, "I couldn't understand how my daughters would laugh and joke with their father as if nothing was wrong."

According to Margery Greenberg, a divorce attorney and court-appointed lawyer for minor children who has had years of experience with abused children, they will suffer abuse, even sexual abuse, and not denounce their abuser because of fear. "Fear is an enormous motivating factor when children keep silent. Another factor is that children believe that the abuse is their fault, or they believe that a parent or close relative would never do anything to hurt them. Therefore, [in their minds] the abuse they suffer is normal behavior and if they talk about it, the blame will reverberate back on them. These particular kids feared that their father would carry out his threat and kill them and their mother."

Eventually, the mother came forward and the father was ultimately convicted of child rape and sentenced to several years in prison.

ACCORDING TO MANY advocates for children, the only thing the child wants is for the parents to get back together so the family can live together under one roof. When there are not horrendous issues such as abuse, ideally the parents could sit the child or children down and explain that they are separating but they still love them and the children will have two homes with liberal visitations to each parent. Obviously, the ideal does not always happen. Instead, children witness one parent or the other being taken out by the police in handcuffs or worse, which only exacerbates the reality that divorce results in trauma and violence for everyone concerned.

There is an irony here. It is a fact of life that lower-income families have less access to professionals who are in a position to make the transition easier for the child, and who are also there to protect the children. When they are fortunate, however, to qualify for intervention on the part of child advocates or therapists, they are far more open to listen and much more respectful of professionals than the upper- and middle-class families.

The other irony is that while the poor and middle-class parents are more receptive to help, there are fewer resources to assist them through the process. Whether the child or children are privileged or poor, schools are not always responsive. The public schools are dealing with so many children with so many other problems that to pay attention to those students whose parents are in the middle of divorce is simply not high on their list of priorities. In private schools, teachers and school psychologists are often too tactful when it comes to discussing with the parents that the signs of a disturbed child could be their fault or responsibility. When and if children do open up, teachers often defend the parent, who actually pays the tuition or who donates money to the school.

Even with the wide range of personal circumstances due to gender and financial standing, there are two instances where the playing field levels out for everyone. One is that all parents, when confronted by professionals in regard to custody decisions, are on their best behavior. They all understand that the professional has the power to decide who the better parent is and what is right for the child. It is often a Solomonic decision.

The other example is that the distress level in all parents going through a divorce and custody case is tremendous. People are not behaving as they would in normal situations. Divorce usually brings out the worst in everyone.

"Husband or wife," Margery Greenberg says, "depending upon who was left, is bleeding from humiliation. When it's the woman, and the husband has a girlfriend, you have to say that this is one thing she cannot control. In a year, it will hurt less and in two years even less. They have to keep their eye on the ball. My job is to keep parents focused on the kids. Both parties are sad and angry, whether they are the leaver or the leavee. My question to parents is always the same: Are you going to allow your sadness and anger to come before your children or have an impact on your parenting?"

There is no ideal equality in the law.

There is no ideal gender equality.

Glorifying motherhood to the detriment of men who often are caring and loving fathers does not result in an accurate judgment of who would be a better custodial parent. Rewarding fathers because their financial situation is better penalizes mothers who have depended on support to continue to raise their children in a loving way.

In divorce cases where there are minor children, both men and women judges are more apt to give custody to mothers or, in less than half the cases, joint custody to both parents. In situations where women are the custodial parent, they are often penalized financially if they are working mothers. According to Margery Greenberg, there is a "cap" on child support, which is detrimental to working women. Any additional monies paid by the father to support his child or children in excess of that cap are given "out of the goodness of [the father's] heart."

In all states throughout the country, there is a table from which to calculate child support. The problem is that the table only provides for six children. What if someone has more than six? There is no way to compute the amount of child support for a custodial parent who happens to have more than a half-dozen offspring.

The other problem for divorced working women is that a man who makes $200,000 a year, for example, is obliged to pay 25 percent of his income to his wife for two children if she is the custodial parent. Twenty-five percent of $200,000 amounts to $50,000 a year.

Take the most common scenario—the husband walked out and has taken up with a younger woman. If his wife is working, and makes $200,000 a year as well, the court takes that into account but still does not calculate the 25 percent that the husband must pay in child support based on their combined incomes of $400,000—rather on 25 percent of $300,000 a year. In other words, because the mother earns a respectable salary, the father is relieved of paying a percentage of his total salary for his children. Instead of taking 25 percent of the parents' combined income of $400,000, the total income is reduced by $100,000. In the end, the custodial parent, in this case the mother, would only receive 25 percent of $300,000.

Margery Greenberg explains the implications of that formula. "What this means," Greenberg says, "is the wife will get less money. Not only will she be paying for the nanny so she can work, but if she has the marital home, she is also paying the mortgage or rent, as well as the majority of expenses for the children. So, instead of getting 25 percent of $400,000, which would be $100,000, she gets 25 percent of $300,000, or $75,000, which is $25,000 less than if the support were calculated based on the parents' combined incomes. A working mother who has custody of the kids suffers more financially than her husband. Most of the time, when women are in that situation, the husband will not give a penny more, especially if he is already cohabiting with or married to another woman."

According to Greenberg, many judges believe that a man's salary is his and he gets to use it the way he wants. "Most judges feel that a man shouldn't be penalized and forced into a financial position where he can't make a new life for himself," Greenberg adds. "If the situation was reversed and the husband got custody, the wife would be in the same enviable position. The point is that most of the time, it is the woman—the mother—who ends up with the kids and who suffers the financial penalty. And, of course, if both parents are working, because of that 'cap' on child support, there is that additional financial penalty to the custodial parent."

There are other glitches when it comes to child support, of which many are unaware. For instance, if a child is already in private school when the parents divorce and the school fees are paid by the father, he will be responsible for maintaining the child or children in private school for the duration of their education. If the mother has the misfortune to be abandoned before her child or children are attending private school, even if private school had been the plan, the father has no obligation to pay school fees. The obvious solution, if possible, is for the mother in this scenario to do everything possible to postpone the divorce until the child or children are already enrolled in private school.

According to Margery Greenberg, once again, when it comes to custody, women are often more victimized than men. "In the parameters of divorce," Greenberg says, "if a man does one thing right, he is a good father. If a woman does one thing wrong, she is a bad mother."

In an average household, even if both parents work, it is usually the mother who researches after-school activities and arranges for the children to be brought there and picked up if she doesn't do it herself. The working mother will also do the grocery shopping, hire the help, and see to it that the children have new shoes and clothing and school supplies. Then there's a divorce. Suddenly, the father, who will be paying child support, complains that his son or daughter is getting piano lessons on his "weekend visiting day," or that the child is playing soccer during the week when it is "his time." After years of never being involved with the children's routine or activities, all of a sudden the father wants final decision or at least joint decision on after-school activities, including time and place. In response, the mother will look at her attorney in disbelief. In all cases of divorce, when there are minor children, the logic of control is suspended regardless of what the situation was before the parents separated. The court will do everything to make sure that the parents have equal say in the life of their offspring. Often, this is where the advocate for the child comes into the picture, when the judge calls upon him or her to make a decision that the court simply cannot or will not make.

Most of these examples concern the privileged. In middle-income or poor families, there is no household help or therapists, or after-school activities. In fact, when there are crises with separation, divorce, or concern over the welfare of children, there is little in the way of help either from the courts or from professionals who are available for the more fortunate.

The system of justice when it comes to divorce is an exception to the basic rights of anyone involved in a legal procedure. In a criminal case, the accused has a constitutional right to an attorney. No such right exists in divorce cases. (Although there are a few exceptions in certain states which have programs to provide lawyers.) Basically, a criminal is far better off when it comes to the provision of legal representation than someone who is simply getting divorced.

Though Margery Greenberg is a specialist on those situations implicating child support for the custodial parent, her real expertise has to do with investigating the home situation to determine what is in the best interests of the children.

The position she holds and the responsibilities she has have changed over the last few years. Where once Greenberg was a "law guardian," she is now called an "attorney for the children." That change was the result of New York's chief judge, Jacqueline Silbermann, who believed that what had historically been the dual role of a "law guardian," as both a representative and an investigator, should focus almost exclusively on representation of children under the age of seventeen who are in the middle of a custody suit, or who are victims of abuse.

"What I do now is represent the child as to his or her wishes," Greenberg explains. "Up until fairly recently, October 2007, when the chief judge promulgated the rule shifting my job from guardian to attorney for the child, the role of law guardian was almost an arm of the court. We were expected to take on an independent investigation of the family and actually advise the court as to what was going on. We were the eyes and ears of the court into the family dynamic. That has shifted significantly over the years, culminating in this actual rule. Now, officially we are not functioning in an investigative capacity but rather we are advocates for children."

Margery Greenberg and others in her capacity believe that children often can't understand the dynamic imposed upon them as the subject of their parents' custody war. She and others who do the same work talk to the family, as well as to teachers, therapists, household help, and the children themselves to understand what would be the best resolution. Most often, they actually tell the court what the children want, or if the children are too young or under the influence of one parent or another, they, through their interviews with everyone involved with the family, make known their own judgment to the court.

"Ironically, there is still a duality of the role we play, even though the primary emphasis has shifted to advocacy," Greenberg continues. "If a child is under the age of six or seven they are not going to be having an on-camera interview and their wishes will not be particularly considered. That said, I've represented children as young as three where the judge would conduct an interview with the child and put stock in what that child says."

The qualifications for an attorney to be appointed as an advocate for children are neither stringent nor complicated. Attorneys can become certified without any training other than on-the-job experience. If three judges are prepared to sign a letter stating that, in their opinion, an attorney would be good at the task, his or her name is put on a list. A panel produces that list and, typically, if two lawyers and a judge believe an advocate is required, the lawyers for each side must agree upon the choice. Once the advocate is called in to the case, as Greenberg describes the process, she "begins her investigation."

Some of the things she looks for are an A student who is suddenly getting Ds, or a child who is late on those days when either the father or the mother has visitation. One of the most important people to talk to, according to Greenberg, is the nanny, as well as other household help. Greenberg cautions, however, that "usually one parent is responsible for hiring the help and paying them, as well as having them report to them, which can mean that their loyalties are not always even."

"One case stands out," Greenberg says. "The mother claimed that the father worked crazy hours and never came home. The father said that he is home but whenever he is, the mother is out. When I asked the children, they said it was their mother who fed them and put them to bed. The problem is, in their minds, it is always the mother, even if a nanny or babysitter is actually doing it. If I learn from the help that they are there from two in the afternoon until nine thirty at night, it is apparent that neither the mother nor the father is home."

Often, the situation is even more complicated when there is a father who does not work but ostensibly stays at home to care for the children.

"In one situation," Greenberg recounts, "the mother said that while her husband is unemployed, she still has to hire a full-time nanny because he does nothing for the children. The husband denied the charge." She shrugs. "But then, people lie all the time."

In fact, both husband and wife have been known to tell outright lies, lies by omission, or simply omit details.

Not only has the law *not* kept up with the changing nature of love, marriage, unusual family combinations, and same-sex couples, but it has not written specific custody laws concerning science and technology as it affects the disposition of frozen sperm, ova, and/or embryos.

One well-known and extremely rich divorced Midwestern real estate speculator put his sperm in a sperm bank. When he fell ill with a fatal disease, his written and express desire was that after his death his mistress use the sperm to give birth to his child. When the man died, the mistress made a motion to the court to release her lover's sperm. The family of the deceased countersued that the sperm did not belong to her since she was not the widow and therefore had no legal right to his unborn children. The litigants went to trial and the mistress won the case. When her lawyer met with the woman after she had successfully gained possession of the frozen sperm, he asked her how she intended to support the child. It was the moment of truth. Unfortunately, the man did not include in his will any financial provisions for his unborn child or his mistress. In the end, she decided that without support, she could not afford to have his child. Surprisingly, neither the mistress nor the deceased considered the future, when she would have to support herself and the child. Nor did her lover take into consideration that he had a legitimate family, including children from several marriages, and that his sperm, once it became a living, breathing child, had the right to support and to inherit under the law.

There have been many other cases where divorced couples have fought over sperm and ova either to gain custody or to have them destroyed so as not to have financial responsibility for future children. One variation of that kind of custody case involved the female half of a couple who couldn't conceive and who paid a woman to provide the eggs. Those issues, however, are usually settled before the deal is made. Two state appeals courts in Washington and California recently ruled that egg or sperm donors do not have the right to parenting the infant unless a written agreement was made beforehand.

Susan Crockin, an attorney and author who specializes in the field of reproductive technology, explains, "Both courts were attempting to add clarity to what can be ambiguous contexts. To do so, the courts asked, 'When the children were conceived, whom did the parties intend to be parents?'"

Another case involving a sperm donor is a curious example of either naïveté or an inability to understand how laws and social guidelines have changed in the last forty years.

Five years ago, two gay women who lived in Florida, Katherine Alicea and her partner of eight years, Ana Sobrino, decided to have a baby. After repeated attempts to get pregnant from sperm they purchased in a sperm bank, they finally turned to a gay friend to provide his sperm. Miraculously, Katherine got pregnant in August 2006 and nine months later gave birth to a healthy baby boy. The negotiations Alicea and Sobrino had made with the friend and his partner before the sperm was donated were casual at best, irresponsible at worst. At the time the baby was born, Katherine put the father's name on the birth certificate, as she wanted the baby to know his identity, though not necessarily to forge a relationship. Unfortunately, as things turned out from a legal viewpoint, that was a mistake. From the beginning, the baby's father made it clear that he and his partner, who also lived in Florida, intended to be a large part of the infant's life though the baby lived with the two women.

The trouble happened when the women wanted to move from Florida to California.

In November 2008, the baby's biological father sued Katherine Alicea for joint custody. "Responsibility for the child should be awarded to the mother and father equally," the father demanded in the suit, "as I am the natural father."

On June 3, 2009, after considering arguments from both sides, Miami-Dade Circuit Court Judge Leon Firtel found that the father was nothing more than "a sperm donor," and had "no rights" as there had been "no contract between the parties before the birth of the baby."

Hugo Acebo, the lawyer for Katherine Alicea, maintained that the biological father had surrendered his role when he let the mothers become primary caregivers.

"Ray has changed his mind about his parental role," Acebo said. "Katherine and Ana feel like their family unit is being attacked."

Probably the oddest case concerning custody of sperm concerns a divorced couple who had three champion bullmastiff dogs valued at $20,000 each—Cyrus, Regg, and Romeo. Karen Scully, who moved to Florida after her divorce, and her ex-husband, Anthony Scully, who stayed in Michigan after the couple split up, went before Michigan Family Court Judge Cheryl Matthews to determine which of them was legally entitled to frozen semen belonging to the dogs. When the judge heard the case, her first reaction was that she was an unwitting participant on *Candid Camera*. In the end, she ruled that the case was not a matter of divorce and the couple would have to settle it in civil court.

Where once there were the usual inequities in cases of custody as discussed, now, with scientific and medical advances in the twenty-first century, some custody cases involve not only overcrowding in the courts, unusual family components, and vitriol associated with divorce in general, but children before they are born as well.

The most heartbreaking and traumatic incidents related to custody are once again because of the hatred and revenge of one spouse toward another. These are the cases where one parent will fabricate accusations of child abuse to wrest custody away from the accused parent. One judge from Chicago admits that it is often impossible to determine which parent is lying. The ultimate victim in these cases, whether the allegations are true or false, is of course the child or children.

18

CHILD ABUSE

Child abuse casts a shadow the length of a lifetime.
—HERBERT WARD

ONE OF THE WORST aspects of custody cases is the abuse of the child by one or both parents. Even more egregious is if the accusing parent is not believed by the court, which continues to put the child at risk. Equally shocking is if the accusing parent is lying and the court believes him or her to the detriment of the accused and of course to the child or children. These accusations and their consequences are incredibly complex and unfortunately are far too prevalent during bitter divorce proceedings and custody hearings.

In the beginning, a judge is incapable of knowing, discerning, or instinctively believing if a child has been abused by a parent. In one particular case, recounted by a Minnesota judge, there were four lawyers and mental health professionals involved in the initial trial, which lasted seventeen days. The entire case dragged on for two years. The child was three when the trial began and five when it finally ended.

The lawyer who represented the mother remains anonymous. According to him, the mother accused the father of sexual abuse of the child. Not only did she want custody, but she did not want the father to see the child. In addition to hiring mental health professionals, the lawyer for the mother hired an art therapist to coax the child into drawing pictures of what the father allegedly did to him.

After the first seventeen days of trial, the court, lawyers, and mental health professionals were no closer to determining the truth. "The child was too young to talk," the mother's lawyer explains. "The art therapists and other mental health professionals were accused of asking leading questions which resulted in the child claiming that 'white stuff came out of daddy.' As a result, the prosecutor's office interviewed the child and told the little boy that if there was anything he ever wanted to say, he could always come back and they would reopen the case. In the meantime, the mother got custody and the father had liberal unsupervised visits with the child."

By then, the child was four. Several weeks after that first interview with the prosecution, the child asked to see the prosecutor again. The mother brought the little boy back to the prosecution but still the child said nothing. The mother was advised to tape all her conversations with her son. The mother complied but unfortunately there was nothing on the tapes that incriminated the father. Oddly, the mother reported that while the child was in the bathtub, he supposedly told his mother that he had "white stuff" on his face during a visit with the father. When the mother reported this to the prosecution, they surmised that the father had ejaculated on the child's face. At that point, the judge ruled that the youngster should undergo regular therapy sessions.

"Frankly, I didn't believe the mother," the judge says, "because I found it odd that the only time the child actually described any incident of abuse was the only time the mother didn't record it. But I told the therapist if ever the child said anything concrete about the abuse, to call me immediately and I would go myself to the therapist's office to talk to the child."

Ultimately, the child did describe the sexual abuse to the therapist and the judge went to her office to hear the recorded tape and to interview the child.

"But because I had become a witness on the case," the judge explained, "I was obliged to recuse myself as the judge. After the evidence was presented to the prosecution, all visitation with the child by the father was terminated until the child was of a certain age. In the end, the father admitted the abuse, and under a plea bargain he did not face criminal charges but agreed not to see his son."

According to the judge, it was a difficult call from the beginning as the mother hated the father and didn't want him involved in the child's life. Her emotional reaction coupled with the difficulty in getting the child to admit the abuse either to the prosecution or to a therapist made it impossible to determine if this was a case of pure revenge and spite, or if the father was actually abusing the child.

"The level of the mother's bitterness and spite," the judge admitted, "colored everyone's belief until the final moment when the child talked and the father finally confessed."

FATHERS ARE ACCUSED far more often than mothers of sexually abusing their children. In the majority of cases, it is the mother who launches the complaint. This charge carries with it the presumption of guilt, not under the law, but by the sitting judge hearing the case. In these cases, it is a question of the "lesser of two evils." Most judges feel that it is better to keep fathers accused of abuse away from the child or children in the event that they are, in fact, guilty. It is far more dangerous to assume innocence and expose the child or children to horrific sexual or violent abuse.

In almost every instance of an accusation of abuse, the father is separated from his children or forced to have supervised visits until a final judgment is rendered, proving the man's guilt or innocence.

Statistically, according to Child Welfare Services in New York City, out of one hundred charges of fathers who sexually abuse their child or children, only 5 percent are actually proven true. The sad fact is that though a man is legally vindicated, the cloud of suspicion never disappears. As for the child, he or she has been put through an unnecessary and painful ordeal, exposed to facts of life that he or she is too young to know, and frequently becomes frightened to see the father, or is brainwashed by the mother to consider the father the enemy.

One father's story is a good example of an accusation of abuse that ended with the involvement of the courts and a for-profit child welfare organization called Comprehensive Family Services in New York City, run by Rick Spitzer, a social worker.

"My ex-wife pressed unfounded charges of child abuse against me," S.T. explains. "I was the noncustodial parent. The justice system listened to her allegations and granted my wife an automatic order of protection before they could even judge that I was innocent. By the time the trial began, I had lost everything, including liberal visitation with my children, because I was forced to have supervised visits only."

In the world of supervised parental visitation, the people who run the organizations who work with the courts to provide supervisors are largely unregulated. Comprehensive Family Services provides supervisors who are paid directly by the company. The social workers employed by Comprehensive Family Services are paid an hourly fee by either the defendant or the plaintiff. They are paid over $250 an hour for their expert testimony and, according to several judges and lawyers, they are often willing to "give the defendant the benefit of the doubt" in making determinations regarding sexual abuse. In the words of Judge Pierre A. Michaud, assistant judge in chief of the Quebec Superior Court in Canada: "In matters of child custody and access rights, the experts would have us believe that science changes as needed to serve the purpose of the prosecution or the defense. Too often, the only objective of the expertise seems to be to knowingly support the point of view of the client."

Lawyers for Children, though similar to Comprehensive Family Services, is a nonprofit organization. When children are in crisis, Lawyers for Children provides protection, support, and free legal and social work advocacy to abused and neglected children, including children in foster care and children in high-conflict custody cases. Founded in 1984, Lawyers for Children is an organization that carries a lot of weight and influence in the courts. According to their mission statement, "Every day, LFC staff can be found in the courtroom and in the community, advocating on behalf of children in New York City whose parents or guardians have voluntarily placed them into foster care, and children who are the subject of abuse, neglect, termination of parental rights, custody, visitation, and adoption proceedings."

The nuance or distinction is important.

Comprehensive Family Services sets the fee based on a sliding scale according to the income of the parent involved. Unfortunately, for those mothers who are destitute, there is no sum, however small, that they can afford to pay to be able to visit their children.

According to the version of the story from the father who was accused of child abuse, Rick Spitzer of Comprehensive Family Services promised him many things that he failed to deliver. We obviously have no way of knowing if what the father claims or his version of events is accurate or not. When we attempted to contact Rick Spitzer, he called back once but never called again, as he promised, to discuss our findings.

"He [Spitzer] bragged that he would deliver reconciliation toward the resumption of unsupervised visits," S.T. says. "The truth is that he doesn't have the power to change the regime of visitations that was ordered by the court. In fact, the court doesn't care what Mr. Spitzer says because the more supervised visits there are, the smaller the risk the court takes with a potential abuser. So I end up, me, the noncustodial father, accused of child abuse, paying the bill for the supervisors while my relationship with my children goes down the drain."

One lawyer who was ordered by the court to deal with Lawyers for Children explains the operation in the following way. "There are cases where the poor qualify to get pro bono work, which are cases that are categorized '18b' cases, and which pay about seventy-five dollars an hour to a court-appointed lawyer. I've been in that situation several times. The court then orders Lawyers for Children to hire a supervisor to be paid for supervised visits. I had to get a 722 order, which is the legal term for getting the court to pay for a supervisor when one is ordered by the court to oversee parental visits. I can give you an example of my involvement with that organization and that type of case. My client had a son who was in foster care. The father was out of the picture. The child was allowed to spend weekends with his mother as an intermediate step toward returning the child full-time to his mother. The problem was that the boy was on antidepressants and the mother didn't believe the child should be taking the pills. Basically, Lawyers for Children escorted the child from foster care to the mother and made sure he took his medication during the weekend."

Clearly, there are organizations that have the monopoly on certain legal services involved with custody, visitations, abuse, and divorce. If the litigants have money, there is emotional hardship but a minimum amount of financial grief. If the litigants have no money, they are faced with emotional issues as well as a potential disastrous financial situation under the current system.

There are cases where mothers have accused fathers of sexually abusing their children but were unable to prove the charges sufficiently in court to the satisfaction of a judge. There are several examples where those mothers actually lost custody of their children when the judge deemed them unfit. They were accused of "manipulating" the children, or "turning the children against the father." One case involved a woman who had children with her married lover.

According to the woman, she and the boyfriend separated during her pregnancy. When the baby was born, he only visited the infant when the woman was present, as a way to get back into her life. When the little girl was three years old, she came back from a visit with her father and told her mother that he had touched her inappropriately. But when the woman went to court to charge him with sexual abuse, the father countersued her for custody of the toddler. For inexplicable reasons, the judge who heard the case decided that the mother was unfit, as she could not prove to the satisfaction of the court that her child had been abused and, therefore, was detrimental to the health and welfare of her little girl by "manipulating and turning her against the father." For more than a year, the woman lost custody of her daughter and was only allowed to see the child during supervised visits.

During the legal battle that ensued, including a media blitz that covered the story from beginning to end, and an appearance before the appellate court, Lawyers for Children, a nonprofit organization, and Comprehensive Family Services, a for-profit organization, spent more than $500,000 trying to prevent the woman from getting custody or even visiting her child without supervision. What stunned many people who followed the story was that during that time another child was abused, starved, and ultimately murdered in her home in Brooklyn. No one intervened to save the child, nor did either organization come forward with funds to prove abuse that ended in murder.

In December 2005, the case of Nixzmary Brown was first opened with allegations of abuse by the Administration of Children's Services (ACS). On January 11, 2006, Nixzmary was found dead in her Bedford-Stuyvesant apartment. It was determined that the cause of death was a blow to the head by a blunt instrument.

After the child was dead, the police investigation finally began. Evidence of bruises premortem indicated that Nixzmary had suffered horrific torture for a long time. The city was horrified and outraged that ACS neglected the case and didn't take swift appropriate action to save the child's life. Subsequently, Mayor Bloomberg revamped and reformed the whole ACS system by firing those who weren't doing their jobs and added six hundred additional social service workers to alleviate the overwhelming workload of an insufficient staff.

Both scenarios are the nightmares of every mother.

The outrage of supervised visits is that only the rich can afford to pay a supervisor from Lawyers for Children, as the cost could reach thousands of dollars for several visits a week. Many women who end up with men who sexually abuse their children have no money or contacts, nor can they navigate the legal system. Some of these women have also made bad choices in their lives. One woman, an admitted sex addict who has sought treatment for her addiction, accused the father of her children of sexual abuse. When she appeared in court, she was inappropriately dressed, which antagonized the female judge. Because she could not prove the abuse charge, the judge took away her children and gave custody to their father. She hasn't seen them in four years.

Another woman who was pregnant was put in jail for making allegations that her husband sexually abused their toddler. She was a Russian immigrant, spoke little English, and had no understanding of the courts. According to a source, the judge charged her with contempt for speaking out of turn and she was sentenced to prison.

The tragedy is that most women who find themselves in that position don't have the money to pay supervisors to be present when they visit their children. As a result, these are the women who haven't seen their children in months and often years.

A law was recently passed in one state that says if a mother makes allegations of sexual abuse in good faith it cannot reflect on her right to custody. Previously if a mother made allegations of sexual abuse and could not prove it, the father did not have to get over the obstacle of "good faith" before the judge penalized the mother.

At the same time, false allegations are made against fathers who, contrary to the law, are assumed to be guilty until proven innocent. Accusations of violence and sexual abuse are notoriously difficult to prove. As a result, there have been gross inequities in the law when such cases have come before the courts.

Other than some of the drastic measures both fathers and mothers take which cause enormous trauma to the children, there are several basic realities which fall under the heading of egregious inequity.

In the United States, there are approximately 1,000,000 divorces granted every year. About 600,000 divorcing couples have minor children, but only about 90,000 have custody disputes. If only 2 percent of disputed custody or visitation cases have allegations of sexual abuse, then only about three out of every one thousand divorces involving children include allegations of sexual abuse.

Why then are there so many false allegations? The answer is simple.

Since most falsely accused persons cannot fight the accusation, all the reinforcements are delivered as soon as accusations are made. Possession of children is secured. The accuser, typically the mother, has full use of the system to get free legal advice, welfare assistance, and emotional support from affirming professionals. Many of the professionals connected to child abuse cases refer clients to each other. In many areas there may well be a formal or informal approved list of professionals established by the county or child protection system or the prosecutors. Most often this approved list includes those professionals who agree with the system and are most likely not sympathetic to the situation of a parent accused of sexual abuse. After all, the Gulag existed for years in Soviet Russia and how many of those prison inmates were ever guilty of anything? Most were totally innocent.

In child abuse, it is the same. There is such a gulag built up in our child abuse system that dictates that "bodies need to be found" and if there is a shortage of real criminals, a false allegation will suffice.

This is an empire-building opportunity for many people in the system who have about as much incentive for finding nonabuse as a dentist has for not finding cavities.

Much has been written about the timing of allegations of sexual abuse. Allegations that arise in the context of divorce are immediately suspect in many people's minds. The belief that women frequently make false allegations to take revenge on their soon-to-be ex-husbands is somewhat entrenched in popular culture.

There are four possible situations that might lead to allegations of sexual abuse during a divorce.

1. Abuse leads to divorce.
2. Abuse is revealed during a divorce.

3. Abuse is precipitated by divorce.

4. False allegations are made during a divorce situation.

Those in a position of authority are not always astute when it comes to determining if the charges are true. If they are aware that the charges are not true, they are often remiss in offering good advice to the nonabusive parent.

Imagine that the custodial parent had knowledge of abuse long before he or she decided to begin divorce proceedings. Once the offending parent was out of the house, the other decided to inform protective services of the abuse, asking that the child be prevented from seeing the accused parent. Imagine that social services informed the parent that unless divorce was officially filed, the child or children could be placed in a foster home until trial determined the guilt or innocence of the parent accused of abuse.

Consider another possibility. The protective parent has known that the child has been sexually abused for months or years and has been too ashamed to report it. Either he or she did not want the child stigmatized as a molested child or the accuser did not want it revealed that he or she had married a child molester. He or she decides to divorce and hopes that it is possible to obtain restricted visitations and custody without having to mention that there had been an ongoing abuse problem.

The tragedy is that the child has been abused. Now the parents are divorcing and the child knows he or she will be forced to spend time alone with the abuser. Once the offender is not around, the child might feel safer in telling the protective parent. When divorce occurs, there is no longer any reason to keep the secret.

Then there are the offenders who sexually abuse their own children as a way of getting back at their spouse for breaking up the home. That is as venal as a spouse concocting a story of abuse for revenge.

According to several lawyers who specialize in parental abuse cases, mothers feel that "no matter what they do, what action they take, they are criticized and penalized by the legal system." One lawyer from Wisconsin says, "If they [mothers] react to their child or children's disclosure of sexual abuse with anger and take measures to ensure their safety, they are called mean, vindictive, and hysterical. Mothers who suppress their rage and calmly go through the tasks needed to protect their children say they are accused of falsely accusing their child's offender. In those cases, the defense claims that if it [the abuse] had really happened, she [the mother] would be enraged and unable to supress her anger." In either case, the child suffers at the hands of either parent as well as the legal system.

While both mothers and fathers have brought false abuse allegations in divorce proceedings, mothers are more likely to be believed. In one noteworthy case, a young child told her father of improper touching by a babysitter. The father reported the allegations to the authorities. When social workers investigated, the mother accused the father of molesting the daughter. The result was a long legal battle during which the father had to fight for even limited access to his daughter. During the father's four-year legal battle, the mother was diagnosed as being mentally ill and was temporarily institutionalized. The social workers investigating the case wrote a report expressing concern that the father might gain custody of the child because of the mother's hospitalization. Eventually, the father managed to convince a court that the charges were false, and he did gain custody of his daughter. The emotional and financial consequences, however, of the false allegations against the father were enormous for the child and the parents.

Margery Greenberg, the attorney for children mentioned in the previous chapter, believes that often mothers are so emotionally dependent and/or subjugated by their child's offender, they are unable to act to protect the child.

"There are so many scenarios," Greenberg says. "An additional subset of mothers believes their child but is disbelieved by those who evaluated the allegations. If such mothers continue to believe and support their child, they are labeled hysterical and paranoid. I know of a case in which a mother was declared insane by the psychologist of the accused [her husband] and court-ordered into psychiatric treatment for believing her toddler had been molested when CPS [Child Protection Services] declared that it had not happened. The sexual abuse of her child was confirmed a couple of years later, but not before the child nearly succeeded in committing suicide. Such mistakes are costly in terms of human suffering."

According to Margery Greenberg, it is as heinous a crime for mothers to make false accusations against fathers as a ploy to win custody as it is for authorities to disbelieve mothers who claim fathers abused the child.

"To avoid situations like these," Greenberg continues, "I try to find out what intervention the family had prior to the time of divorce and custody disputes. At first, I see the child, usually at my office, and explain who I am and why I'm involved. I also explain to the child who the players are and how they are in place to help the parents through the divorce. The child is told that anything he or she says is totally confidential unless they give me permission to repeat the conversation to the judge."

The marriage contract by tradition and history has been twofold. Historically, men provide women with financial compensation for the care of children and the home in exchange for loss of virginity, an end to reproductive fitness during the marriage, and loss of youth, all, or at least some of which are marketable qualities. Traditionally, in the human species, it is assumed that the mother rears the children. If there were a divorce court for sea horses or shorebirds, the male of the species would receive maintenance or alimony, as it is the male of the species who cares for the offspring. In today's world, despite the fact that some men have better mothering skills than women, it is still considered anathema to take children away from the mother. There are numerous horror stories. The most horrific is when either parent ignores a court order concerning custody and simply abducts the child or children.

Abduction is every parent's nightmare.

19

CHILD ABDUCTION

The abduction of a child is a tragedy. No one can fully understand or appreciate what a parent goes through at such a time, unless they have faced a similar tragedy. Every parent responds differently. Each parent copes with this nightmare in the best way he or she knows how.
　　—JOHN WALSH, HOST OF THE TELEVISION SHOW *AMERICA'S MOST WANTED*. WALSH IS KNOWN FOR HIS ANTI-CRIME ACTIVISM, WHICH BEGAN AFTER THE ABDUCTION AND MURDER OF HIS SON, ADAM, IN 1981.

THE ONE SITUATION that occurs across economic and gender lines is child abduction. Though it does not happen frequently, when it does, it is the most complicated and difficult circumstance to rectify. It is bad enough for one parent to abduct a child from one state to another, but it becomes a nightmare scenario when a parent who holds foreign nationality abducts a child to another country. The result, without exception, leaves the parent who searches for the child in complete psychological disarray. Children who are abducted are in a perpetual state of confusion, anger, and fear, and are ultimately scarred for life. Margery Greenberg, advocate for children, maintains that abduction is the worst thing anyone can do to a child.

Unfortunately, the role of the law guardian or advocate is very limited. "The most we can do," Greenberg admits, "is to get the custody order for the remaining parent asserted in court. The solution, or at least the one thing we can do—and the courts should be aware of before it happens—is the pathology of a parent in order, hopefully, to predict that such a thing can take place. If the parent is foreign, for instance, and holds foreign nationality, or if that parent has tried to convince the child that the other parent is evil and is single-minded in his or her mind that the child, regardless of the repercussions, should be taken far away from that parent, the alarm bells should go off. In the mind of the parent who steals the child, he or she will feel justified. There are so many examples of either the mother or the father leaving the country with the child, often resulting in years before the child is returned home."

Women who have abducted their children often file sexual abuse charges against their husbands, which they either can't prove sufficiently to the courts, or they "know" the father is unfit and simply take the law into their own hands. In a perfect world, the advocate for the children has a responsibility to listen and assure the woman that there are people and organizations in place to help. Of course, that is not always the case, especially for lower-income families, and in certain legal venues when judges will punish women who they believe have made false accusations.

According to statistics taken from the branch of the Hague Convention that deals with international abductions of children, men who abduct their children are most often foreign, and their actions are steeped in their cultural and religious beliefs—for example, the man has the sole right to the children in the event of divorce.

The Hague Convention is an international treaty currently in effect between the United States and fifty other countries, enacted in 1988. One of the rules of the convention is that a civil proceeding must be brought in the country to which the child was abducted within one year of the abduction. When that happens, the judge must order the child returned to the custodial parent and the country of residence. Curiously, all Hague Convention cases are not about "the best interests of the child," but rather about returning the child to the jurisdiction that should hear the custody matter. They adhere to the letter of their own statutes or law, which often means the child is not returned to their home country, but rather to the jurisdiction that is determined to be responsible by law to hear the custody dispute. The problem, of course, is that abduction is kidnapping and not anything to do with a custodial disagreement.

The success of finding abducted children and returning them to the custodial parent varies, depending upon whether a country is a member of the Hague Convention. In reality, finding a child or children and bringing them "home" is far more difficult if the offspring is kidnapped by a parent to a country that is not part of the Hague Convention, or if the country has joined the convention after the child was abducted.

In those cases when a child is abducted to a country that is not a member of the Hague Convention, the parent left behind has very little recourse. To countermand this eventuality, the United States has made parental abduction a crime. If a state felony warrant has been issued and the abductor has fled the state, it is possible to get a warrant for "unlawful flight to avoid prosecution" under the federal Fugitive Felon Act.

In 1993, the United States also enacted the International Parental Kidnapping Crime Act, which made abduction of a child to a foreign country a federal felony. The problem is that there are many barriers to this act—some states do not want to spend the money to extradite the guilty parent and many countries do not have this offense on their list of extraditable crimes.

Of the fifty nations that adhere to the treaty, the only South American countries that are members are Chile, Columbia, Ecuador, and Venezuela. With the exception of Israel, no countries in the Middle East are members.

Statistics gathered from the Hague show that Latin American countries accounted for one-third of all aductions, and Middle Eastern countries accounted for one-fourth. Overall, one-third of all abductions were to countries that were parties to the convention.

Abduction of a child by a parent is usually a well-planned operation. Family members and friends are aware and in place in the country of destination. The abductor also puts money in savings, liquidates assets, quits a job, and waits for tax refund checks. More long-range plans include gathering the child's school documents, passport, birth certificate, health records, and securing a place to live or locating a family member or friend who is prepared to receive the abductor and the child. The abductor is cunning. Many will keep the child during visits past the designated time of return to create a pattern that does not signal danger. As a result, when the child is not returned on time from a parental visit, the custodial parent will wait longer than he or she should to report the child missing. After all, he or she knows or assumes that often the child is brought home late without dire consequences.

Often a distraught mother or father will resort to self-help. Men's magazines carry advertisements for soldier-of-fortune types who will hire out for a commando-style re-kidnapping of the child complete with a midnight raid or snatch on the way to school to a waiting private plane. Sometimes it works. More often it leaves a disappointed—and poorer— parent waiting fruitlessly for a child who is not coming home.

Every case is horrific.

The outrage is that parental abduction is widely regarded as a private family matter. According to statistics taken from the American Prosecutors Research Institute in 2009, more than two-thirds of left-behind parents encountered individuals and organizations who told them that their situation did not require legal intervention. One-third of parents reported that law enforcement officials would not take information about their cases as they considered the abduction to be a "domestic situation."

Mothers and fathers are equally likely to be the abductor. The patterns of destination, however, differ between mothers and fathers, and account for a lack of success in finding the child. Mothers usually take the child to a South American country, while fathers take the child to the Middle East.

In 1991 the book *Not Without My Daughter*, by Betty Mahmoody, was published. It was the first time child abduction was described in a nonfiction book. Ultimately, the book was made into a film starring Sally Field, bringing the subject to international attention. This particular abduction was different than the usual, as the mother was held hostage along with her daughter.

In 1981, Betty Lover met an Iranian doctor, Sayyed Bozorg Mahmoody, in a Michigan hospital. They married and had a daughter they named Mahtob. Though their union occurred shortly after the U.S./ Iranian hostage crisis, and relations with Iran were significantly strained, Betty and Sayyed were happy until the summer of 1984. It was then that the family traveled to Iran, ostensibly to visit Sayyed's family. For eighteen months, Betty and her daughter lived as virtual prisoners in the Mahmoody home, as Sayyed had decided to embrace the fundamentalist teachings of the Shiite religion. Betty found herself alone, despised for being an American, and treated as a slave by her husband's family. The only hope was her escape from Tehran with the help of an underground network that helped Iranian nationals escape the brutal regime of the Ayatollah Khomeini. Never before had the organization involved itself in helping an American escape with her child.

As the book title indicates, Betty risked her life and that of her child when she ultimately found a way to flee the country with Mahtob. Mother and daughter now live safely in the United States.

An example of a more typical case involves an American mother, Janet Greer, who lost her three-year-old daughter, Dowsha, more than twelve years ago. The father of her child, an Egyptian, though not her husband, kidnapped the little girl from their home in Hawaii and took her to Egypt.

Greer had already separated from her Egyptian boyfriend by the time the baby was born. Going to court, she pleaded with the judge to give her sole custody as she feared he would flee the country with Dowsha. The judge refused and Greer's fears became a reality when her daughter never returned from a weekend visit with her father. Greer fought for years to see her daughter, and at one point, she even won a ruling in the Egyptian courts for a visit with the girl. But because of an error her lawyer made in filling out the legal paperwork, the judge overturned Greer's right to visit the child. After constant appeals and an intervention by Secretary of State Hillary Clinton to the Egyptian foreign minister, Greer was finally able to see her child in Egypt. As for the Egyptian authorities, they forbade Greer from taking the little girl back to the United States. The case is still pending in the Egyptian courts.

Another case involves Jennifer Siefke who, along with her mother, Margaret Cholewinski, was arrested in Livingston, Montana, for custodial interference and unlawful flight to avoid persecution. Siefke, with the help of her mother, abducted her son, now six years old, and his half sister, because she claimed she "had to protect their lives from their father."

This case is typical inasmuch as many women accused of abducting their own children claim they escaped domestic violence or their children had been subjected to sexual abuse by the father. At the core of many of these claims is that the courts did not believe the women during custody battles, which prompted them to take the law into their own hands. Another explanation is that mothers never reported the abuse during a custody trial because they feared either that they had no proof or that they and their children would suffer violent repercussions at the hands of the father/husband. The problem occurs when the courts, law enforcement officers, and child protective agencies, along with family lawyers, accuse the women of lying to get revenge because their husbands left them. It is always a difficult judgment to make. In the case of Siefke, when she was finally apprehended, her son and stepdaughter were taken into custody by child welfare services until her allegations could be proven and her husband's defense could be heard.

Even after questioning the children, it was difficult to ascertain who was telling the truth. A lawyer from Colorado who often represents mothers in custody cases says, "The legal system is trying to stop this phenomenon of mothers going underground. In the fifteen years I've been working in the field, repercussions keep escalating, from a slap on the wrist to starting to try to put these women in prison. In every custody case, someone is unhappy, but something has to be drastically wrong for a mother to take her children and go into hiding."

As of this writing, the Siefke children are still in foster care.

One of the most spectacular cases is that of a mother who was willing to give up her freedom rather than divulge the whereabouts of her daughter. Elizabeth Morgan, a plastic surgeon from Washington, D.C., claimed her former husband sexually abused their two-and-a-half-year-old daughter. When Morgan separated from her husband, Eric Foretich, a Washington, D.C., dentist, she defied a judge's order to allow her daughter, then five years old, to see her father. Instead, Morgan sent her little girl into hiding. The court held Morgan in contempt and sentenced her to prison until she produced the child for the father's court-ordered visitation. Morgan refused and remained in prison for twenty-five months, the longest time on record that anyone had been incarcerated for civil contempt in a custody case. Though Foretich vehemently denied the charges, Morgan and her attorneys remained adamant in their accusations. It was only after a public outcry over her long imprisonment that President George H. W. Bush hastily signed a congressional bill limiting to twelve months the time a person can be jailed for civil contempt in the District of Columbia. In effect, the bill had been written especially for Elizabeth Morgan.

Elizabeth Morgan is now free, though her daughter still remains in hiding. According to Morgan, she still remains a psychological prisoner of the most celebrated custody case in the nation. During numerous television appearances and other media interviews, Morgan claimed that the battle was not over. She criticized the legal system for having sent a "raped child back to her rapist." In response, Eric Foretich questioned his former wife's sanity and demanded that federal authorities locate his daughter. Once released by Congress, however, Dr. Morgan left the country and has lived with her daughter in New Zealand for the last six years. Last year, congressional allies of Dr. Morgan announced that she wanted to return to the country. A bill was introduced to remove the jurisdiction of the court in the case and to block the standing court order in the case. The bill directly endorses the allegations of Dr. Morgan that Dr. Foretich represents a danger to his daughter and that his current parental rights prevent her safe return to the country.

In Tasmania, there was a different reaction from a judge in family court when it came to accusations of child abuse. In that particular case, the mother accused the father of her children of "violent, abusive, and controlling" behavior. Though the couple was not married, the father sought to share parental responsibility, including visitation every other weekend, one overnight during the week, half of all school holidays, and "special occasions."

The judge ruled that the mother and her two young children could go into hiding and change their identities to escape the violence. It was a rare decision in which the court not only upheld the woman's complaints, but also granted an order of protection that the man could not go within one hundred feet of the woman and her children.

MANY OF THE TRADITIONS and laws governing marriage, divorce, and custody are steeped in historical standards. Despite the changes in customs and morals, gender equality, and science and technology, the law has not kept up with the enormous strides, assumptions, and expectations that people have today when it comes to coupling and family. In fact, the law is not based on logic or social advances, but rather on precedent. Precedent, by definition, stymies progress. The law is one of the only systems or professions that looks backward in time rather than forward to keep up with social growth.

In the past sixty years, since the 1950s, social and cultural changes account for the rise in divorce; an increased life span, the presence and power of women in the workforce, and society's acceptance of unconventional relationships and single-parent households. Notwithstanding that the patterns of commitment are changing, basic human instincts such as love, sexual attraction, and jealousy, which have been either repressed or expressed throughout the centuries depending on social customs, have done little to change human beings since the days of the caveman.

PART FOUR

HISTORY OF LOVE, MARRIAGE, AND DIVORCE

sense of magic and superstition. The circle of unity signified that wher-
ever the bride or groom ventured, they would always return to the home
and hearth. The first wedding band dates back to 7 B.C.E. Egypt, where
the never-ending band made of twisted plant materials such as hemp
signified eternal love between two people. The Egyptians placed the
rings on the fourth finger of the left hand, based on a belief that the vein
from that finger led directly to the heart, thereby linking the couple's
destiny.

The Romans were a little less romantic. Their iron wedding bands
were not a symbol of love, but signified a binding legal agreement of
ownership by husbands who regarded rings as tokens of purchase. The
Romans, like the Egyptians, also believed that the vein in the left ring
finger, or the vena amoris, led directly to the heart, symbolizing that the
hearts of the bride and groom were joined forever.

Ancient Spartan soldiers were the first to hold stag parties. On the night
before the wedding, the groom would host a party for his male friends during which he would swear allegiance and loyalty to his comrades, who
would forever come before his bride.

Bridal showers were also given to solidify the bond between the bride
and her friends, who would be there to give her moral support, advice,
and to prepare her for the rigors of married life. Unlike her intended
spouse, however, she would bid a symbolic farewell to her friends with
the understanding that her husband and his family would always have
priority in her life.

When the father of the bride in ancient Egypt gave his daughter to
her husband, he would include a pair of sandals to symbolize that she
officially and legally belonged to her husband. Shoes were apparently
important in Anglo-Saxon times as well, when the groom would tap the
heel of the bride's shoe to show his authority over her. In later times,
people would throw shoes at the couple, which eventually gave way to the
tradition of tying shoes to the back of the car.

(For more on marriage, its symbols and origins, consider *A Natural
History of Love* by Diane Ackerman.)

During early Anglo-Saxon times, the color of the wedding dress reflected values. Blue meant constancy, and green symbolized youth, while
a blue ribbon worn on the shoulder of a dress meant purity, fidelity, and
love. The two colors never worn by a bride, especially during weddings

20

THEN AND NOW

*Marriage, n. A community consisting of a master, a
mistress, and two slaves, making in all two.*
                    —AMBROSE BIERCE, *THE DEVIL'S
                                DICTIONARY, 1911*

IN TODAY'S WORLD, many laws governing marriage, custody, separation, financial settlements, and divorce are steeped in history and replete with archaic moral judgments. In the twenty-first century, in certain ethnic, economic, and social circles, marriage has almost become a sociological myth, while divorce has frequently become a miscarriage of justice.

Some of the traditions of love, courtship, and marriage are symbolic. Most don't impinge on women's rights. Some have been amended or modified to keep up with modern times. Others are dire as they continue to influence many of the harmful social mores that are still in place today. Even those customs which could be considered frivolous still have undertones of ownership of the wife by the husband.

Dating back to Greek and Roman times, the expression "tie the knot" comes from the Romans. The bride wore a girdle that was tied in knots which the groom had the pleasure of untying.

The tradition of giving a diamond engagement ring began with medieval Italians, who believed that the diamond was created from the flames of love. The wedding ring became part of tradition as well, meant to instill a in medieval times, were yellow, which was associated with jealousy, and gold, which denoted avarice or greed. Young women from the lower classes wore only white dresses to their weddings, a public statement that the brides had nothing to bring to their marriages, which made their husbands exempt from their debts. It wasn't until 1499 that the white wedding dress, worn today by most brides, was made popular by Anne of Brittany, forever changing the notion that white was for the impoverished.

Less frivolous customs during the Greek and Roman era accorded women fewer privileges. Greek men allowed their wives to leave their homes for only limited occasions and then, always in the company of a female relative. Women had no legal standing and could not own property, nor were they permitted to learn how to read and write. Before marriage, women were owned by their fathers and only after marriage did that ownership transfer to their husbands. Their opinions, dreams, and goals went unheard, if at all spoken, and women were relegated to a subservient place in their husbands' lives.

In Xenophon's *Oeconomicus,* Socrates asks his friend Critobulus, "Is there anyone with whom you talk less than your wife?" The friend replies, "There are few or none, I confess."

In A.D. 585 the Council of Macon debated whether women truly had souls, and, by only one vote, concluded that they did.

Until fairly recently in Western cultures, marriage was also regarded as too important a family matter to be entrusted to inexperienced youths. Having a marriageable girl or boy was a financial asset. It had nothing to do with the feelings or sexual attraction of the potential partners and everything to do with making a contract that was beneficial to the families. About the only way the poor had considerably more freedom than the rich was because they had few assets to negotiate a marriage. As a result, people had more freedom to marry whom they pleased. Only during difficult economic times were the rich able to marry whom they chose and without seeking parental approval.

The process of an arranged marriage began with the involvement of only the parents or guardians of the prospective bride and groom. In ancient Rome, Augustus legislation assumed girls would marry at the minimum age of twelve years, while their husbands would be much older. There was only one law that protected minors from marriage. Legislation during the reign of the Emperor Augustus did not allow girls under the age of ten to be promised or betrothed to their husbands. He also limited the time of betrothal or engagement to two years. Augustan marriage laws of A.D. 9 also penalized women who did not have a baby before the age of twenty. Other laws during that era allowed young girls to marry much older men. The rationale was that so many girls and women died in childbirth that husband and wife, despite the disparity in age, would die within several years of each other.

After financial negotiations between the parents of the prospective bride and groom were completed, a banns was posted in the town square. If anyone had a prior claim or contract with either party, they were invited to come forward before the marriage took place. If there were no objections, there was a handfasting, or an engagement, at which time the couple would become betrothed and the marriage contract was signed and witnessed. To become officially betrothed, the future bride and groom would join hands, his right to her right, his left to her left, resembling a symbol of infinity. If the woman was a virgin, her hands would be bare. If she was a widow, she would wear gloves. Handfasting was always done at the church door in front of witnesses, which made the couple "married" for one year and one day. Following that period of time, they could renew their vows for another year and a day or end the contract.

In a variation of this tradition, in 1953, anthropologist Margaret Mead suggested that marriage vows should be renewed every decade as the home situation changed and the husband and wife had different goals and needs. Mead also advocated two different types of marriage—the "individual marriage" for couples not intending to have children, and "parental marriage" for those desiring offspring.

In ancient Rome, fertility was the most important reason for marriage. An infertile woman would be shipped back to her father and guaranteed to go through life not only childless but also without a husband. There was no such concept as marrying without having children. The purpose of marriage was less about the couple and more about the family they would create.

Fertility was always considered the responsibility of the woman. Ancient Romans baked a cake made of wheat or barley and broke it over the bride's head to ensure that she would be fertile. In some circles in ancient Rome, tradition dictated that small cakes were piled one on top of the other as high as they could be balanced without tipping over, after which the bride and groom would kiss over the tower of cakes without knocking them down.

Currently, in some extremely poverty-riddled areas of the Middle East such as Gaza and the Occupied Territories, the Muslim religion dictates that women who marry and cannot conceive are sent back to their families. One case was that of Wafa Idris, the first woman suicide bomber in Jerusalem, who gave birth to a stillborn infant and was told that she would never be able to have children. Recruited and brainwashed to believe that her life was meaningless, she fell under the influence of Hamas, and strapped on an explosive belt. Barren, her life on earth was meaningless.

In the ultraorthodox Jewish religion as well, brides who are not able to have children after a certain period of time are also shipped back to their families. Unless they are able to break free of the strict edicts of their religion, they too are destined to a life alone.

In ancient Rome, the father possessed unlimited power within the family. He even had the power of life and death over his children. At birth he could choose to raise them or kill them, and when they got older and disobeyed or fell out of favor, he could have them executed. The celebrated legendary founder of the Roman Republic, Junius Brutus, had his sons executed for disobedience. Less draconian, the early Roman father owned all property, and his children, regardless of their age, were unable to own anything in their own name as long as the father lived. The father also had the power to make or break his children's marriages. Women and girls had even fewer rights than their male siblings.

As a child, a girl was under the complete control of her father. When she married, she could be handed over to her husband or married *in manu*, which again was at the discretion of her father. If she was not married *in manu*, she remained, though married, under her father's protection. Her father owned everything with the exception of property that came with her husband, which belonged to his father until death, when it was passed on to the groom and his siblings. The only good news for the independence of Roman women was if their husbands died, they could, as widows, come into their own and become *sui iuris,* or able to own property in their own names—but only if their own fathers were dead. That changed, however, by the end of the rule of Augustus, who made it easier for women to become *sui iuris*. Augustus proclaimed that women could own property if their own fathers died, and did not have to wait until the death of their husband. Since fathers were presumably older than husbands, women became financially liberated while still married.

As it concerned divorce, those women who did not marry *in manu* had the right to divorce. Frequently, the woman's father might not only instigate the divorce but also demand the dowry be returned. If her husband initiated divorce proceedings, the dowry of his wife would be returned to her father unless he was dead. Only then would it be returned to her personally, with several exceptions. If the wife behaved unbecoming to a married woman, or if there were children from the marriage, the husband could keep a good portion of the dowry, as well as full custody of the children.

Despite those exceptions that rendered women unable to have their own money or custody of children in the event of divorce, during that era Roman men complained that women had become too independent and liberated. In those cases when women had independent means, men lamented the fact that their wives could not only own property, but they could sell it, or give it away without their permission. Male writers during that era also expressed their disapproval that women were less obedient to their husbands. In fact, a rich woman could divorce her husband and take all her assets with her, which posed a threat to the husband's ability to maintain his standard of living. Those husbands who depended on their wives' wealth would not dare ask for a divorce. Back then, there was no alimony or maintenance for men. This newfound financial liberation of women resulted in an increase in adultery and promiscuity. Roman men reminisced about the "good old days" when women spent time with their children, rather than focusing on their bodies and luxuries. The trend back then was to turn over infants to wet nurses, usually the lowliest slave in the household, who would nurse babies and further free women to pursue their own pleasures.

The laws governing marriage and divorce changed throughout Roman history. As ancient Rome expanded into new areas, social classes, and businesses, customs also varied to keep up with the beliefs of many different citizens of the Roman Empire.

Throughout the Roman Empire, divorce was not uncommon, and

ancient Roman law gave men the right to divorce their wives for such grounds as adultery, making copies of the household keys, consuming wine, and of course infertility. When Rome entered the "classical age," women were finally allowed to divorce their husbands with the same impunity and freedom as men could divorce wives. In the upper classes, marriage was often viewed as a political move to join two powerful families who could benefit from each other's political connections and opportunities. If and when a political opportunity became possible, husband or wife could divorce and remarry. Some Roman men and women during that era married and divorced several times as power shifted from one important family to another.

Curiously, the notion of fault and no-fault divorce existed in the classical age in Rome. Both men and women could divorce simply because they no longer had a desire to be married. That could be interpreted as incompatibility or constructive abandonment in today's divorce laws. The reasoning behind those new "no-fault" grounds was that marriage was defined as a will or desire by the couple to view each other as man and wife. When the desire disappeared, the marriage could end. During that era, it was only necessary for one spouse to decide that the marriage was no longer viable and a divorce would be granted—similar to uncontested divorce in the twenty-first century. In fact, divorce where only one spouse decided the marriage was over did not necessitate that the other spouse be notified. Divorce during the classical age in Rome was always a private affair. There were no laws that dictated that either church or state should be notified. The problem, of course, was that there were no public records, and with so many marriages and divorces, there was often a problem of bigamy.

IN THE MIDDLE AGES, troubadours traveled throughout Europe spreading the message that love and marriage were incompatible and even destructive, as seen in tales such as Tristan and Isolde, Abelard and Heloise, and Troilus and Criseyde. Emotion interfered with the original purposes of legally joining two people together—economic security, children, companionship, and propriety. The main reason to marry was to procreate. The man was meant to be the provider and the woman to bear his children. Toward the end of the Middle Ages, things changed slightly, and wives were allowed to divorce husbands convicted of certain crimes or if they were away at war for a long period of time. That change in divorce law did not, however, change the fact that wives were the legal property of their husbands. A man was allowed and even expected to beat his wife, as long as he did not inflict mortal injury.

FROM 1400 UNTIL 1800, from the end of the Black Death to the beginning of industrialization, marriage seldom lasted more than twenty years. The notion that marriage would join people until they were old was inconceivable. Almost all marriages ended because of the death of either husband or wife. Marriage contracts, therefore, were primarily provisions for widowhood. Since the beginning of time, whether by death or divorce, some form of marital dissolution has always been part of the human experience.

The French Revolution signaled the end of many customs that had regulated marriage. Romanticism, a philosophical movement, became the new wave throughout Europe. Against the evils of society, the tyranny of reason, and middle-class respectability, the Romantics were similar to anarchists inasmuch as they believed that society should not adhere to manmade laws. Instead, they believed that society should worship nature, the unspoiled and mysterious pastoral fields and forests, and ancient ruins from distant and exotic lands. The Romantics believed that emotions, sensations, and feelings should mimic nature, which naturally changed from season to season. To the romantic, love was not limited to married couples and should not have to be sanctioned and blessed by the church. Manmade conventions and morality were a contradiction to the natural feelings of human beings.

The French citizen revered poets, painters, musicians, composers, and writers. Almost all lived their artistic fantasies and made no secret of them. An artist had license to live and love as he or she wished without adhering to the morals that man inflicted upon his fellow man. Married men referred to their wives as the "angel in the house," and passion was made pure through matrimony, while lust for another woman or women was transformed into sentimentality.

Things changed throughout the rest of the Western world by the seventeenth century. Parental control was slowly waning; child betrothals, a favorite means of controlling marriage, had been abolished; and the minimum age required for marriage was raised. The lack of parental control did not mean that love was the preferred reason to marry. Women were thought to be victims of their emotions. To make the distinction, men often sneered at love to prove they, unlike women, were pragmatic and rational.

On September 20, 1792, divorce became legal in France. In 1816, when Catholicism again became the official religion of France, divorce was abolished. If a couple had the right connections and social standing, however, they could get special dispensation from the pope and get an annulment. Grounds included impotence, if the marriage had not been consummated, and spouses related by blood. One of the problems with annulment, however, was that it rendered the children of the union, if any, illegitimate. Further, if the grounds for an annulment were based on consanguinity, the children of that union were forbidden to marry and have their own children.

In France, despite many attempts by legislators to legalize divorce, it was only reestablished in 1884 under the Third Republic, which adhered to the Napoleonic Code. Based on Roman law, rather than church law, divorce once again became legal and was gender neutral. Women, as well as men, could divorce, and children of that union were legitimate and could marry with impunity.

The first divorce in America was recorded in 1639. From then until 1698, there were only 98 divorces in the United States. From 1850 until 1910 there were more than 210,000 divorces in the United States.

Following the Civil War and with the invention of the typewriter and the growth of the garment industry, women found jobs and contributed to the support of the family. This new status of women and the emergence of a women's movement resulted in much more independent and vocal women. Also in the nineteenth century in the United States, the chaperone system of supervised visits between the sexes was becoming less frequent due to the invention of the bicycle in 1855. Lovers could pedal away to a secluded spot for secret trysts. With the invention of the telephone, the lovers could make arrangements for those meetings without anyone knowing. Finally, in the early twentieth century, love in America became a prior condition for marriage rather than a hoped-for sequel to the wedding. Alice Preston noted in *The Ladies' Home Journal* in 1905, "No high-minded girl, and no girl of truly refined feeling . . . ever . . . admits the advisability of marriage without love."

The 1908 introduction of Henry Ford's Model T, the first mass-produced, affordable automobile, allowed more Americans the freedom and privacy associated with car ownership. Then, as now, the car often became a bedroom on wheels.

With inventions and industrial progress, customs changed. Predictably, it took a much longer time for attitudes to adjust and even longer for laws to adapt to those changes.

During the early history of the United States, a man virtually owned his wife and children as he did his material possessions. In Mississippi it wasn't until 1839 that a woman could sue her husband. In 1848 New York followed, and in 1854 Massachusetts passed laws that allowed women to own property separate from their husbands. From the earliest migrations to the New World, American pioneer women had achieved more independence than many European women when it came to marriage. Out of necessity and hardship, American women shared with their husbands the burden of forging and building a new life in the prairies. Progress was still slow when it came to women's rights in the area of owning their own assets and attaining a divorce and custody of their children. In the event of divorce, the husband gained control of all property and custody of the children.

During the latter part of the nineteenth century, women gained the right to vote in some states, to hold and sell real property, to maintain personal property, and to retain custody of children in case of marital breakup. After the Civil War and the rapid industrialization of the country, including the invention of the typewriter, women were able to work as secretaries and as factory workers. Though women had a more important economic role in the family, they were still exploited when it came to earning equal pay with men. Women's working conditions were also mostly horrific. The elevated status of women, however, and the continued demand for justice by the women's rights movements, helped create a climate for the emergence of a "new," much more independent woman. By the beginning of the twentieth century, many men were willing to accept the social equality of women, though they balked at granting them economic equality in terms of jobs and pay.

Following the end of World War II and the war effort, American society in the 1950s was increasingly centered on the family. Marriage and children quickly became part of the national political agenda in the Eisenhower and Kennedy administrations. The Cold War was in part a culture war with the family at the center of the struggle between American good and Soviet evil. The accepted image of the Communist woman was one who dressed in drab clothes and toiled in wretched factories while her children were cared for in anonymous day-care centers. The American woman was portrayed as feminine and well dressed, tending to the hearth and home as she and her family enjoyed the fruits of capitalism, democracy, and freedom.

In the 1950s, marriage rates were at an all-time high. Women who weren't married by thirty years old were viewed with suspicion. The feminine ideal of the 1950s was the perfect wife and mother who would help and encourage her husband to achieve in his chosen career. Her views or aspirations, if she had any, simply had no place in the equation. In 1955, Mrs. Dale Carnegie wrote in *Better Homes & Gardens*, ". . . when Mr. and Mrs. set their sights, it is on a happy home, a host of friends, and a bright future through the success in HIS job."

As important as home and family were during the 1950s, the rate of failed marriages was increasing. Despite the emphasis on domestic life that characterized the decade, the institution of marriage actually lost ground. One reason for the higher divorce rate was the successful economy, which made it possible for more women to consider leaving their husbands. The problem that women had—those who were courageous enough to seek divorce—was that they did not have access to as competent lawyers as did their husbands. It was far easier for a man to hire his corporate legal counsel to represent him, often at minimal cost. Even if a woman had a job and some independent means, the cost of hiring an attorney was prohibitive, and the ability to find one who knew divorce law was limited. The majority of women going through divorce were represented by legal aid lawyers. In fact, before the Legal Aid and Advice Act of 1949, few women could afford divorce. By 1955, according to the Legal Aid Society, approximately 78 percent of all legal aid cases were about divorce.

In 1950 there were 1.66 million marriages. In 1960, there were 1.52 million marriages. At the same time, the divorce rate rose slightly, from

385,000 in 1950 to 393,000 in 1960. In 1950, one in every 4.3 marriages failed. By the end of the decade, the most family-oriented ten years, that ratio had changed to one in every 3.8 marriages ending in divorce.

By the 1970s through the turn of the century, divorce has been part of the human experience. If half of all marriages end in divorce, then statistically if not culturally, divorce is the norm. By 1985, the divorce rate had steadily increased to over 55 percent. As the human life span increased, the duration of marriages decreased.

Today, those who are at mid life have the prospect of another forty or fifty years with decent health. The possibility of spending another forty or fifty years in an unhappy marriage presents a very different perspective from the time when the average life span was far shorter. Added to that reality, women play a deciding role in the increase of divorce. In addition to a longer life span, their income is higher and their financial independence has increased, which gives them the freedom of choice and opportunity, allowing them the luxury of reassessing their desire to marry and stay married.

Throughout the centuries, the expectation of living "happily ever after" has become somewhat of an unreality, as divorce has become an occurrence in more than 50 percent of all marriages. The problem, however, is that often divorce remains a stigma to some, and laws have remained static rather than keeping up with the changing nature of family and coupling.

21

Marital Rape and Crime
of Passion

Any woman who claims she has been raped by her
spouse has not been properly bedded.
     —A Maine Legislator, 2009

There are crimes of passion and crimes of logic. The
boundary between them is not clearly defined.
     —Albert Camus

BEFORE MARRIAGE, rituals to do with sexual initiation meant that a male had reached adolescence. Because medieval moralists believed that lust dominated the adolescent mind, they considered it their duty to protect both boys and girls from their own sexual urges. As advice on how to avoid tempting situations, girls were instructed not to speak to men or boys in the streets while boys were encouraged to satisfy their sexual needs with prostitutes.

Though marriage was the ultimate goal and chastity was revered, rape was very common in the Middle Ages. If the rapist could be found, he would only stand trial if the victim would offer testimony, which of course presented a myriad of other problems. Girls or women who had been raped or lower-class females who had been forced into prostitution by their masters were likely never to marry. In some cases, slaves would be sold into prostitution by the women of the house. The only women who married early and who could expect to have sex only with their husbands were those from the upper classes—and even then, there was no guarantee.

During the Middle Ages in London, there were stories of forced sexual initiation of young women. One tells of Elizabeth Mappulton, a maid, who had been forced to have sexual relations with the master of the house. Though she complained to her parents, who wanted to protect her, they were unable to do anything, as they needed her weekly wage to help support them. In the end, the parents of the girl petitioned the court that the man marry their daughter. When he refused, the court ruled that from then on, the girl would be referred to as a "maiden," or an unmarried woman without her chastity. Laws in the Middle Ages maintained that sexual relations did not change a woman's status to adulthood unless she married. If she remained single, she was a "maiden," and the community understood that she had been either violated or had succumbed to her sexual desires.

A document written by Andreas Capellanus in 1184 states: "If you should, by some chance, fall in love with a peasant woman, be careful to puff her up with lots of praise and then, when you find a convenient place, do not hesitate to take what you seek and embrace her by force." Peasants were not the only women being raped during the early Middle Ages. Noblewomen were often taken advantage of in the crowded passages of the castle. It was also common for a woman to be raped in her own bed while her husband was out attending to family business.

A game for knights in training was to seduce and abduct the woman of the castle. This was only a game to test the young knight's valor, but its setting was real life and sometimes ended in the forceful taking of the lady, followed by her rape.

Then as now, in castles or on college campuses, acquaintance rape was and is more common than frequently assumed. According to the National Rape Center at the University of Minnesota in 2006, 70 percent of all rapes reported were acquaintance rapes. There are other similarities as well between then and now. Again, throughout history and continuing today, blame for the attack is frequently placed on the victim, whether because of her attire, her availability, or simply because she had previously been intimate with her assailant. There is what is called the "kick, bite, scratch, and scream" rule. That merely means that the burden is upon the rape victim to fight off, or attempt to fight off, the attacker. The exception is if she is in immediate danger of bodily harm, such as a knife being put to her throat.

In the 1980s, the term "date rape" was introduced by Mary P. Koss, a psychologist who used the term in an article she wrote for *Ms.* magazine. Currently, there is not only an awareness of date rape, but also concrete measures have been taken on many college campuses to protect women. Antioch College, for instance, developed the "verbal consent" code that required a question/answer scenario seeking verbal consent during sexual activity.

Though the legal definition of rape varies from state to state, the prerequisite proof of resistance is still based on a seventeenth-century tradition from English courts that the victim's testimony cannot "be trusted," as she would lie to protect her honor. Even more complicated and cloudy is the issue of marital rape.

Then and now, the law assumed that husband and wife were melded into one legal entity and, therefore, a husband could not rape a wife. Somewhere in the idiocy of the law, there is also a rule that states one "can't rape a statue." Both assumptions are ridiculous. Husband and wife are separate people with different desires, feelings, moods, and personalities.

The first study conducted of marital rape was in 1978. Nine hundred married women were interviewed by sociologist Diana Russell, who revealed that 14 percent had been sexually assaulted by their husbands. Of those, 50 percent had been raped more than twenty times by their husbands over the course of a two-year period.

In 1978, the first marital rape case was tried in New Jersey. Daniel Morrison was found guilty of raping his estranged wife. Six months later, however, John Rideout became the first husband charged with the rape of his wife while living with her. Rideout was acquitted, but the case garnered national publicity and made people aware that rape can and does occur in marriage. Many states, including Minnesota, defined marital rape as forced sexual intercourse committed by a man against a woman. It wasn't until 1981 that Minnesota changed its statute to include rape of a wife by her husband. Ramsey County in Minnesota was the first to charge a case of marital rape against a husband, but later dismissed it. In general, these cases are hard to prove and to win, given that the question of consent is clouded by societal beliefs about marriage.

How can a husband be guilty of taking something that belongs to him? In reality, much of what has been learned and written about marital rape originated in the legal community. Throughout history, it has been acceptable for men to force their wives to have sex against their will.

On July 5, 1993, marital rape became a crime in all fifty states, at least under one section of the code of sexual offenses. Currently, in seventeen states, including the District of Columbia, there have been zero prosecutions against husbands who rape their wives. In thirty-three states, however, there are still some exemptions—when a wife is mentally or physically impaired, unconscious, or asleep, a husband is not exempt from prosecution. Notwithstanding those exceptions, there is still no state that lists marital rape as grounds for divorce.

From the ancient belief that women are the property of their husbands, to the accepted premise that husbands can't rape their wives, there are still historical and cultural beliefs that are seriously detrimental to men and women. Some are even written into law in the United States and in Europe.

THE CRIME OF PASSION is both cultural and legal in the minds and on the books in many South American countries, in France, Spain, and Italy, as well as in certain states in the United States. One of the most egregious examples of crime of passion used as a defense occurred in two separate murder trials in France in 2000 and in 2004. The first trial, in 2000, received less media attention than the one held in 2004, as those involved were high-profile international celebrities.

Before the first case is recounted in all its horrific details, it is important to understand the definition of a "crime of passion" as it is used to describe the defendant's state of mind when he or she commits murder. "Crime of passion," as defined in legal terms in France, is a "crime due to sudden anger or heartbreak in order to eliminate the element of premeditation."

This usually arises in murder or attempted murder cases, when a spouse or sweetheart finds his or her "beloved" having sexual intercourse with another and shoots or stabs one or both of the coupled pair. To make this claim, the defendant must have acted immediately upon the rise of passion, without the time for contemplation or allowing for "a cooling of the blood." This definition is sometimes called the "Law of Texas" since juries in that state are supposedly lenient to cuckolded lovers who take the law into their own hands. The benefit of eliminating premeditation is to lessen the charge of homicide to manslaughter so there is no possibility of the death penalty but rather the probability of a limited prison term. An emotionally charged jury may even acquit the impassioned defendant. Crime of passion is nothing more than murder as an alternative to divorce.

In 2000, in France, Jean Pierre S., a successful doctor, had been married to Pascale S. for twenty years. They had four children. When Pascale fell in love with another man, she told Jean Pierre she wanted a divorce. The couple agreed to the terms, including that Pascale would live in the marital home with their four children, ranging in age from six to fifteen. Jean Pierre would have liberal visitation, one day a week and every weekend. For months, the arrangement continued without any problems, as lawyers for both parties went through the necessary bureaucratic details to finalize the couple's divorce. The tragedy happened on a Saturday when Jean Pierre arrived at Pascale's house to take the children for the weekend.

When Pascale opened the door, Jean Pierre shot and killed her at point-blank range. He then proceeded to shoot and kill three of his four children. The only child who survived was a girl of eleven who hid in a closet until her father, disoriented and bloodied, left the house. When arrested, Jean Pierre claimed that his actions fell under the heading of a *crime passionnelle,* or "crime of passion." He had been driven "mad" by the fact that his wife was with another man and his family was broken. His lawyer, one of the most reputable in Paris, managed to get him released on bail until his trial. While free, the court awarded Jean Pierre custody of his surviving child. After the trial, Jean Pierre was sentenced to five years in prison for the murder of four people. His surviving child was placed in the custody of her maternal grandparents, with the understanding that she could have liberal visits with her father while he was in prison.

In 2006, Jean Pierre S. was released from prison and his surviving daughter was placed in his custody. As of this writing, he still practices medicine as if he never lost his license. Life goes on. . . .

The other case which garnered huge media coverage in 2004 involved Marie Trintignant, a French actress. Trintignant was the daughter of Jean-Louis Trintignant, who starred with Anouk Aimee in the classic French film *A Man and a Woman*. Marie Trintignant was beaten to death by her lover, rock star Bertrand Cantat.

The murder occurred in Lithuania, where Trintignant was filming a movie, one of fifty that she had made as one of France's most talented young stars. Cantat, the lead singer in a group called Noir Désir, or Black Desire, was arrested in Lithuania and held in prison there to stand trial. His lawyer, Virgis Papirtis, pled his client guilty of manslaughter, the result of "extreme emotion," which under Lithuanian law is tantamount to a crime of passion. Cantat was sentenced to eight years in prison but was released after serving four years. As of this writing, Cantat is out of jail and back performing with his rock group.

In the United States, a crime of passion is one committed under the influence of sudden or extreme passion. A man might attack another with an ax that was within reach if the victim had insulted the attacker's wife. The most frequent use of crime of passion as a defense is in situations where there is adultery. Catching his wife in bed with another man, a husband might, in the heat of passion, kill the man at the scene where the sexual act occurred. As a result, the law could and often does reduce the charge of homicide to manslaughter. The rationale is that the person whose passions are provoked is incapable of premeditation. The most pivotal proof would be the length of time between the provocation and killing, the manner of the killing, and the relationship of the people involved. Women, as well as men, commit crimes of passion.

In American civil courts, a crime of passion falls under the heading of temporary insanity. This defense was first used in 1859 by United States Congressman Daniel Sickles of New York. When he discovered his wife with her lover, he killed the lover at the moment of discovery.

Domestic violence prevention organizations are applauding the conviction of a businessman who murdered his former lover on her wedding day, a case that divided the Dominican community in New York and New Jersey and raised the controversial issue of whether the defense of "crime of passion" mitigates a murder.

On September 26, 1999, Gladys Ricart was shot and killed as she stood in her wedding dress, surrounded by her wedding party, preparing for her marriage at her parents' home in New Jersey.

The man who murdered Ricart was a former boyfriend who was also a respected businessman in the Dominican community in New Jersey. According to his defense lawyer, Ricart had only announced her marriage to him the night before. Ricart's family claimed she had informed Garcia two months earlier and had been the victim of Garcia's abuse and harassment until he ultimately murdered her on her wedding day. Had the jury accepted Garcia's defense of "passion provocation" manslaughter, he would have received a minimum jail sentence.

The reactions from people during the two years leading up to Garcia's trial for murder varied drastically. Many throughout the Dominican community blamed the victim for having provoked Garcia during the six years they were together before unceremoniously leaving him to marry someone else. They described Ricart as a traitor who may have invited her own death. In essence, they and Garcia's defense attorney blamed the victim for her own murder, for causing Garcia to be "led to a state of high emotional distress because he was unaware that she was marrying someone else."

The accusations and innuendos were broadcast and reported by many media outlets, which caused unspeakable grief to the victim's family. At least some in the New York and New Jersey communities who became familiar with the case, mostly men, gave credence to the portrait of Garcia as a spurned lover, with the right to avenge his wounded pride and blemished honor. In New York's Dominican neighborhoods, six candidates for New York City Council were questioned about the case and the validity of a crime of passion defense. Most hesitated to condemn the crime. The defense was further validated when the judge, William Meehan, ruled that they could use crime of passion as a defense.

In the end, Garcia was convicted of murder and sentenced to life imprisonment.

This sensational case demonstrated how the notion of crime of passion as a defense—a defense which should have been obliterated from the criminal code long ago—is still being used. The fact that a judge could allow such a defense speaks volumes for the need for change.

In 2007, Lisa Hartwick, the director of the Center for Violence Prevention and Recovery at Beth Israel Deaconess Medical Center, was in an elevator with two men. It wasn't difficult to overhear their conversation. One man was complaining that with legal fees and child support that were overwhelming during a divorce, it would be a lot easier and cheaper to kill his wife. The other man agreed that though the divorce was certainly costly, and he knew from personal experience since he was going through one himself, murder was a bad option, especially since there were "kids involved."

The conversation was certainly disturbing even if it was only talk. But conversations like that are not always just "venting," or talk. Men—and it is more commonly men—kill their spouses as a way to end an unhappy marriage without having to divorce, deplete their assets, ruin their reputations, or wreck an idyll that just wasn't that idyllic. The surprise is that the majority of men who kill their wives were not criminals before they committed murder, but rather, average, ordinary men whose neighbors and friends are shocked when they are arrested.

David Magraw, a real-estate investor, strangled his wife, Nancy, in the living room of their Walpole, Massachusetts, house. Magraw was distraught over the six-figure divorce settlement he had been ordered to pay Nancy. At first, his defense was crime of passion due to his distress at having to break up his home. In Magraw's case, though the act was spontaneous, the jury brought down a verdict of homicide because they believed that he had a long time to consider murder as an alternative as he went through the stages of a divorce.

Bill Mason, an elected prosecutor in Cleveland, states that in his district, in the last five years, three law-abiding men ended their marriages not by divorce but by murder. "This method of divorce," Mason says, "has become so common that I've coined a phrase for it—divorce substitute. Why men choose to kill their wives rather than just leave remains a mystery to me."

David Adams is a psychologist and cofounder of Emerge, a Cambridge, Massachusetts, program that offers counseling to violent men in and out of prison who abuse or murder their wives. According to Adams, men who kill fall into five categories: jealous; hopped up on drugs; career criminals; suicidal or depressed; or, most commonly, what Adams calls "materially motivated."

"Those men," Adams explains, "had something to lose, whether it was fine cars, nice homes, reputations, or lives they considered to be perfect to the outside world. Typically, these men keep secrets. Either they have affairs, or have financial problems, including tax problems, or have a dream that their wife is stopping them from realizing. These men will do anything to protect their secrets."

The Joseph Pikul case was perhaps the strangest of all. One of the coauthors of this book represented Mrs. Pikul. Joseph Pikul, at the time of his trial in 1987, was fifty-four years old. He was a former Manhattan securities analyst. The Pikuls had first met at an Alcoholics Anonymous meeting and subsequently married in July 1978. By 1986, there was trouble in the marriage and they were consulting a therapist. Ultimately, the couple separated. During divorce negotiations, Mrs. Pikul told her lawyer a bizarre story. At the time of one of his visitations with the children, Pikul blindfolded them so they would not be able to see where he was taking them. The first reaction from Mrs. Pikul's attorney, as well as several other attorneys in the office, was to get an order of protection for her and the children. She refused to allow them to do so. Her last words to her lawyers before she left the office that day were "I can handle it."

On the weekend of October 24, when Mrs. Pikul was murdered, the couple had made arrangements to meet at their summer home in Amagansett to prepare the house for sale, the proceeds of which were to be divided in the divorce. Mrs. Pikul, who was an assistant to the publisher of *Harper's* magazine at the time of her death, arrived at the house at about one in the morning, long after she was expected. When she arrived, Mr. Pikul confronted her with an unfamiliar brand of condoms he had found under their bed. According to him, he told his wife that she "broke up the family by bringing men back to sleep in my bed." He told her he would seek custody of their children. Earlier, under questioning by his lawyer, Mr. Pikul said that when they met at the Amagansett house, his wife had shown him pictures of himself in women's clothing and that she had threatened to use them as "blackmail" during the divorce proceedings. Further, during testimony at his trial, Pikul actually admitted killing his wife after an argument over her alleged infidelity but claimed that his wife had attacked him with a kitchen knife and he was "defending himself."

"I turned and saw I had been cut," Pikul testified under oath, "and that she was coming at me with a knife." He claimed he had "grabbed for her neck, while struggling with the other hand to get the knife.

"I started to squeeze her neck," he said. "I squeezed her neck as hard as I could, trying to get the knife away. Her body went limp. She dropped the knife. She was dead."

A pathologist had testified that death was caused by strangulation by hand and by cord as well as by at least ten "blunt force impacts" to the head.

After the murder, Mr. Pikul said he wrapped his wife's body in the car cover and took it to the beach at Little Albert's landing, where he "covered the body with sand." Later, leaving the children with friends, he dug the body up and drove throughout New England. It came out in earlier testimony that he had asked his first wife if he could bury the body in her backyard in Massachusetts.

Mr. Pikul then returned to New York and filed false missing-person reports with the Easthampton Police and the New York City Police Department, to "cover my trail," as he said on several occasions. He was doing so, he said, because he was "afraid" that if he was "arrested" he would not see "my children again."

The next thing that happened was that Mrs. Pikul's lawyer received a phone call from Robert Morgenthau, the New York district attorney, who told him that Mrs. Pikul was found in a culvert in Upstate New York. She had been strangled and wrapped in a car cover. Apparently, the police had arrested Joseph Pikul for murder and Morgenthau wanted to know his (the lawyer's) thoughts on what should be done about the two children.

Reconstructing the events, it seemed that after Pikul and his wife argued, he left the house and bought duct tape and rope. Returning to the house, he strangled her, wrapped her up, and put her in the trunk of his car. Pikul then proceeded to take his children and drive them to Upstate New York. According to the children, they claimed they heard something banging around in the trunk of the car, but when they asked their father about the noise, he concocted an excuse to quiet them. What they had heard was the body of their mother rolling around in the trunk of the car.

When Pikul and the children finally reached their destination in Upstate New York, he dropped the children off with a former girlfriend who lived there, and proceeded to dump his wife's body on the side of the road. After that, Pikul went to a car wash to clean out the trunk. When he tipped the attendant one hundred dollars, the man got suspicious and called the police.

After an investigation where the police connected all the dots, Pikul was arrested and charged with first-degree murder. According to the police, when they arrested Pikul, he was wearing a bra and women's panties under his clothes. The problem, as District Attorney Morgenthau indicated, was what to do with the children. Pikul was out of jail on bail and the lawyer for the deceased Mrs. Pikul was now representing her cousins, a childless couple who were more than happy to take the children. The lawyer began a custody case, which on its merits—the couple were both scientists at a prestigious hospital—turned out to be extremely difficult. The judge was hostile and antagonistic, even when the lawyer and expert witnesses claimed that Pikul was dangerous and could even kill his own children in a final Götterdämmerung.

When Pikul was in jail, before being bailed out, he told someone he had AIDS, which at the time was a death sentence. This alerted Mrs. Pikul's lawyer that he was capable of committing a murder/suicide. Curiously, the judge denied a motion that Pikul submit to an AIDS test. Things became even stranger when during the course of the custody trial, the lawyer for the deceased wife's cousins found a videotape that Pikul had made, and played it in court. On the tape, Pikul is reading *The Wall Street Journal,* dressed in a bride's dress, and masturbating to a recording of "Here Comes the Bride."

The judge who heard the case, though outwardly hostile, took the children away from Pikul and gave them to his late wife's cousins—but only after Pikul threatened his new wife with a knife. Mr. Pikul married Mary while awaiting his trial for murder. Mary was a "fan" of Pikul's, a woman who had followed his case meticulously and considered him a "celebrity."

Pikul was convicted of first-degree murder in Westchester County. While awaiting sentencing, he died of AIDS in prison. Because he died before his appellate processes were exhausted, technically he was never convicted of murdering his wife. The money he inherited from the woman he murdered (since under the law he had not been proven to be the murderer) went to Pikul's new wife. On August 22, 1987, Judge Thomas Byrne of Orange County Court signed an order erasing Mr. Pikul's conviction from court records.

WOMEN ARE NOT THE ONLY victims of spousal murder. The main difference is the defense of domestic violence when a woman murders her husband, as opposed to the use of crime of passion when a man murders his wife.

On a recent trip to Bedford Hills Women's Prison in New York, during interviews with sixteen women incarcerated for spousal murder, all gave as their defense that they had suffered from domestic violence for a period of at least ten years prior to murdering their husbands. Upon examination of the evidence and testimony from witnesses—boyfriends and family members—it was subsequently learned that ten of those women had poisoned, stabbed, or run over their husbands with a car with the help of a boyfriend. None of the ten committed the murders in self-defense or while in the process of being sexually or physically abused. In fact, in all but two cases, the women had six-figure insurance policies on the lives of their husbands. In the two cases where money was not the motive, there was always another man.

Even in murder as an alternative to divorce, there is inequality. According to Alan Dershowitz, statistics supplied by the criminal justice system show that wives who kill their husbands were acquitted in 12.9 percent of the cases studied, while husbands who killed their wives were acquitted in only 1.4 percent of the cases.

A close cousin to a crime of passion is an honor killing. Used as a cultural defense in specific cases of murder, it is most prevalent within certain immigrant communities and ultraorthodox religions throughout the United States and Europe. In Germany, for example, there have been sixty honor killings during which young women were murdered by their husbands because the women wanted a divorce. They have also occurred when young women are killed by male members of their family for allegedly tainting their honor because they refused to live within the rules of "arranged marriages." Those that occur in Germany almost always involve victims of Turkish, Kurdish, and Afghan origin with strong ties to extreme Muslim communities. Surprisingly, many German judges have reduced sentences because they have accepted the cultural defense that calls for honor killings when a family is disgraced within the confines of those conservative religious groups. There is an unfortunate similarity between the laws in Germany and those in the United States, a country with a long tradition of legal pluralism, where several honor killings have occurred over the past years. Muzzammil and Aasiya Hassan founded Bridges television network in November 2004 to counter anti-Islam stereotypes. They touted the network as the "first-ever full-time home for American Muslims." On February 6, 2009, Aasiya Hassan filed for divorce, citing numerous incidents of domestic violence. On February 18, 2009, Muzzammil Hassan beheaded his wife rather than go through the disgrace of being the defendant in a divorce case. He was charged with second-degree murder. Though many in the community defended Hassan's actions as an "honor killing," his defense attorney, James Harrington, maintained that he would not cite culture or religion as mitigating circumstances. Although he was convicted of a lesser crime, the question remains why Hassan was not convicted of first-degree murder in his wife's beheading. According to one criminal lawyer, the jury believed that Hassan beheaded his wife without premeditation.

Progress has been made concerning many social and political issues in the United States and throughout the world. These issues include votes for women, gender equality in the workforce, and to a large extent, an official absence of racism. That said, there are still far too many who continue to resist gender equality and integration under the guise of religion or historic precedent.

Laws concerning equal rights for same-sex couples have changed to benefit the gay and lesbian communities in some states as well as in certain foreign countries. It is curious how people can expend so much energy, virulent feelings, and opposition to gay marriage and yet not exhibit the same level of outrage when it comes to honor killings or marital rape. The reality is that several archaic laws governing marriage and divorce and certain sexual practices are still officially "on the books." Those laws that forbid an individual over twenty-one to choose how he or she will conduct his or her sexual life with another consenting adult thwart political and social progress for everyone. Other laws which permit men to get away with murder under the guise of extreme emotional distress are still prevalent in some states. Less dangerous but equally archaic are those laws which ultimately cause society to stigmatize divorced women far more than divorced men. Though it is impossible to change certain cultural beliefs in foreign countries where honor killings are accepted and encouraged, or the concept of marital rape is nonexistent, the outrage is that these barbaric practices are not definitively renounced and expunged from the canons of law in America, which only proves that the notion of ownership of wives by husbands is still embraced by some under the guise of religion or social customs. It is even more incomprehensible that those who rally against a woman's right to choose, gay marriage, and a woman's independence even if she is married, almost always use God and the Bible as their reason and reference. Focusing on marriage and divorce only, it is imperative for all these social judgments to change in order for the law to catch up with the reality of the twenty-first-century family.

PART FIVE

HAPPILY EVER AFTER

22

PREPARING FOR THE END
IN THE BEGINNING

Before you sit down with lawyers, talk to your honey
about what you want to include in the prenup. There's
a lot you can talk through when you're not getting
billed by the hour.

—SUZE ORMAN

A LONG-TERM SUCCESSFUL MARRIAGE is an exception to the rule.
A bitter and nasty divorce is the rule. Still, there are certain actions that
individuals can take to eliminate the financial fallout from a divorce. There
are other actions people can take to diminish the control that courts have
over litigants in a divorce. Finally, there are suggestions that can help people move on after a divorce to establish happier and healthier lives. Given
the statistics of failed marriages, and the stigma society puts on divorced
people, it is far more important to learn how to have a happy divorce rather
than a happy marriage.

When the French apply for a marriage license, the law says they must
choose at that moment whether they want to combine or separate their
assets. If couples opt to have what is called a *"separation de biens,"* or separate assets, all they bring into the marriage, whether it is earned or inherited during the marriage, is kept separate from the assets of their spouse.
If there is a divorce, there is no danger of protracted fights over which assets are commingled and which are individual. If, at the time people apply for a license, they choose to combine their earnings and assets, as
well as future earnings and inheritances, it is understood that if there

is a divorce, the marital pot is divided in equal shares between the husband and wife. There are several addendums or exceptions to the French law.

If there are children at the time of divorce, and the assets have been separate, a judge decides which parent, according to his or her net worth and income, will pay the bigger portion of child support. If the assets were combined, the judge will award a certain amount of child support to be shared by both parents regardless of which one has permanent custody or they have shared custody. Concerning inheritance, the law in France dictates that the order of "succession" or inheritance goes first to the children and then to the wife. A spouse may always disinherit a spouse but never biological children.

During the course of the marriage in France, whether couples have chosen to combine their assets and income or keep them separate, they have the right to change their minds during the course of their union. There is no time limit on when they rewrite their original agreement. All they have to do is go before a notary and rewrite or amend the agreement they signed before they married, and the financial rules of their union automatically change. Both must sign the new agreement.

What this law succeeds in doing is twofold. People don't have to go through the agony of asking for a prenuptial agreement, nor do they have to pay lawyers or mediators to forge that agreement. It is built into the marriage license as a law of the French Republic. If divorce happens, there is no drawn-out bitter battle over money. People also have the ability to revisit the financial arrangements that they made right before they married, and rewrite them without penalty.

There is no such law in the United States. In fact, separate and marital property laws vary from state to state. In the event of divorce, the laws of the state where the couples reside apply, not the laws of the state where they were married. If the law changed and prenuptials were a requirement at the time a marriage license is taken out, there should also be a uniform law throughout America that recognizes the prenuptial agreement regardless of where the couple married, resided, or filed for divorce. Short of building in the prenuptial as part of the law when applying for a marriage license, as it stands now, even those couples who want a prenuptial agreement often have serious problems asking for one. Before any solution or protection from costly and emotionally draining divorces can be put into the place, the conflicts and dilemmas of asking for a prenup should be aired, discussed, and understood.

Historically and religiously, society encourages marriage, and yet because of the difficulty in the legal system to dissolve a marriage, laws have taken over which force people to spend an inordinate amount of time wallowing in a structure that is overcrowded and complicated. Even more complex is that the law has not caught up with the changing nature of marriage between same-sex couples.

One way to level the playing field is for couples to resolve financial disputes before there is a rupture in the relationship. That can be done in several ways, the most common of which is to enter into a prenuptial agreement. If couples are not planning to marry, they can enter into a cohabitation agreement. Some lawyers believe that even more efficient than either a prenuptial or a cohabitation agreement, in matters of entitlement in the case of death, is a will. It should be noted, however, that a prenuptial agreement will usually trump a will. For instance, if a prenuptial agreement provides for a wife or husband to receive 70 percent of the estate, this would not be affected by the fact that a deceased partner leaves a will with a bequeath of only 50 percent. This should not be confused with the fact that in most jurisdictions in the United States, a spouse cannot be disinherited in a will, and is entitled to "elect" against a will unless they have specifically waived this right in either a pre- or postnuptial agreement.

Agreements made between same-sex couples who are not married are usually much more sophisticated when they prepare for any eventuality that could threaten their union. More than unmarried heterosexual couples, same-sex couples craft agreements which are designed to protect each other, as well as to protect them from the outside world.

Same-sex couples, much like those involved in second and third heterosexual marriages, make sure they are armored within the limits of any state law against attacks from relatives or current spouses. The will must be well written in a way that states that anyone who challenges it will be automatically excluded. Such a provision is called an in terrorem, or no-contest clause, and is frequently utilized by lawyers. Frank Sinatra's will was a case in point where he stipulated that if any person attempted to contest his will or the bequeath to his wife, Barbara, they would lose any benefit they would have received under the will.

One man, Joshua T., a noted writer, had a relationship with his partner for more than twenty years. When his partner fell ill, Joshua cared for him night and day, and paid for all the medicines and other treatments that weren't covered under his health-care plan, as well as caregivers who helped administer medication and other palliative treatment. During the man's protracted illness, Joshua called his partner's family, advising them that their son was terminally ill, and invited them to come visit. The reality had been that the dying man hadn't seen his family since the time he had announced that he was gay, years earlier. Still, Joshua believed that whatever enmity existed between the family and his lover, they had the right to know that he was near the end of his life.

Joshua received no response. It was only after the man died and Joshua was making funeral arrangements that the mother, sister, and a cousin arrived in New York. They were hysterical with grief, mourning the loss of their son, brother, cousin, to the point where at the funeral service, those who did not know the backstory believed that Joshua's lover had been incredibly close to his family.

After the burial, when everyone gathered at Joshua's apartment, his deceased lover's mother approached. "She wanted to know if her son had made a will," Joshua explains. "She told me clearly that she knew her son had certain antiques and family heirlooms, like silver and a set of cobalt dishes, as well as cufflinks his late father had given him, along with a gold Rolex watch. If there was a will, she would challenge it. If there wasn't a will, she was the next of kin and would claim all of her son's possessions."

The truth was that Joshua's lover had sold everything years before when he was out of work. There was nothing left. Indeed, he had made a will, which he had never changed, and in that document had left everything to Joshua. Though the family did not actually sue Joshua, they harassed him for years with threatening letters and phone calls. At one point, they even called his editor and threatened to sue the publishing house for Joshua's royalties. In the end, nothing happened, but the aggravation added to the anguish of losing a loved one made Joshua forever mindful of protecting himself in the future.

———

PEOPLE SAY THAT ASKING a partner to sign a prenuptial agreement before the wedding takes the romance out of marriage. If couples really want to see a lack of romance, all they have to do is wait until the divorce battle begins. Fearing damage from a prenup is nothing compared to the damage experienced by both parties if they don't have a prenup. The best argument for having a prenuptial agreement is that if a couple is going to break up over money, it is better to find out *before* rather than *after,* when it's too late.

Another pragmatic reason for the inclusion of a prenuptial agreement is that if and when divorce happens, the fate of the couple is not solely in the hands of the court. Prenuptial agreements level the playing field, eliminate the power of the courts and judges, and reduce legal fees.

As it stands now, prenuptial agreements are not required before people marry. It is fair to say, however, that while they are not required, they are impacted by socioeconomic factors. Based on statistics gathered from the American Bar Association in 2007, the attitude toward prenuptials varies based on the age of the couple, whether it is a first marriage, and if there are children from a previous union. Some couples believe that the connection between a prenuptial and a wedding is an oxymoron. Others believe that if the relationship is strong, it should survive the act of drafting an agreement.

One woman explained, "A wedding is an act of faith and a prenup implies an act of fear. If my fiancé insisted upon a prenup, I would prefer to call the marriage a partnership or a contract and the wedding a farce."

Another woman explained that she wanted a prenup at the time she married and her husband refused, threatening to leave her if she insisted. "I was married for twenty-one years," she explains. "My marriage was proof that you don't know someone until something happens. My husband became someone I didn't know and had I known him to be as cruel and dishonest, I never would have stayed with him. Love is blind. Women must protect themselves. I was badly burned." She regretted not forcing her husband to sign a prenup.

Prenuptial agreements should be made when couples are the most enraptured with each other, and they should be reviewed every five years as finances and other variables in the marriage change. Though these agreements have been around for thousands of years under different names and under the guise of various religions (ketubah in Judaism and mahr in the Muslim faith) they are more essential than ever given increased life expectancy, the high rate of divorce, and the amount of wealth that young people accumulate today. Prenuptial agreements leave no surprises when "happily ever after" is suddenly not an option. One of the absolutes for writing a prenuptial is that each partner, when revealing assets, income, real estate holdings, stock, and anticipated inheritance, must be completely and totally honest. When people lie when listing their assets in an agreement of this kind, it is assumed that they would hide assets or minimize their net worth. The irony is that often men, far more frequently than women, will lie by inflating their net worth to portray themselves as richer and more successful.

One man who was considerably older than his fiancée falsely listed his net worth in the millions of dollars. When the time came to divorce, he was forced to admit that he had lied. At the time he signed the agreement, his assets were far less than he had claimed. The judge ruled that the prenuptial would be upheld and ordered the man to pay his estranged wife exactly what had been written in the falsified agreement. Which leads to the next question: are prenuptial agreements ironclad?

Any contract is subject to attack under the law. Prenuptial agreements, however, are the only contracts that people can challenge in court, and lose, and still never get less than what was written in the original contract. That said, prenuptials are one of the most difficult contracts to sign, and even more difficult to propose to the one who will presumably be a loving partner for life. Many believe that asking a future spouse to sign a prenuptial agreement is tantamount to planning a divorce at the time of marriage. If people looked at a prenup as a kind of insurance policy, the emotional fallout might be less severe.

Almost everyone buys insurance, signs the policies, and then hopes they never have to use them. When people buy a house, they don't expect it to burn to the ground. When people buy a car, they don't think it will be stolen. Making provisions to protect tangible assets, however, like a house or a car, is not an emotional decision. Making a will is difficult because it deals with death. Making a living will is perhaps even more difficult because people don't want to imagine themselves existing in a vegetative state or in a state where there is no hope for recovery. When it comes to love and marriage, people are far more resistant to prepare for the possibility of divorce than for any other eventuality in life.

Who will forget Donald Trump's reaction when he heard that Paul McCartney did not insist upon a prenuptial when he married Heather Mills? Trump called him, in less polite terms, naïve and irresponsible. In truth, the absence of a prenup was shocking. The former Beatle is a so-phisticated man who has been in the most cynical and complex business for his entire life. His net worth was upward of $1 billion, he had four children from a previous marriage, and a coterie of financial and legal advisers who were there to counsel him. Yet, with all the variables of McCartney's life, good sense, and tons of warnings, he failed to do what would have protected him and his children. Only one explanation comes to mind. This was a man, regardless of his immense wealth, experience, and talent, who had only one reference when it came to marriage. And that was an idyllic and happy union with Linda, the mother of his chil-dren, who died and left him with only the best memories of what a solid and loving marriage could be. McCartney, like many others, undoubt-edly imagined that he was one of the lucky ones—which he was when it came to Linda. His mistake, of course, was that he imagined his luck would continue. He counted on his own goodwill, decency, honesty, and the erroneous notion that he alone had the power to make his second mar-riage as wonderful as his first. Signing a prenuptial with someone who had the same intentions as he did when he proposed marriage would not have hurt their mutual goals for a long and happy life, but it would have spared him the embarrassment, publicity, inordinate legal fees, and ultimately a horrendous settlement, which harmed not only him but also his children.

A more pragmatic reason why Paul McCartney did not sign a prenup-tial agreement is because those agreements are not held as binding in an English court of law. The vast majority of McCartney's fortune was earned before his marriage to Heather Mills. According to English law, the most she could receive would have been approximately 15 percent plus support for their child, Beatrice. Though McCartney initially offered 15 percent to Mills, she chose to use the media to accuse him of physical and emo-tional abuse and in the end, mainly because the former Beatle was not willing to adopt a slash-and-burn attack, Mills received $47 million in-stead of the $32 million that McCartney offered.

Even for those who are not worth billions or even millions, there are still potentially dire consequences in not signing a prenuptial. For instance, if one spouse does not report all of his or her income, the Internal Revenue Service can come after the other spouse for unpaid taxes. Even a savings account in the name of one spouse will be counted as marital property. As for a will which leaves all assets to children, the law says that one-third automatically goes to the surviving spouse. Consider there is a divorce proceeding during which one or the other spouse dies. Without a prenuptial, one-third goes to the widow or widower who had the good fortune not to have changed his or her marital status because a divorce was not yet finalized. Also, a joint mortgage debt might last longer than the marriage if the ex-spouse who gets the house cannot qualify for a new mortgage alone.

JUST AS SOME deranged people opt for murder rather than divorce, there are also horror stories concerning prenuptial agreements. Some people have murdered their prospective spouse or broken off with them rather than sign. One man in Idaho was just convicted of murdering his fiancée when he found out that she had sought legal advice about getting a prenuptial agreement. Another man from New Jersey simply didn't show up at his own wedding after being asked to sign a prenup on the evening before.

There are lessons to be learned from every story cited about people's reactions to divorce and just as many about signing a prenuptial that protects husbands and wives from the horrors of financial litigation. Love and money are both highly emotional issues. Curiously, women have an easier time broaching the subject of a prenuptial agreement at the moment when love is at its most intense. Men, especially those marrying for the first time, often lack the nerve to bring up the subject when the wedding is being planned, especially since it is usually being planned and paid for by the bride's parents. Men are more fearful about hurting their fiancée's feelings, or implying that they lack trust, or are only thinking about money. Several young executives who were interviewed on the subject of prenuptial agreements recount their fears when broaching the subject.

Just a few years out of college, Zack is pulling down a six-figure salary working at a hedge fund. He has been dating the same young woman since his junior year in college. Several months ago, he proposed. When he announced his engagement to his friends, they all asked if he intended to do a prenup. Two of those friends were older and had been divorced and paid a heavy financial and emotional price. Two were his contemporaries and were also about to become engaged and were wrestling with the idea of getting a prenup signed before the wedding.

"I knew it was something I should do," Zack explains, "and there was no doubt that I'd heard plenty of nightmare stories about executives in my firm, and friends of my father's, who had gone through hell because they didn't have a prenup. But knowing what I should do and actually doing it was a huge dilemma that scared me."

One evening after a beautiful dinner with champagne and flowers, Zack and his fiancée returned to their apartment. He asked her to sit down in the living room because there was something he wanted to discuss.

"I figured she had the engagement ring. We had a great rental apartment that was in both our names. Our parents knew we were getting married, and wedding arrangements were in the works. It wasn't that I was rich, but I was on my way up. She worked as well and had a decent salary. Everything was aboveboard. We loved each other and knew each other for years. So I broached the subject of a prenuptial."

Though Zack expected his fiancée would be surprised or even upset, he was unprepared for what ensued.

"She took off the engagement ring and threw it at me. She started crying hysterically and screaming that obviously I wasn't sure the marriage would work and wanted to protect myself. She accused me of having second thoughts but being too scared to come out with the truth. It ended up that she packed a bag and left for her parents' house. Even her parents tried to make sense with her, but she broke up with me. In the end, I gave in and we got married without a prenup. Now, when guys ask me about getting their girlfriends or fiancées to sign one, I tell them that I'm the last person to come to for advice. When I tell them my story, they get scared and end up not bringing up the subject."

A contemporary of Zack's who knew the story about his request for a prenuptial agreement found herself in the same position. She was engaged and wanted to make sure that if the marriage didn't work, neither she nor her fiancé would suffer irreparable and unfair financial penalties. Without any doubt that it was the right thing to do, she sat her fiancé down one evening and brought up the subject.

"The way I look at it," Eleanor explains, "everyone who marries has a prenup whether they like it or not. If you don't sign something before you marry, you're doomed to accept a prenup which is known as divorce law. I just didn't want my life in the hands of the government or the courts. I worked too hard for everything I'd acquired and earned in my life to leave things up to chance in case the marriage doesn't work. I was lucky. At first my fiancé was hurt, and then he came to understand that it wasn't just for me but for us. We both agreed that after five years we would revisit the prenup and make the appropriate changes, especially if we had children."

According to Bernard Clair, a divorce lawyer who has represented fashion designer Carolyne Roehm and socialite Jocelyn Wildenstein, his prenup business has more than doubled in the past five years, and one-third of his clients are couples entering their first marriages.

"People are starting to look at marriage like a business relationship," Clair says. "It's sort of amazing to think that it's taken until this century to realize that's what it really is."

Actually, it hasn't taken until this century for people to prepare for eventual divorce or even to rule from the grave about how they want their widows or widowers to live the rest of their lives.

American Patriot Patrick Henry stipulated in his will that all his worldly goods would go to his wife on the condition that she did not remarry. If she did, she would forfeit everything. "It would make me unhappy," he explained, "to feel I have worked all my life only to support another man's wife." Mrs. Henry remarried anyway and did not lose any money.

An eighteenth-century Australian cattle baron stipulated in his prenuptial agreement that in the event of divorce, his wife would receive only one shilling for "tram fare so she can go somewhere and drown herself."

Broad-based statistics on the secretive, spouse-to-spouse agreements do not exist, but divorce lawyers and marital therapists maintain that there is an increased amount of curiosity and interest in prenuptial agreements. The Equality in Marriage Institute, a nonprofit that advises couples, reports that the number of prenuptial inquiries more than tripled from 2003 to 2005 to five thousand a month. That is not to claim, however, that all inquiries lead to actual writing or implementing of the agreement.

Bernard Clair, however, insists that today, more than ever, everyone is "hedging their bets."

"It's almost like there's a split-personality syndrome that's going on with the younger prenup couples right now," Clair has recently said. "It's equal parts optimistic hope and resigned pragmatism. They've seen what divorce and its destruction can do, and they want to armor themselves to avoid any collateral damage. In fact, one of the reasons younger couples are seeking prenups is that it's nearly impossible for people today to maintain an 'it-won't-happen-to-us' attitude. This prenup boom is also because couples are waiting until they're older to marry, which means they've had time to acquire more wealth."

Robert Stephan Cohen, an attorney who has counseled Uma Thurman and James Gandolfini through their divorces, says, "There's so much money around, and so many divorces, when you put the two together, you get an explosion."

In the past month, Cohen has been retained by five clients who came to him to write prenuptial agreements. Two worked on Wall Street, an investment banker and a trader; the others were a real estate broker, a female advertising executive, and an heir to a family fortune. Cohen explains that New York is one of only a few states to allow potential future earnings to be tied to professional licenses (as in the case of doctors and lawyers), partnerships, or degrees to be considered marital property.

Alton L. Abramowitz, chair of the New York City Bar's Matrimonial Committee, claimed that he would never allow his twelve-year-old daughter to be married in New York without a prenup.

"My daughter sings with a local opera company and wants to become a major opera singer. If she married without a prenup she could be subjected to an enhanced earnings claim someday. I wouldn't want anyone entitled to half of her talent."

One of the best arguments for drawing up a prenuptial agreement is that it facilitates either partner's ability to live up to each other's expectations. When an ugly divorce is in the negotiation stage, it is not unusual that one litigant will demand the most precious possession his or her spouse holds dear, merely for spite. If there is a prenuptial agreement, it eliminates that potential agony if, before the marriage, each can list what each considers his or her most precious asset. A prenuptial agreement requires people to respect each other's possessions and assets earned or inherited before marriage. It also sets the rules of the marriage in advance and helps to guarantee that a relationship based on reality—and money is reality—has a better chance of success than one based on illusion.

When writing a prenuptial agreement, it should be fair. If not, many judges will discount the agreement at the time of divorce. Also, husband and wife cannot state how much each will contribute to child support. That will automatically be removed by a judge hearing the divorce and will ultimately be decided by the court based on formulas already set.

Common sense dictates that prenuptial agreements should be written with an acknowledgment that things change—finances, physical conditions, needs, space—and included might be a guarantee to revisit the prenuptial every five years. The best advice is that a prenup should be signed at least six months before the wedding. Waiting until the last minute might give a judge the impression that there was pressure put on either party, forcing them to sign when invitations were already sent out, the caterer paid for, and gifts received. Some lawyers will refuse to begin the process of a prenuptial agreement less than ninety days before a wedding is scheduled.

Given what many reactions are from those who are asked to sign a prenuptial, some veterans of the process give the following advice: Pick the right place and time, obviously in private but not before, during, or after an intimate moment. Also, ask in a way that is not interpreted as a demand, but rather as a discussion about what is best in the long term for both. Obviously, the worst thing to do is present an agreement that has already been drafted, along with a pen with which to sign.

Perhaps the best reason for bringing up the subject is to understand future expectations in the spirit of having a marriage where things can be talked about openly without fear of recrimination or regret.

However and whenever the subject is broached, the one bringing it up should be prepared for his or her partner to express dismay. "Don't you trust me?" is one question that is frequently posed. Another is, "Are you questioning if our marriage will work out?"

The trick to any negotiation is flexibility. If one or the other is unwavering in certain demands, whether it is sharing assets or owning a particular painting or dish, the entire exercise will be sabotaged from the beginning.

If one person is adamant about signing a stringent prenuptial, it is advisable to build in "sunset provisions" that stagger the terms over time, or nullify the contract after a certain number of years, or at least amend it after children are born.

Wisdom dictates that people should not respond immediately.

Wisdom also dictates that people should consider a prenuptial agreement as an opportunity to settle potential disagreements before they happen, if at all.

A prenuptial is really the first test a couple might face to know if they are able to handle other conflicts that will arise during the marriage. If the subject results in the relationship breaking down, there's a good chance there was more to settle that had never been addressed.

It is usual that the one who proposes the prenuptial pays the attorneys for both parties. The cost can range anywhere from five thousand to fifteen thousand dollars, with more prestigious firms charging more, for three to five attorney/client meetings. Another option is to hire a mediator, which is far less costly, between fifteen to twenty-five hundred dollars, to draft the agreement. After that, the parties, as in divorce negotiations, still have to hire separate lawyers to review the document for signature. (See Appendix B for a sample prenuptial agreement.)

Personal wealth is not the only concern of those who opt for a prenuptial agreement. One of Bernard Clair's clients is a twenty-eight-year-old attorney who currently earns almost $200,000 a year and is on the fast track to making partner at a large firm. The reason this particular young man wants a prenuptial is not only to control the amount of money his wife-to-be would be awarded in the event of a divorce, but also and primarily to protect his firm against a barrage of discovery motions.

"Companies often send off-the-radar messages to their partners and managing directors to avoid exposing the company to a carpet-bombing of documents," Clair explains. "Executing a prenup that specifically keeps the company out of the matrimonial mix is something that more and more large firms insist upon from their employees."

Corporations, law firms, investment banks, and many other businesses are becoming increasingly aware of the turmoil divorce causes for their employees. They are also more cognizant of the potential involvement they could face if financial records are subpoenaed during the investigative part of a divorce. Those who face the legal dissolution of a marriage often find themselves unable to function in their job. Depression or lethargy accounts for less productivity at the office. Seeking professional help, therapy, or counseling is a viable alternative, but appointments have to be made and kept, costs are not always fully covered by insurance, and people still find themselves depressed or anxious on the days they are not seeing their therapist. Calling the lawyer rather than visiting him or her at the office is an automatic bill, as attorneys, without exception, charge by the hour for everything, including telephone conversations.

One remedy to help people through the turmoil and to assure more efficiency and less absentee time would be if every corporation and company had a relationship counselor on staff and salaried. Only then could people who have problems with a divorce, separation, or any other psychological issues afford the luxury of talking to someone when the need arose, and without having to miss work or leave the office.

In the United States, people can get a driver's license, but until they have insurance, they can't drive legally. People can get a law degree, but they can't practice law until they pass the bar exam. A barber cannot cut hair, nor a plumber fix a toilet, without proving they are qualified for a state license. In almost every example, the prerequisite is a civil requirement, which the state has the full authority to regulate.

What if the state said Jews were not allowed to be lawyers unless they were bar mitzvahed? Or, Catholics couldn't be doctors unless they could take Communion?

The law says one is entitled to certain benefits that are provided to all citizens—the right to marry, make a prenuptial agreement, and divorce. The law does not say, however, that you have to practice a religion according to rules set by the state. Nor does the law dictate that you have no right to the benefits of the law that govern marriage and divorce. In every instance, there are two words to remember: protect yourself. The law does not cover every potential problem or misinterpretation.

23

WILL THE REAL ME PLEASE STAND UP?

When people divorce, it's always such a tragedy. At the same time, if people stay together it can be even worse.
—MONICA BELLUCCI

THE WORST THING YOU could imagine has finally happened. You are getting divorced. Whether or not your spouse left you or you left your spouse is irrelevant. Whether or not your spouse left for someone else or you left for another is immaterial. What matters is that life as you knew it will never be the same again.

The day of reckoning has arrived. Your matrimonial lawyer is suddenly the most important person in your life other than your children if you have any, or your parents, or friends, at least those friends and family who haven't taken sides and gone over to the enemy camp.

If you have been left for another, you are filled with anger and recriminations. Anger because you have given years of your life to your spouse, or because the marriage was too short to make the necessary adjustments to give it a chance to survive. Recriminations because of all the things you could have done but did not do, such as losing those extra pounds, taking better care of yourself, being more attentive, going on those silly fishing trips or jaunts to a spa, learning how to play chess, being more ambitious, cutting out the nagging when he or she worked overtime or stopped for a few drinks with friends. You hate your spouse at the same time that you tell yourself you should have been more vigilant and not assumed that he or she would never leave because of money, children, reputation, or just because of all those years of shared history.

If you are the one who walked out for another, you, too, are filled with rage, but also with guilt and remorse that you could be so selfish to follow your heart while your spouse is destined to suffer days and nights of loneliness and fading memories. The rage you feel might come from remembering all that you wanted and expected and all that your spouse did not do to satisfy your expectations. You conjure up your grievance list: you should have left years before; you should never have married him or her in the first place; you resent the system that will meddle in your life and often take months or years to free you from that person who stands between you and a new life.

If you or your spouse has no one waiting to step up to the domestic plate, and you broke up because you fell out of love, decided you hate each other, have nothing in common, or simply realized one day that the "death" in "till death do us part" was a certainty that carried with it a sense of dead-end doom, there are still a myriad of mixed emotions.

Whatever the scenario for the rupture, and there are too many different reasons to list, you now find yourself embroiled in emotional turmoil and involved in what is politely called "negotiations."

The usual advice and solutions to making divorce less traumatic externally, or making people less traumatized on the surface as they deal with the various legal and logistical challenges that come up, are sensible and straightforward.

1. Understand that divorce can and often does lead toward a new and better life.
2. For women, it is not necessarily a new man.
3. For men, it is not always finding the fountain of youth.
4. Alimony should not prevent a man from going on with his life.
5. Alimony should not rob a woman of the incentive to make a new life.

Many marriage counselors and matrimonial attorneys maintain that when divorce is a reality, couples tend to focus on the history, the reasons why they are facing a failed marriage—betrayals, frustrations, disappointments. During the often bitter negotiations after each has consulted a lawyer, people also tend to relive their years of misery, anxiety, and hurt. When the divorce is final, there is often residue of those emotions which hampers people from moving on to new lives, loves, friendships, and challenges. When and if people seek counseling, they are often told to forget the past in order to move on to new lives. Forgetting the past is a tough order, unless someone suffers from amnesia, or undergoes a lobotomy. Letting go of years of history without searching for their meaning is tantamount to treating a protracted illness with aspirin.

From a purely superficial viewpoint, there are activities, changes, and goals that people can do and prepare for after a divorce to begin a new life and form new habits. For example, people could focus on themselves, and that includes physical exercise and a commitment to a healthy diet, both of which signal a new beginning to mental and physical health. Changing habits might include contacting old friends, having a willingness to make new ones, and even joining support groups for recently divorced adults—a reassuring way to understand that they are not alone and there is something similar in everybody's reaction to divorce.

Blame is deadly. The best advice is to stop blaming yourself or your spouse. Life is not static. People change. There is always something new on the horizon, which can be discerned when people stop obsessing about the past. Engaging in frivolous activities is another way to start anew, for those who have the means. For instance, for those who don't have financial problems, they might redecorate what had been the marital home, buy a new wardrobe, take a trip to a place they have never been, consider plastic surgery, get a trainer, take two weeks in a spa, join a health club, and if they don't have one already, consult a therapist to help them see all that they have, rather than all that they've lost.

A LOVELY AND CHARMING Frenchwoman was married to an equally attractive attorney in Paris. They had an interesting and active life, two children, and everything to make them happy. One day, the husband fell in love with a woman half his age. He carried on an affair for several years until his wife finally asked him to leave the marital home. The problem was that his law office was in their enormous apartment near the Parc

Monceau. They made an arrangement so that each owned one-half of what had been their apartment, and the wife and the children agreed to move out. The husband would be responsible for the rent and all other expenses for his family. In the event of sale, the proceeds of the apartment would be divided between the couple. Though some thought it was odd, the husband found his wife and children a large flat directly across the street, so that his living room windows faced her bedroom. Apparently, there were no issues and the wife moved in. Despite the fact that the husband was still involved with the young mistress, he would constantly stop at his former wife's house, not only to see his children, but also to see her, have dinner, and discuss his business, as she had once been his closest adviser. At the time that the divorce became final, several American friends of hers in Paris asked the woman if she would seek therapy to get through the trauma of officially ending her marriage. She laughed. "Why on earth would I get therapy?" she asked. "I intend to go to Zermatt, ski, and find another husband."

The trip was a success. The snow was perfect and there wasn't a cloud in the sky for the entire two weeks she was ensconced in the Mont Cervan hotel. On her third night, she met the man who would become her second husband.

The moral of that story is that everyone has different goals and coping mechanisms. Often, people are able to construct techniques that work. Often they can't. Not everyone chooses to dwell in the past. Some prefer to believe divorce has erased the past. There are many methods for both scenarios that are tried, tested, and work. Others don't work.

Some men and women become involved in good works. Concentrating on global misery or other peoples' tragedy often diminishes personal pain. Being single and without the daily routine of married life can liberate spare time, and there are some who use those newfound hours to help others.

For those who have a career, it is equally important to set new goals at work and to begin mingling with coworkers. Often, people who are living in unhappy marriages tend to resist communicating with people at work for fear they have nothing to say except to recount the tribulations of their own personal lives. Once people at work know someone is divorced, or on their way to divorce, often they will offer their experiences as a way to make new friendships. Changing a professional routine is another sign that life will be different. Some people get in early and stay late at the office, while others begin their day later or leave earlier. Work could be less of an escape and more of a mission or a passion.

For those with limited financial resources, frivolities don't always have to be costly. Surrounding oneself with familiar friends and family or involving oneself with children's activities after school is another way to break old patterns. Living in a bad marriage often drains people emotionally or renders them inert. Removing the source of unhappiness frequently gives people more energy to engage in social and physical activities. In fact, seeing old friends might mean going to high school or college reunions. According to the Association of Matrimonial Lawyers, 60 percent of divorced adults connect romantically with someone from their distant past.

The air is free, as are the parks. There is nothing more invigorating and thought-provoking than a daily routine of walking every morning or evening before or after work. Making plans in advance for the weekends gives people something to look forward to. In good weather, outdoor activities with children and friends are healthy, or indoor get-togethers where everyone brings something to the table—emotional and edible—is a way to focus on others.

When something ends in life, something else begins. Divorce is an end to only one aspect of life—a relationship that did not work for whatever reason. Fault is irrelevant. Mourning a bad or deceitful relationship will never bring inner peace. Understanding the deceit and negative aspects of the relationship is a first step. Letting go of the anger and resentment is the only way to have freedom to move on and begin a new and better life.

It is important to remember that without divorce, people would be doomed to survive without another chance at happiness—whether they choose living alone or finding another partner.

Activities, physical changes, and acquiring new habits and disciplines are all important to breaking out from under depression, anger, or remorse. But there is something even more crucial to surviving divorce without fear and dread that life will never be the same again.

Looking at the big picture of a marriage by sifting through the small snapshots of what had been a life allows those going through divorce to put things in perspective. There is no rule that getting divorced at thirty makes it easier than being divorced at sixty. Though youth brings with it optimism when it comes time to start again, middle age carries with it the benefit of experience to know the pitfalls before they happen.

Though it is a statistical fact that men will live with someone new or marry faster and more frequently than women after a divorce, that ability carries with it a price. Women who manage to find a husband or partner immediately after a marital rupture also face obstacles. Those who try to build a relationship while still in the process of ending one often encounter more complications and problems. The healing process is not altogether clean.

Every marriage and divorce has its own story. Reviewing the story is a process that people either choose to face or decide to ignore. Even if there are no regrets about the divorce, it is nonetheless a loss, similar to a death, where mourning is part of that process. To repress the story or to conveniently tuck it away in the recesses of the mind is not always the most productive way to achieve freedom to build another life.

Whatever the circumstances of the marriage, divorce, or whether or not people have moved on to new partners, there are sporadic images, memories, and fragments of the past that appear without warning. Those who allow the stories of their past to invade and interrupt their present are often able to cope with the loss better than those who erase the history. Mary Martin, who played Nellie in the Broadway play *South Pacific,* sang the song "I'm Gonna Wash That Man Right Outta My Hair," about the breakup of a love affair. In a similar way, after a separation and divorce, there are those who destroy photographs, mementos, objects that were bought by their departed spouse, gifts, souvenirs, or other items that cause them to remember a trip, vacation, a specific store, or a celebration. These are the people who cut themselves off from stepchildren, friends, and in-laws, who give away pets, and are determined to throw out every last reminder of the wives or husbands who are no longer in their lives. Ask those who take this approach to healing and most will respond that the only way to forget and get over the pain is to obliterate every trace of their ex-spouse's existence.

"Clean house," one woman explained. "Get rid of his carbon footprint is the only way I can go on." Another woman said, "Why should I look at something that was once so meaningful and now just brings all the rage to the surface? I even threw out our bed." A man whose wife left him and their two children finds himself fighting to care for his son and daughter without feeling resentful toward his former wife. "I look at my kids, and though I love them, I see her in their eyes and want to punch out the wall. . . ."

Choosing to allow the sporadic thoughts to enter or the images to appear, or moments of memory to invade their consciousness when they recall a word, expression, or incident, is far more painful in the short term than erasing every trace of a former spouse. But allowing memories to invade their hearts and minds gives people a better chance of letting go of a life that has already been left. In the long term, it is the only way to achieve total freedom.

The litmus test of moving on is how often a past partner appears, how frequently thoughts turn to a past partner, how recurrently do those thoughts interrupt a current and new life. The only way to achieve freedom from memories, whether they are bad or good, is to face the tunnel of pain head-on, and sift through them at every turn, until the tunnel recedes into the distance and the exit is visible.

In the end, there are no foolproof formulas or ironclad rules that guarantee a painless divorce or an aftermath devoid of suffering. Suggesting changes in the law that make the legal process more fair and less costly and lengthy is one piece to make divorce less traumatic and to level the playing field. Citing cases of how violence and revenge achieve nothing except pain and anguish is not always successful, nor does it serve as a cautionary tale for those who are so emotionally damaged. Even discussing those divorces where people have proven that life goes on in a happier and better way for all concerned does not always work, because they are not examples that everyone will believe or follow.

Freedom is precious. Political freedom is not always a choice that people can make. Psychological freedom is also not always an option for those who suffer debilitating mental illness. Freedom from guilt, rage, hate, and revenge as it concerns divorce, however, is mostly a matter of intellectual access and discipline.

Just as Leo Tolstoy opened his book *Anna Karenina* with the words "Happy families are all alike; every unhappy family is unhappy in its own way," so is every divorce different. In the final analysis, Rudyard Kipling's thought that "the Colonel's Lady and Rose O'Grady are sisters under the skin," the troubles, tribulations, and ultimate salvation can be universal. (This could just as easily refer to men.)

There are many remedies for a failing marriage, none of which have to be extreme, whether it's random infidelity, emotional withdrawal, or Lorena Bobbitt's infamous surgical approach. Ending a marriage should be a conscientious and rational decision. Behavior during the various steps people are obliged to take in order to end a marriage should also be conscientious and rational.

There is the law—both what it is, and what people believe it should be.

There is common sense.

There is introspection and fair self-discovery of root causes. And there is hope and, ultimately . . . salvation.

There is wisdom to learn from one's own mistakes and to move on.

Appendix A:
Sample Intake Questionnaire

History of this Marriage

DATE OF MARRIAGE: _____

PLACE: _____

INCLUDING THIS MARRIAGE, HOW MANY TIMES HAVE YOU BEEN
MARRIED? _____

INCLUDING THIS MARRIAGE, HOW MANY TIMES HAS YOUR SPOUSE
BEEN MARRIED? _____

ARE YOU AND YOUR SPOUSE LIVING TOGETHER NOW? _____

IF NOT, WHEN DID YOU SEPARATE? _____

WHERE WERE YOU LIVING AT THE TIME OF YOUR
SEPARATION? _____

WHEN WAS THE LAST TIME YOU HAD SEXUAL RELATIONS WITH YOUR
SPOUSE? _____

OTHER THAN WHAT IS LISTED ABOVE, HAVE YOU AND YOUR SPOUSE
LIVED TOGETHER CONTINUOUSLY THROUGHOUT THE MARRIAGE?

_____

INFORMATION ABOUT YOUR CHILDREN

FULL NAME, DATE OF BIRTH, RESIDES WITH: _____

_____

ALL ADDRESSES THE CHILDREN HAVE LIVED IN FOR THE PAST FIVE
YEARS AND WITH WHOM THEY LIVED: _____

_____

_____

DO ANY OF YOUR CHILDREN HAVE ANY PHYSICAL OR OTHER
PROBLEMS THAT WILL BE A FACTOR IN THIS CASE (I.E., LEARNING
DISABILITY, PHYSICAL IMPAIRMENT, ETC.)? IF SO, PLEASE EXPLAIN:

_____

_____

_____

DO YOU ANTICIPATE A DISPUTE ABOUT CUSTODY OF THE CHILDREN?

_____

INFORMATION ABOUT YOUR EMPLOYMENT

ARE YOU EMPLOYED? _____ IF YES, STATE YOUR EMPLOYER:

_____

JOB TITLE: _____ TYPE OF JOB: _____
EMPLOYED SINCE: _____ GROSS YEARLY SALARY: _____
PLEASE STATE YOUR EDUCATION AND VOCATIONAL TRAINING
(INCLUDING NUMBER OF YEARS YOU ATTENDED HIGH SCHOOL AND
COLLEGE, IF APPLICABLE): _____

_____

INFORMATION ABOUT YOUR PRIOR MARRIAGE(S)

If you or your spouse has been married before this marriage, state
name(s) of prior spouse(s) and how, when, and where prior marriage(s)
were terminated: _____

_____

IF THERE ARE ANY CHILDREN FROM PRIOR MARRIAGE(S) OF YOU
AND/OR YOUR SPOUSE, PLEASE LIST THE NAMES AND AGES OF ANY
CHILDREN AND STATE WITH WHOM SUCH CHILDREN LIVE: _____

_____

_____

Prior Proceedings

HAVE THERE BEEN ANY LEGAL OR OTHER PROCEEDINGS BETWEEN
YOU AND THE OPPOSING PARTY? IF SO, PLEASE DESCRIBE: _____

_____

Reconciliation

DO YOU HAVE AN INTEREST IN RECONCILIATION? _____
DOES YOUR SPOUSE, AS FAR AS YOU KNOW? _____
HAVE YOU TRIED MARRIAGE COUNSELING? IF SO, WHEN AND WITH
WHOM? _____

Other

HAS YOUR SPOUSE CONSULTED AN ATTORNEY REGARDING THIS
MATTER? IF SO, PLEASE INDICATE HIS/HER NAME AND ADDRESS, IF
KNOWN: _____

_____

HAVE YOU CONSULTED OTHER ATTORNEYS REGARDING THIS MATTER?
IF SO, PLEASE STATE WHOM YOU HAVE SEEN AND WHEN:

_____

_____

DO YOU HAVE A WILL? IF SO, WHO ARE THE BENEFICIARIES?

_____

_____

_____

DO YOU HAVE AN ACCOUNTANT OR HAVE YOU EVER USED AN
ACCOUNTANT? IF SO, PLEASE STATE HIS/HER NAME AND ADDRESS:

_____

_____

ARE THERE BANK ACCOUNTS, LINES OF CREDIT, STOCK AND
INVESTMENT ACCOUNTS, OR OTHER ACCOUNTS TO WHICH YOUR
SPOUSE HAS ACCESS? IF SO, PLEASE CLARIFY: _____

_____

_____

DOES YOUR SPOUSE HAVE IN HIS OR HER POSSESSION CREDIT CARDS
FOR WHICH YOU ARE RESPONSIBLE? IF SO, PLEASE SPECIFY: _____

_____

_____

HAVE YOU EVER SIGNED ANYTHING WHICH MAY AFFECT THE CASE,
INCLUDING A PRENUPTIAL OR POSTNUPTIAL AGREEMENT(S), OR
OTHER DOCUMENTS PRESENTED BY YOUR SPOUSE? IF SO, PLEASE
DESCRIBE WHAT YOU SIGNED: _____

_____

HAVE YOU OR YOUR SPOUSE SOLD ANY REAL PROPERTY IN THE LAST
FIVE (5) YEARS? IF SO, PLEASE SPECIFY: _____

_____

_____

*DO NOT DISCUSS THIS CASE, OR ASPECTS OF IT, WITH ANYONE OTHER
THAN YOUR ATTORNEY. REMEMBER THAT YOU ARE MARRIED UNTIL THE
FINAL JUDGMENT IS SIGNED BY THE JUDGE AND ENTERED IN THE
COUNTY CLERK'S OFFICE; YOU SHOULD COMPORT YOURSELF ACCORDINGLY.

Appendix B:
Sample Prenuptial Agreement

AGREEMENT made this _____ day of _____, 20_____, between _____, residing at _____ (hereinafter sometimes referred to as "_____") and _____, residing at _____ (hereinafter sometimes referred to as "_____").

WITNESSETH:

A marriage is contemplated between _____ and _____, each of whom is of full age. The parties desire to fix and determine by this Agreement, pursuant to and in accordance with DRL 236(B)(3), certain rights and claims that each of them may have arising out of the marital relationship and to accept the provisions of this Agreement in lieu of and in full discharge, settlement and satisfaction of such rights and claims under the laws of any Jurisdiction.

WHEREAS, the parties are entering into this Agreement because of a mutual desire to resolve prospective disagreements in advance, and acknowledge that this Agreement is entered into without duress or promises other than those stated herein or expectations other than those reflected herein.

IT IS THEREFORE MUTUALLY AGREED BY THE PARTIES THAT, if the parties at any time in the future marry one another, then, in such event:

ARTICLE 1.

CONSIDERATION

The consideration for this Agreement is the mutual promises and agreements herein contained, and the contemplated marriage of the parties.

ARTICLE 2.

ESTATE WAIVER

2.1   Each of the parties hereby waives, renounces, grants, remises and releases to the other, forever and for all purposes whatsoever, any and all right, title and interest, and any and all claims whatsoever, under the laws of any state, territory or jurisdiction whatsoever, including dower, curtesy and community property rights and interests, which he or she now has or may hereafter acquire, in the real or personal property or estate of the other, wheresoever situated and whether acquired before or subsequent to the marriage of the parties or before or subsequent to the date of this Agreement, by reason of inheritance or descent, or by virtue of any decedent estate law or any other statute or custom, or arising out of marital relations, or for any other reason whatsoever, including without limitation, any trust or annuity created by the other and any power to dispose of or appoint property of the other arising under or pursuant to any Will, Trust or other instrument now or hereafter made or amended. Each party hereby expressly waives and releases any rights of election as may now or hereafter be provided for under or by virtue of the laws of the State of New York, or under the laws of any other state, territory or jurisdiction, against any Last Will and Testament or Codicils thereto, of the other whatsoever (whether heretofore or hereafter executed), particularly the right to elect to take as against the same the intestate share to which he or she would otherwise be entitled, and each party hereby renounces and waives any right to act as administrator or other fiduciary of the estate of the other party. This mutual waiver shall, of course, not prohibit either party from providing for the other in his or her Will or otherwise as he or she may wish to do.

2.2   Except as otherwise provided in this Agreement, the parties shall each have the right to dispose of his or her property by his or her Last Will and Testament, or otherwise, as if the other had died during his or her lifetime. The parties agree that if the other should die intestate, his or her estate, whether real or personal, shall belong to the person or persons who would have been entitled hereto if the Husband or the Wife, as the case may be, had died during his or her lifetime. The parties shall each permit any Last Will and Testament of the other to be probated and shall each allow letters of administration upon his or her estate and personal effects to be taken and received by any other person who would have been entitled thereto had the Husband died during the lifetime of the Wife or had the Wife died during the lifetime of the Husband. However, the foregoing shall not bar a claim on the part of either party against the other for any cause or causes of action arising out of a breach of this Agreement during the lifetime of the deceased party against whose estate such claim may be made.

2.3   The provisions of 2.1 and 2.2 hereinabove are intended to and shall serve as:

i. A waiver and release of the waiving party's right of election in accordance with the requirements of Section 5-1.1 and 5-1.1-A of the Estates, Powers and Trusts Law of the State of _____, and any law amendatory thereof or supplemental or similar thereof, or of the same or similar law of any other jurisdiction which may be applicable.

ii. The right to an intestate share in the other party's estate.

iii. The right to act as or be designated administrator or administratix of the other party's estate.

iv. All claims or rights of curtesy or dower that such party now has or may hereafter acquire in and to any and all real or personal property now or hereafter owned by the other party.

v. All rights to widow's or widower's allowance such as that provided by Section 5-3.1 of the New York Estates, Powers and
Trusts Law.

ARTICLE 3.

EVENT OF MARITAL DISCORD

For all purposes of this Agreement, the term "Event of Marital Discord"
shall be defined to mean:

A.   Commencement of an action or proceeding by either party seeking
a separation, annulment, declaration of nullity, divorce, or dissolution of
the marriage, for any reason whatsoever; or

B.   Delivery to the other party of a signed, written notice of one party
to the other stating that he or she desires to effectuate a permanent separation. Said notice may be delivered by mailing it to the last known address of the other party by certified mail, return receipt requested, or by
personal delivery.

C.   If there is an "Event of Marital Discord" other than commencement
of an action for divorce, or separation or support between the parties, they
agree that they will have a thirty (30) day "cooling off" period wherein
they would live together during such period and make a good faith effort
to work out any differences that may exist.

ARTICLE 4.

PROPERTY

4.1   For purposes of this Agreement, it is the parties' intention that
each party's separate property and estate shall include, without limitation,
all property owned outright by such party at the time of the marriage,
including, but not limited to property acquired by gift or inheritance,
testamentary substitutes of any kind, revocable living trusts, all property
held in trust for such party's benefit at the time of the marriage or in the
future, all property distributed or distributable before or after the marriage to or for the benefit of such party from a trust for such party's ben-

efit, all businesses of any nature, professional licenses, practices, enhanced earning ability, and any additions of property thereto, all stocks, including any later stock splits, mergers, stock distributions and/or spin-offs, all income earned thereon, any increase in value of such property, whether or not fully or partially the result of monetary contributions and/or efforts of the other party, any property acquired in exchange for such property, or increase in value of such property, and/or purchased with funds resulting from the sale of separate property, all income earned on such exchanged property or property acquired from sale of separate property ("Separate Property"). Separate Property shall remain the party's in whose name it is held or, if there is no document of title, the party who has had sole use and possession of the property, for example, a party's jewelry, watches, furs, personal clothing and effects. Each party shall own, control and possess such party's Separate Property, free of any claim or right of the other, with full power to dispose of the same as fully and effectively in all respects and for all purposes as if unmarried.

4.2   The parties desire that title shall control as to all property acquired during the marriage. All property acquired during the marriage in _____'s name shall remain _____'s separate property. All property acquired during the marriage in _____'s name shall remain _____'s separate property. All property acquired in joint name shall be owned by the parties jointly, with each party having a fifty per cent interest therein.

4.3   Upon the happening of an Event of Marital Discord, separate property contributions to joint property shall be returned to the contributor prior to distribution of joint property. Property acquired during the marriage used by the parties for their household such as home furnishings, artwork and antiques ("household articles"), shall be deemed to be the property of the party in whose name the dwelling where the household articles are located is owned. If the dwelling is held in joint names, such household articles shall be equally divided as with all of the other joint property.

4.4   Gifts given by one party to the other party which cost less than five thousand ($5,000) dollars, or any gifts of jewelry, personal clothing or effects, shall be the Separate Property of the donee.

4.5   It is understood and agreed that any payments from a party's separate property towards the parties' expenses or lifestyle shall not affect the characterization of property set forth hereinabove. Nor shall contributions from marital property towards the upkeep, maintenance or improvement of a separate property asset change the character of that asset as separate property.

4.6.   It is anticipated that the parties will reside in an apartment in _____ and at a home located in _____.

4.7   Notwithstanding paragraph 4.2 above, the contents of the _____ apartment will be shared by _____ [both parties] as they may decide in the future. However, _____'s personal property, including artwork, jewelry, dishes and silver shall remain her property.

4.8.   Any dogs that are possessed by _____ and _____ at the time of an event of termination shall be the sole and exclusive property of _____. _____ shall have the right to visit said dogs until such time that either _____ and _____ decide not to speak to each other.

ARTICLE 5.

REPRESENTATION BY LEGAL COUNSEL

5.1   _____ confirms that she has been advised by legal counsel of her own choice, _____, about the matters referred to in this Agreement, including any and all rights which she is or may be surrendering pursuant to this Agreement.

5.2   _____ confirms that he has been advised by legal counsel of his own choice, and/or he has declined to have separate counsel, but has read, fully understands and agrees to the terms of this Agreement, including any and all rights which he is or may be surrendering pursuant to this Agreement.

5.3   Each of the parties agree that they shall each be responsible for any and all legal fees incurred by each of their attorneys.

Article 6.

DISCLOSURE

6.1   Each party confirms that he or she has made a complete disclosure of his or her financial information in the form of Statements of Net Worth which are annexed hereto, and the other party acknowledges that she or he has received such information that the other party offered to respond fully and directly to all questions such party and such party's attorneys might have concerning such financial information, that such party regards such information as full, fair and complete disclosure, both in form and substance, that such party is under no duress or other pressure to refrain from obtaining detailed written disclosure and that, upon advice of such party's independent counsel, such party is fully aware of and understands all of the rights that such party is surrendering or releasing pursuant to this Agreement.

Article 7.

DEBTS

Each of the parties will be solely responsible for any debt, charge, obligation or liability that party incurred or contracted, or which arose or was imposed, whether before or during the marriage and shall hold the other party harmless and indemnify the other party for any such debt, charge, obligation or liability.

Article 8.

MATRIMONIAL DECREES

The provisions of this Agreement shall not be construed to preclude either of the parties hereto from maintaining a suit for absolute divorce, separation or annulment against the other in any jurisdiction upon any grounds recognized as lawful in such jurisdiction. If any final decree of divorce, separation or annulment shall be entered in any action, the provisions of this Agreement shall be incorporated by reference in and made a part of such decree, but shall survive and not merge therein. Both parties agree that no judgment, order or decree in any action for divorce, separation or annulment, whether brought in _____ _____, or in any other state or country having jurisdiction of the parties hereto, shall make any provisions inconsistent with the provisions of this Agreement, but if any provision be made in any judgment, order or decree which is inconsistent with the provisions of the Agreement, or imposes a different or greater obligation on either of the parties hereto than provided in this Agreement, the provisions of this Agreement shall take precedence and shall be the sole obligation of both parties hereto.

ARTICLE 9.

VOLUNTARY EXECUTION

Each party acknowledges that this Agreement is fair and equitable, that it is being entered into voluntarily and that it is not the result of any duress or undue influence. Each of the parties has read the Agreement prior to its execution, understands it and is fully aware of the rights that he or she is releasing pursuant to the terms of this Agreement.

ARTICLE 10.

ENTIRE UNDERSTANDING OF THE PARTIES

This Agreement sets forth the entire understanding of the parties and supersedes all other agreements, written or oral, between the parties including, without limitation, any implied or other agreements arising in connection with any period of cohabitation. The parties affirm that no agreements presently in effect have been entered into between them prior to the date of this Agreement. Neither party has relied upon any representation of the other party or any other person, except such as are specifically mentioned in this Agreement.

Article 11.

AMENDMENT OR REVOCATION

This Agreement may not be amended or revoked except by a separate instrument in writing, signed by _____ and _____ and mutually acknowledged, expressly modifying or revoking one or more or all of the provisions of this Agreement.

Article 12.

BINDING EFFECT

All of the provisions of this Agreement shall inure to the benefit of and be binding upon the respective heirs, issue, distributees, executors, administrators, successors and assigns of the parties.

Article 13.

PARTIAL INVALIDITY

If any provision of this Agreement is held to be invalid or unenforceable, all other provisions hereof shall nevertheless continue in full force and effect.

Article 14.

GOVERNING LAW

All matters affecting the interpretation of this Agreement and the rights of the parties shall be governed by the law of the State of _____.

ARTICLE 15.

JURISDICTION

For purposes of this Agreement, "Jurisdiction" shall mean the United States or any state, subdivision or territory thereof, including without limitation the State of New York, and any foreign country or any state, subdivision or territory thereof.

IN WITNESS WHEREOF, the parties have hereunto set their respective hands and seals as of the day and year first above written.

SUBSCRIBING WITNESS: _____

SUBSCRIBING WITNESS: _____

ACKNOWLEDGMENT

STATE OF _____)

                      :   SS.:

COUNTY OF _____)

On the _____ day of _____, 2010, before me, the undersigned, personally appeared _____, personally known to me or proved to me on the basis of satisfactory evidence to be the individual whose name is subscribed to the within instrument and acknowledged to me that she executed the same in her capacity, and that by her signature on the instrument, the individual or the person upon behalf of which the individual acted, executed the instrument.

_____

NOTARY PUBLIC

CERTIFICATE OF SUBSCRIBING WITNESS

STATE OF _____   )
                                  :   SS.:
COUNTY OF _____   )

On the _____ day of _____, 2010, before me, the undersigned, a Notary Public in and for said state, personally appeared _____, the subscribing witness to the foregoing instrument, with whom I am personally acquainted, who, being by me duly sworn, did depose and say that she resides at _____, that she knows _____ to be the individual described in and who executed the foregoing instrument; that said subscribing witness was present and saw said _____ execute the same; and that said witness at the same time subscribed her name as a witness thereto.

_____

NOTARY PUBLIC

ACKNOWLEDGMENT

STATE OF _____   )
                                  :   SS.:
COUNTY OF _____   )

On the _____ day of _____, 2010, before me, the undersigned, personally appeared _____, personally known to me or proved to me on the basis of satisfactory evidence to be the individual whose name is subscribed to the within instrument and acknowledged to me that he executed the same in his capacity, and that by his signature on the instrument, the individual or the person upon behalf of which the individual acted, executed the instrument.

_____

NOTARY PUBLIC

CERTIFICATE OF SUBSCRIBING WITNESS

STATE OF _____   )

                                :   SS.:

COUNTY OF _____   )

On the _____ day of _____, 2010, before me, the undersigned, a Notary Public in and for said state, personally appeared _____, the subscribing witness to the foregoing instrument, with whom I am personally acquainted, who, being by me duly sworn, did depose and say that (s)he resides at _____, that (s)he knows _____ to be the individual described in and who executed the foregoing instrument; that said subscribing witness was present and saw said _____ execute the same; and that said witness at the same time subscribed his name as a witness thereto.

_____

NOTARY PUBLIC

INDEX